> Dear Simon
> I'm not sure, I told you
> in any event here is
> piece of it
> It's kind of a summary of what I'm --
> about.
> All the best, Elliot 3/3/07

One of Eight

Getting the most out of life isn't all laughs..... but luckily a lot of life is.

By: Elliot E. Heit

© Copyright 2006 Elliot E. Heit.
All rights reserved. No part of this publication may be reproduced, stored in a retrieval system, or transmitted, in any form or by any means, electronic, mechanical, photocopying, recording, or otherwise, without the written prior permission of the author.

Note for Librarians: A cataloguing record for this book is available from Library and Archives Canada at www.collectionscanada.ca/amicus/index-e.html
ISBN 1-4251-0444-4

Printed in Victoria, BC, Canada. Printed on paper with minimum 30% recycled fibre.
Trafford's print shop runs on "green energy" from solar, wind and other environmentally-friendly power sources.

TRAFFORD PUBLISHING

Offices in Canada, USA, Ireland and UK

Book sales for North America and international:
Trafford Publishing, 6E–2333 Government St.,
Victoria, BC V8T 4P4 CANADA
phone 250 383 6864 (toll-free 1 888 232 4444)
fax 250 383 6804; email to orders@trafford.com

Book sales in Europe:
Trafford Publishing (UK) Limited, 9 Park End Street, 2nd Floor
Oxford, UK OX1 1HH UNITED KINGDOM
phone 44 (0)1865 722 113 (local rate 0845 230 9601)
facsimile 44 (0)1865 722 868; info.uk@trafford.com

Order online at:
trafford.com/06-2201

10 9 8 7 6 5 4 3

Acknowledgments

My heartfelt thanks to Susan Goldworm, one of my three daughters, for an endless effort and un-abounding patience in creating manuscripts, re-editing, and a source of comfort, from start to finish.

We were partners (If the book, One of Eight, could talk, it would agree)

Table of Contents

Prologue 1
Meet the Family of Eight Brothers and Sisters 1

Chapter 1 17
Growing up One of Eight 17

Chapter 2 29
World War II and Learning to Fly 29

Chapter 3 37
Amherst College and West Point 37

Chapter 4 65
Post West Point and Return to Flying 65

Chapter 5 73
Flying Atomic Bombers in England & Return to Civilian Life 73

Chapter 6 79
Climbing the Corporate Ladder in New York 79

Chapter 7 127
Traveling the World as a Corporate Vice President for Greyhound 127

Chapter 8 171
Leaving Greyhound & A New Career 171

Epilogue 205

Prologue

Meet the Family of Eight Brothers and Sisters

My name is Elliot Eclipse Heit. Eclipse?? Yes, my birth took place 8:30 in the morning on January 24, 1925 in the Lying-In Hospital, located in the borough of Manhattan, New York City. Furthermore, my mother insisted that all Heit "birthings", and there were many; had to have madam provided with a proper suite, which in this case, was the suite used a year earlier to launch Gloria Vanderbilt of the Vanderbilt dynasty. Back to my middle name, at precisely the time I was born all of New York went completely dark and thus in darkness, Elliot Eclipse Heit joined the living world. My father, who was a very bright individual would, during my early years, frequently remark "Yes sir son; you were born in the dark, but I had my fingers crossed, that someday, you'll see the light".

I was the fourth child of my parents, who were married in 1919. I being born six years after their marriage had no idea; there would be two brothers and a sister already walking around. Four children in six years, and she isn't even a Catholic! Where was she heading for? Answer - she wanted twelve!! Due to some medical problems, she was forced to settle for eight. So now, you have some insight on at least, half the title of this book - "One of Eight".

Before I concentrate on myself, as "The One of Eight", it would help to gain a better understanding of how the eight Heit children differ from any other large family I have ever known. To do this effectively, I request you join my step back to the early family history when characteristics were forming to make the Heit family what it became. I will not dwell on my father's part other than to say that he was an exceptional kind, honest, educated, hard working parent: the kind of person you could at any time, come to with your troubles (that is, just in case, he did not already know what was bothering you). Despite his total dedication to us, the real source of our energy, imagination, and inspiration came from our mother. We will get to mother shortly; before doing so, I ask myself, where did this little woman get all the combustion and determination to move forward with all her ambitions. (Little woman means she was five feet tall). To the best of my recollection it was her father, David Kramer that was the most important beginning element in the shaping of Anna Kramer, his first of three children (her father, incidentally was the same five feet tall as my mother). David Kramer at the very young age of fourteen with only a apprentice knowledge of carpentry learned from his father sets off, alone, from Kiev in Russian Ukraine late in the nineteenth century to voyage to the United States of America - alone!!

Soon after arrival, he manages to secure a push cart then tosses in a few tools brought over from Russia and he pushes his cart from the lower east side in New York City to Wall Street! Here he is in the very heart of the world-renowned financial district of New York City. Wall Street is a surprisingly small and narrow street and made it possible for him to go back and forth several times a day, yelling out to the business offices located at street level, "repair furniture". Here and there, he gained a few customers, who were so impressed with his expertise, that word got around, and the same few suggested he open a shop. He did and that was the beginning of David Kramer Office & Desk Company. His business grew and grew. His biggest leap ahead occurred with his contracts to install interior walls made of very fine mahogany. This decor was made for many New York companies particularly the large branch offices of Manufacturers Trust Company and National City banks. David Kramer was most effectively established. He became a millionaire at a very young age and stayed wealthy for the rest of his 95 years. It was not his accumulation of wealth that I underscore; it was his amazing determination and steadfast purpose. These were the qualities that were "fed" to my mother and carried further on with her children. Let it be said that David Kramer's own life deserves to be a story in itself, but for the purpose of this book, it does illustrate the seeds of inheriting strong will that he formed in his life, and then the fallout to his daughter Anna, and finally from her to the flock of eight children. While you will read several times, the mention of wealth in her family, it is misleading.

Mother was not interested in money of itself. She was brought up with out having any regard for the almighty dollar. When she married and began her plan to raise the largest family possible she focused herself on discovering in each child, the self-interest that they could build on for their future, rather than the concern for building wealth.   When she was a young adult she worked for the well-known Henry Street Settlement organization, which was a social workers paradise. Perhaps this further put aside the importance of wealth for Anna Kramer. Despite what was just said, Anna should have been more thankful for the many things her wealthy father made possible for her and the family. During the family grow-up period, it was my father who had the toughest time. Too proud to accept working for my grandfather, he "ploughed ahead" to eek out a living and doing what ever he could do to afford his wife's eccentric ways of raising us. (Inwardly, I am certain, he took great satisfaction of the way we all turned out.)

Let us take a look at Raymond, Anna Heit's first child. Although he grew up physically small like his grandfather and mother, my mother quickly noted he definitely, while very young, also displayed a high degree of similar skills quite like that of her father's natural ability for carpentry. As a child, Raymond was very good at putting together toy log cabins and quite clever with erector sets as well. This was all Anna Heit needed to start acquiring for Raymond an extensive set of hand tools. By the time he was ten years of age, he became one of the very few children his age that also had electric tools like lathes, jigsaw, circular saw, etc.

It is important to pause now about Raymond's early youth and spend some time telling you about the house we lived in, because the house played a very significant part of the family activity. It was a perfect environment for a very large family with parents, particularly a mother, who had this explosive search within her to seek each child's talent that would set the course for each child's life. In her mind, there were certainly eight children, but more to the point, each one was brought up as though he or she were the only child. To do this, she left her friends behind, and relatives for the most part, as well. Prior to my mother and fathers marriage, she lived with her own father, mother, two younger brothers and a sister in a fifteen room mansion located in Boro Park, Brooklyn, one of the five boroughs of New York

City. Boro Park, Brooklyn, at that time was considered to be the most desirable location for many of the wealthiest Jewish families in New York City.

It so happened that my mother's mother died early in life and the same also happened to her sister. This left Anna caring for her two brothers. After the family deaths, her father gave her and my father the house and my grandfather moved to Central Park West in Manhattan. It was not very long before her two brothers also moved out to establish their own homes and family. Now the house became hers to raise the many children she had, and was going to have. At one time prior to the kids taking up quarters, the property itself had a sumptuous lawn with lovely gardens and bushes. On the corner of our block was a lake filled with ducks and graceful swans. The house had three floors and a large basement. The basement housed a coal burning stove, huge storage for the coal, some laundry items, and a little room with a big cross bones on the door and the threatening letters "KEEP OUT", (this I later discovered when as a young child, I came on the scene and found my two older brothers, Raymond and Allen had their exclusive hide out in the basement of the house). Along side the house was the garage and in the back yard was this very unusually large cherry tree that rose so high, it was above the third floor of the house. (We will revisit the cherry tree when we talk about Anna's second son and Raymond's brother Allan). On the first floor there was a large kitchen and pantry, a large dining room, a music room, and a large parlor. The second floor had my parents' bedroom; next to them was my small bedroom with a bunk bed for my younger brother, David. Also next to my parents room was another bedroom for Sally-Jane and Arlene. Then next to their room was another large bedroom for two other sisters, Marilyn and Lucille. There was still one more room on this second floor, which we called the utility room containing all laundry equipment and sinks. Finally, we journey up to the sacred third floor. Here my two older brothers Raymond and Allan had their own bedroom and their own very large bathroom (theirs, except in the early morning, my father would make use of "their" bathroom, to began his day).

On the third floor there was also a small maids room and another small room, which ultimately became the chemistry lab of the second oldest brother Allan. Finally, next to the lab was a very large room, which became my oldest brother's workshop.

Previously, I referred to the third floor, as sacred. Other than my father's early daily visit to the bathroom, Raymond and Allen forbid any of the kids to wander up there. Raymond and Allen just plainly did not want anyone going into their "hobby rooms". Although their reason for this was self-serving, it was also possible the "trespasser" could hurt them selves in the workshop, or worse yet, accidentally cause a fire in the lab. With the house now in the story, let us return to the early childhood of Anna Heit's first child Raymond.

The Heit Family Residence that withstood the turbulence of bringing up eight maverick children

At about the same, time he received his full set of hand tools and put his workshop together; he became fascinated with model airplanes. If my memory serves me correctly, I believe this new area of interest originated some time in the early 1930's during one of our annual two months summer vacation spent in a quaint seashore resort along the New Jersey coastline called Belmar. Belmar was one of a group of "restricted" towns along a section of the "Jersey Shore" such as Ocean Grove, Spring Lake, Point Pleasant, and Bay Head, (Spring Lake actually had a chain barrier across the road). A Jewish family had a tough time getting a house for the summer but mother loved Belmar and that made it final. We had summer homes in Belmar from 1927 to 1940. My father would come down, weekly from New York. On one occasion he took Raymond and me to the Spring Lake golf course. There on one of the flat fairways was parked an old two wing biplane called a Travelair. The front cockpit was big enough for one adult and two small children. The pilot sat in the back seat and flew the plane. My dad did not ask any questions of us. All three of us squeezed into the front cockpit and off we went. The ride was mostly for Raymond and I was just fortunate to go along. I was about seven years old and "Ray" was about twelve. He went raving wild and my reaction was just absolute awe. After the thriller, at the first opportunity, mother bought him a type of model airplane kit called in those days a "solid model". It was a box about ten inches long and it contained one solid block of balsa wood for the body and varying sizes of "sheet balsa", for the wings and tail surfaces. A simple plan was included and "Ray" shortly completed carving out a reasonable facsimile of Charles Lindbergh's plane called "WE" (used for the first solo flight across the Atlantic in 1927). Ray was now "out of the gate" and building all kinds of kits with rubber band powered propellers. Then, on to his own designed planes, that were actually powered by tiny internal combustion engines. Most of his progress occurred before he was fifteen! At that time he started competing in regional and national flight endurance contests, and won a good share of the contest prizes.

It was these model plane flight contests, that Elliot Heit marks his entrance to the Ray Heit picture. For several years prior to this point of time, I had become Raymond's "stooge" (I was actually referred to him by that nickname when, several years prior, he allowed me to be the only other family member to enter the sacred closed door of his work shop, on the third floor of the house. I sat perched on a chair next to his workbench and was completely at his beck and call for assistance. I was never allowed to talk; one word out of my mouth, and I was kicked out for several days until I promised not a word would come from "the Stooge"). While some might think this menial servitude made no sense; actually it did allow me to concentrate on "the magic" he was constantly creating that eventually led to my own skills as a model builder.

Let's get back to the flight endurance contest. My grand father, who felt very close to Raymond, would on many contest occasions send Steve, his fully uniformed chauffeur to our house, completely equipped with a late model Packard limousine to pick up Ray, his models, and his stooge. The limousine was absolutely elegant; the passenger section had two "fold away seats", a very comfortable rear seat, and remarkably, a telephone to call Steve who was separated from us by a glass window that closed off the passengers from the driver. Now you have to visualize an unforgettable scene. One particular contest was held at Bradley Airport in New Brunswick, New Jersey, a good distance from the Heit house in Brooklyn; our limousine arrives at the field with Ray, the Stooge, the model planes and obviously Steve the chauffeur. Keep in mind, this takes place in the early thirties right "smack" in the middle of the depression! It was a mystery how the other contestants were able to get there. Very few parents or friends had cars and there was only limited public transportation available. It would not surprise me if some contestants walked from nearby New Brunswick. People were "all over' the limousine, daring to touch here and there. It was like we were from another planet.

Each contestant ready to fly, was assigned a timer who first weighed the plane and based on an eighth of an ounce of gasoline per pound of plane, the contestant would receive the proper portion of fuel. The trick was to build the planes big and make them heavy but still aerodynamically designed to have a steep rate of climb. The heavier planes thus received more fuel than the lighter ones. When the engine ran out of fuel, the glide capabilities, properly designed, take over to lengthen the endurance of the flight. My brother's planes usually had a six-foot wingspan and weighed about six pounds. That meant three quarters of an ounce of fuel gave him a five to six minute engine run. This could give the plane an altitude of six hundred feet before engine runs out of gas and then the gliding aspect takes over for the rest of the flight. (In those days there were no radio control or engine timers). This detail for the flight contest is important to the reader, so you understand the complete flight phenomenon, which included what each person connected with the airborne model had to do. For example right after take off, the Timer and Ray "hopped into the limo" and with Steve at the wheel, raced off, in style, to follow the plane as best as possible along the roads. Left behind is the Stooge. He was told to start running in a straight line toward the plane, whose rudder has been, adjusted slightly, so that the plane is circling. The problem is wind drift. At six hundred feet in the air the wind drift can move a plane about ten to fifteen miles per hour. The other problem/opportunity are thermals; these are vertical rising air currents that can take a model to 900 feet or more even after the empty fuel tank stops the engine! When I started my humble pursuit of the model in the air, my path took me through cornfields, cow pastures, forests and streams. Some of these runs went on for four or five miles of really mean cross-country. I was usually lucky; it was though I was a Beagle dog chasing the elusive fox. Some times the plane just flew out of sight, and we would have to depend on a message with all address and reward information, as well, placed on the wing. I must admit that despite the physical difficulties, two important achievements were made. First, I usually came back with the plane and, secondly, I found myself developing a very muscular physique, which led to my athletic accomplishments later on in high school and college. (We will return to this fact later in the story).

Raymond continued his progress in the model builder's world. During his fifteenth and sixteenth year, he designed model airplane plans for air model magazines and plans for model airplane kit manufacturers. He then went on to a special public high school called Harran, where he actually worked on full size construction of airplanes. Mother thought he would go on to college to become a aeronautical engineer, but he was set on becoming, at that time, involved with the manufacturing process of military aircraft, for the war. During the early part of World War Two, Ray worked for Republic Aircraft on fighter planes until he was drafted into the army. I will bring Ray back into the picture as we get into the heart of "One of Eight".

The second son of Anna and Louis Heit was Allen. When launched, he weighed thirteen pounds (with a shove, he could have walked out). Even as a small, but physically big child, he was a voracious reader of all kinds of literature and textbooks. Mother's intuitive senses reacted to Allan's expressed interest in chemistry, and she provided him with his own laboratory, complete with chemicals and apparatus. Allan also has a strong interest in playing piano he was particularly fond of Beethoven. Incidentally, learning classical music was a compulsory part of basic training to be a Heit. My father played violin, Raymond did a short course in violin I had an eight-year stint, with more detail about my violin later on. Mother, Marilyn, and Allan played piano, Lucille is next to be born after me; she played the "triangle". I am not sure what the little Heit's of the family played, i.e. David, Sally-Jane, and Arlene, but the big Heit's made sufficient noise. Mother had music orchestrated so that we could have family recitals with Mother and Allen duet on piano, Dad, Raymond and myself respectively played first part, second part, and third part on violin; Lucielle on the triangle. God, it was awful, but we did it until it was recognized to be useless.

Returning to Allen: at the age of six, he wrote a primitive thesis on life. At seven, he ran away from home and was found nine miles away at Fort Hamilton Army Post. A few years later, he became so intellectually advanced with his vocabulary and deep thoughts he could not be fully understood by most of the family. This created some distance with his brothers and sister. (He was definitely one of a kind; and that is saying a lot, when you consider the individualism of each of us). Personally I was attracted by his intellectuality and thus we were quite close.

During World War Two, he served in the navy, then afterwards, went to Columbia University. He graduated with a Bachelors of Science degree and majored in chemical research. He was employed over his career, by several modestly large chemical firms, as a research chemist. He won six or seven U.S. patents on desalinization of seawater in the early days of that process development. While he was highly regarded by all of the companies he served, once again, as was the case with Raymond, seeking material benefits was not a priority in their lives. Mother overlooked that aspect, and instead, devoted her energy and resources to giving Raymond, Allan, and in fact all of us, overwhelming support in pursuing our individual interests. As stated previously, Allan's chemical "lab", was located on the sacred third floor of the house. It was adjacent to Ray's workshop. This arrangement allowed them, to be practically separated from the rest of the house (those two, occupied by themselves the entire top floor of the house). Many times they pretended to go upstairs to bed, but it was not very long before the pitter-patter of feet took them to their hobby nests. (The rest of the family including my parents knew little of the long hours they spent deeply engaged in their obsessions).

Allan had many peculiar habits. One of them was priceless. Wherever there was a tree that was difficult to climb, Allan had to conquer the tree. I also mentioned that in the backyard we had an unusually tall cherry tree. The height of the tree put it up as high as the three-story house. This tree was Allan's favorite. He would put a book to read inside the shirt he was wearing, then climb to the top of the tree, secure him self, and read! Mother would prepare the dinner and the only one missing from the table was Allan. Mother would then turn to me, and say, "Go upstairs and tell Allan to come down to dinner". I would then go upstairs to Ray and Allan's bedroom on the sacred third floor, open the bedroom window and yell to Allan swaying in the top of this cherry tree. Allan reluctantly would climb down the tree and would enter the house for dinner.

Next to come on the scene is my sister Marilyn, and here again at a young age, mother observed an inclination in Marilyn for ballet. Off she goes to the Neighborhood Playhouse. This was a learning center that our mother knew of, where they focus on the children who show a talent for the arts. Mother "hits the mark again"; Marilyn does so well, she is given scholarship after scholarship and was well on her was to becoming a ballerina. In those days, entering the professional art of dancing was something my mother was against. Marilyn continued with modern interpretive dancing, but not professionally. She also was very good in school, to the extent that she graduated Brooklyn College at the age of 18! She then fell in love with a great fellow, Sam Leibovitz. They marry; she tries to imitate her mother by raising six children while Sam remained in the Air Force for twenty years. After World War Two, and while in the Air Force, the Leibovitz family roamed the world yet; all children attended college and earned their degrees. Marilyn did not pursue her dancing professionally; instead she did a wonderful job with her husband in bringing up six very productive children, one of whom is Annie Leibovitz; one of the worlds greatest women photographers. Marilyn can be thankful that she was so endowed with her mother's fierce determination to devote herself tirelessly to her family in the same unusual way we were all brought up.

Chronologically, Elliot should be the next member of the family to arrive. Although I did arrive, I choose to remove myself from the prologue of this book until all other members of the Anna and Louis Heit family have duly been described. Pursuing this approach will help you have a better understanding of the book "One of Eight".

Therefore, allow me to introduce Lucielle. Lucielle and I were pretty good pals growing up. During that phase, she showed a strong interest in art, and as before and before and before, Mother "catches the scent" and suddenly Lucielle has her easel, canvas frames, paints and all other accoutrements. She too went to the Neighborhood Playhouse institution and Mother proved once again to have the proper judgment for Lucielle's aspirations to be an artist. She continued by getting accepted to the very first class of New York City's newest specialty school, The Fashion Institute of Technology. After graduating she went into the business world as a fashion illustrator and was on the staff of a very well established Brooklyn department store, Abraham & Strauss. She was doing very well in this capacity, but after marrying and, being old fashioned, she turned away from fashion illustration, and kept the house and two children in order. Some years later the urge to get back to her skillful past returned and she became a high school art teacher until she retired.

I have always referred to the first five Heit children as the Big Five. Now comes the Small Three. This is not done in any way to discredit them; each one of them contributed themselves to being an integral part of the Heit clan. Each has a story to be told, but what was becoming apparent was that mother was growing older with every new addition, (my father was as well sharing that change of life). Mother particularly was losing her high level of energy. Actually toward the last birth of the small three contingent, suffered a stroke before the last child, Arlene was born. I also strongly believe she felt the Big Five would act as an inspiration for the Small Three, to find and establish their own direction to follow. As a case in point, my brother David, the oldest of the Small Three "shadowed" both Raymond the oldest and his Stooge. In fact when Ray fell in love and got married at a young age, he left home. I took over his shop and my younger brother David, became a reasonable facsimile of myself, as I was with Raymond, in helping me with my model building etc.

David and I got alone very well and shared a small room with a double-decker bed. My mother allowed me to paper all walls with road maps I collected from various gas stations. It was indeed very different and quite unique, but so was I.

Afterwards Sally-Jane joins the gang. Mother, still trying to be what she was with the Big Five, saw a spark of the theater in Sally-Jane, and of course, she was rushed off to her favorite home for the arts, the Neighborhood Playhouse. Sally-Jane was magnificent, and frequently won scholarships. She went on to the High School for the Performing Arts, in New York City, where she won acclaim after acclaim, (students who were allowed to enter had to be carefully screened). Then to Hunter College, where she continued to "sharpen up" her theatrical talents. While at Hunter, she won all kinds of kudos. Relatively soon after graduating from Hunter, she married. Her husband became a tax lawyer and secured a job with the Internal Revenue Service. This made it necessary to move to Washington, D.C.. It did not take Sally-Jane too long to get into a "theatrical group". She began appearing as a comedienne at several supper clubs in the Georgetown area of Washington and became quite popular in the capital. At one time, she was invited to the White House by President, Lyndon Johnson to entertain his dinner guests.

During her exciting career in the capital, she invited the whole family to her own comedy production called Separate Checks. At the time in Washington *Theater in the round* was very popular. This production was performed in such a theater. It was a monologue done individually by a couple experiencing a difficult marriage. The actors were seated in high chairs at a small round table, set in the center of a large room and surrounded by the audience. Each actor would speak aloud their monologue, describing the things that went wrong with their married lives. Sally-Jane's monologue was quite critical of our mother and some of our relatives. Bare in mind, this was only done, to contribute to the plot of the play. Never the less, all Heit's were seated together and when Sally-Jane brought up her criticism of her mother, my older brother Allan, the genius and sometimes quite eccentric, leapt to his feet and yelled, "this is a lie, and that was not my mothers fault". Sally-Jane proved her experience as an actress and handled the situation professionally. Needless to say, Sally-Jane and the rest of the family were mortified, although, I believed the rest of the audience must have thought my brother Allan was actually part of the act.

The youngest and final member of the Small Three that joins the Heit family is cute little Arlene. I am surprised she was not scared out of her wits when she looked up from her crib and saw this crowd of brothers and sisters curiously looking down at her. Cute little Arlene stayed to this day, cute and little. It is interesting to note, that despite being the last to join the Heit flock, and despite my mothers weakened attention to her unique parental formula for bringing up children, Arlene seemed to be in many ways representative of us all. Except for our chemist brother Allan, who marched to a different drummer with personality and character that was exclusive to him. Arlene is funny, and quite theatrical and remains so to this day. She also was "artsy" and graduated from the Fashion Institute of Technology. When she married Ronald Krum, she had no idea what the future held for her. Ronald's family was one of the best-known candy manufacturers in New York City. Krum's Candy was best known for kosher candy and it had a very strong loyalty among Jewish families in New York City and throughout the neighboring boroughs. When Ronny Krum left the service after Korea, he reported to his fathers candy plant for a totally different kind of duty. He also involved Arlene in the business by taking advantage of her artistic talents. Krum's Candy went through a difficult period due to a change in the market for candy. Sugarless, diet and population shifts, and more integrated areas had a lot to do with the business taking a downward turn. Even so, Ronny was the President of a National Confectionary Organization for several terms, and is still very active in the business. The reason for detailing a bit about Ronny is because my sister Arlene has been by his side playing a very active part during all the difficult candy business ventures they have been involved in to date. Her expertise, tracks back to her "artsy" instincts mentioned earlier. With her training and innate ability, she has worked tirelessly with candy designs, store displays and wrapping preparations, making a significant impact on the business.

With Arlene Krum finally "on board", we have come to the end of the prologue, which hopefully will help the reader understand the environment that made it possible for Elliot Eclipse Heit's arrogance in titling this book, One of Eight. I will now begin to trace my life which, was "jam packed" with stories that may seem to you, exaggerated or hard to believe. This will be your choice; as for me, at eighty years of age, I am just happy that I was blessed with being involved with such a wide variety of life's experiences. Come along with me as I review as much as I can of what fell on my plate.

One of Eight, The family in full bloom - 1938, Atlantic City, New Jersey

One of Eight

Chapter 1

Growing up One of Eight

From the age of five, or as far back as my memory will serve me, I commenced violin lessons. I was equipped with a very small violin and a suite of black velvet. This suit consisted of short pants, a white ruffled shirt along with white high socks and patent leather shoes. Professor Louis Persinger, who taught Yehudi Menuhin and the Ricci twins, was recommended to my parents for my audition. The result was Professor Persinger told Mother and Dad I was a child prodigy. He also told them, he would like to be my teacher, supervise my practice, and make sure my weekends were taken up with attending violin concerts. At these various concerts, we would go back stage where the professor made it possible for me to meet and speak to some of the most famous violinists in the world, such as Fritz Kreissler, Yasha Heifitz and Yehudi Menuhin. All this sort of thing went on for eight years! While I am sure there was some talent in my little body, the truth of the matter is it made me a loner, and furthermore, I did not like the over indulgence with the violin. (I will say to this day, I do have a strong passion for classical music, but that is all that remains.) You will recall in my prologue, how I emphasized the perspicacity of Mothers measurement of each child's inclinations. I am sorry to say for me, she and my father were dead wrong. This will become obvious as we proceed, keeping in mind what I mentioned about the violin obsession having a sort of reverse effect on my personality. In my early years I preferred to do things alone, just as I was alone a lot being a violin soloist. As an example, I do not believe I was more than nine years of age, when I told my mother I was going to take a very long walk, by myself to the George Washington Bridge. The bridge is located in the northern end of the borough of Manhattan. (She already knew I was capable of doing something like this, because several times, as a stooge for brother Ray, I would receive change for the subway to Manhattan and instructions to go to Polk's Hobby Shop on 32nd Street and Fifth Avenue, to pick up some material he needed for one of his airplane models.) Walking to the George Washington Bridge from Boro Park, Brooklyn was like climbing Mount Everest, especially for a nine year old. It was at least 25 miles to my final destination, where I eventually stopped for the night. I got the green light from Mother and early the next morning I set our, alone, for my destination. My mother gave me a dollar "in change" for phone calls; she also packed me a few sandwiches. Off I went, on to Fort Hamilton Parkway, and on to Prospect Park. I continued to Flatbush Avenue, over the Brooklyn Bridge, and up Broadway to the George Washington Bridge, (If you have a map of New York City handy, you will find this was already quite a feat for a small tot).

After crossing the bridge, I decided to go further north until darkness. Suddenly, it seemed that darkness was upon me without notice. Where was I, and where could I stay? I found out I was in Alpine, New Jersey, a small town, located more or less, across the Hudson River from the city of Yonkers, New York. I called home collect and explained that I would stay overnight in Alpine, New Jersey and return via the subway (located on the New York side of the George Washington Bridge). To get to the subway, the following morning I had to retrace my route by foot from Alpine, to the bridge and then back across to New York. Do you know where I slept in Alpine, NJ? Alone, in a graveyard, behind a church and I was FRIGHTENED TO DEATH! Needless to say, at nine years of age, this experience of walking a total of about forty miles by myself, gave me a great deal of confidence for my future exploits. (Keep in mind my grandfathers determination and the will of my mother).

Elliot Eclipse Heit, child prodigy at age five

The book's prologue describes our summers of fun at the Jersey shore resort of Belmar. One summer I got "the itch" to see if I could bike in one day to my grandfather's farm in Connecticut. I was about eleven years old. I set forth on this one-day bike ride, covering 65 miles from Belmar, New Jersey to New York City. Then another 65 miles further to my grandfather's farm in Southbury, Connecticut. I would ride a total distance of 130 miles. I had already been making bike trips during the fall and spring of the previous years, from Brooklyn to my summer shore friends who lived in Jersey City and Newark, New Jersey. These trips were about 25 miles each way. I always stayed overnight and that made the routes easier to navigate in the daylight.

I must express to you how I felt about my bicycle. This was not only my means of transportation; to my young imagination it was a motorcycle. This motorcycle fantasy started when I tried to imitate my brother Raymond. Like everyone else in the family Ray had a bicycle, but he became determined to convert it to a motorbike. To do this, he bought and old piece of junk lawn mower motor, and completely overhauled the engine. He then put a wood roller on the engine crankshaft and mounted the motor above the rear tire of his bike. A shifting system was devised, where by he would pedal the bike to get a certain amount of speed, then a lever he made could lower the motor so that the wood roller he put on the engine crank shaft, rubbed against the bike tire. The speed of the peddling rotated the engine, which then starts it, and Ray is on his way at a hot 10 to 15 miles per hour. He once allowed me to try it, and from them on I pretended my bike was a motorbike.

I believe the bicycle I had was a Columbia, which at the time was a very reputable manufacturer. Every time I had a birthday or wanted something badly enough for my bike, my parents would indulge me. Bikes in those days were basic and simple. They, of course, had two wheels, handlebars, a seat and brakes…PERIOD. My bike had one of the earlier versions of a three-speed shift, and brake drums on both wheels for hand brakes, instead of brakes that simply rub against the rims of each wheel to stop the bike. It was also equipped with an electric generator, for headlights and taillights. The generator, when turned on, would rub against the tire to generate electricity.

Finally, I had balloon tires and a very sturdy rack at the rear of the bike. The balloon tires gave the bike a comfortable "ride" and the rack was used frequently to carry my clothes needed for my overnights. There was no question it was a heavy bike! Why all the bike detail? When I was thirteen years old another adventure began. On the last half day of the school, before the Christmas vacation, two of my classmates bet me a quarter each that I could not make it to Washington D.C. from New York in time to see President Roosevelt light the Christmas tree on the White House lawn. The lighting was to take place the next night! We "shook" on the bet, and I ran home, told my mother, and her reply was "If you are going to do it, you better leave now or else your father will forbid you to go". I ran up to my room, took my little satchel with some clothes, and toiletries: tied it on to my sturdy bike rack and told my mother I was ready to go. She gave me fifteen dollars and a note. I asked what the note said? She said, "Read it". I did, and this is what she wrote, "To whom it may concern. This is my thirteen-year-old son Elliot. He is an experienced rider, and therefore he has my permission to ride his bicycle to Washington to see the President light the Christmas tree". It was signed Anna Heit, but I still did not understand the purpose. I shrugged my shoulders, shoved the piece of paper into my pocket, and kissed my mother goodbye. On December 23rd at 2 p.m., I was on my way to the 69th Street ferry, which crosses New York harbor to the borough of Staten Island. Everything was going well. I arrived on Staten Island and peddled to Hylan Boulevard, where it started to snow! On top of this, I am bucking head winds. This tired me a bit, so I pulled off the road to rest on the ground next to the bike. About five minutes go by, and two policemen, who must have assumed I was some kind of runaway, awakened me. One of them asks in a gruff voice "Where do you think you are going?" I simply replied, "I am going to Washington to see the President light the Christmas tree". The policemen then replied, "Forget it kid, you are going to the station house".

I knew if this happened I would lose the bet, and then I remembered the note Mother gave me. Quickly, I took it out of my pocket and said, "Here is a note from my mother about this bike trip". Both policemen read the note, looked at each other, scratched their heads and said, "Would you believe this? Letting a little kid do something like this".

They thought for a moment and then agreed to let me go on. I arrived 20 miles south of Trenton, New Jersey by about 9 p.m. I found what we used to call a Tourist Home. I remember the rate was two dollars and fifty cents and that was fine with me. The next morning I was under way by 4 a.m. The only highway south from where I stayed was number 130. It took me all the way down to the end of New Jersey. Then I crossed the Delaware River and went further south past Wilmington, Delaware, in order to get on highway 40 to Baltimore. Thirty-eight miles to go! I arrived at Washington's YMCA at 4:30 p.m. I pleaded with the front desk to send a telegram to my parents that I was safe, and of course, the time on the telegram will be shown as evidence to the other "bettors". The front desk accepted my bike as collateral, and the best news was that I only had a short run to make it on time for the lighting of the Christmas tree. After the "lighting ceremony", I returned to the YMCA thoroughly exhausted, but I had one more chore, which was to have Railway Express ship my bicycle collect to the Brooklyn house, then I went to bed. After breakfast the next day, I took a Greyhound bus home. It was an interesting and varied reaction that I received back at the Heit house. My brothers, my sisters, and my parents totally believed this thirteen-year-old child peddled all by himself, 238 miles to Washington to see Franklin Roosevelt light this Christmas tree. Some of my relatives just plain and simply did not accept it as true. One had the audacity to suggest I "hitched" a ride with a truck and the driver threw my bike in the back of his truck. I was very surprised after such an effort; to think some people did not believe me. I know two more people beside my brothers and sisters and parents who did believe me, and it was the two friends from school who paid the bet with a quarter each.

Reaching thirteen was certainly one of the crossroads in my life. The bike ride to Washington was a top feature of the year. Another critical happening was I insisted on ending my musical career as a violinist. My parents reluctantly accepted this, although in someway, they believed I still had the capability also, they were finding it difficult to keep up with the expenses of running a family of eight children, especially our family with their individual pursuits. This change allowed several shifts to take place in my growing up. I could spend more time as Ray's stooge; in so doing, I was getting fully acquainted with all tools and model equipment in his workshop. Ray could see I was making progress in model airplane construction, and in the design of my own model plans; so much so, he allowed me to talk while in the workshop! Secondly, at this time, I was also developing a very strong interest in really flying a plane. This took my trusty bike and me to many local airports, were I scouted all different kinds of planes. In the meanwhile, Ray and I did a lot of talking and working together on his various projects, which were almost too numerous to mention. But a few are worthy of describing. There was the old Model 'A' Ford that he bought and completely disassembled down in Dad's garage. Then he took each part, piece by piece up to the third floor workshop. Over a period of a year Raymond, "takes them down" to bare metal and overhauls the engine, the same way. When finished he takes it back down piece by piece to the garage; paints, reassembles, and the Model 'A' looked like it just rolled off the Ford assembly line. After that he built a boat, on his third floor shop. It was an eight-foot racing shell. For power he bought a "beat up" four-horse power Everude outboard motor. This Ray rebuilds and it is in perfect running condition. There was only one thing he forgot to consider, how were we going to get this monster out of the shop and get it down three flights of stairs leading to the front door? Incidentally, my father and mother did not even know he had already built the boat!! One idea was to remove the double window in the shop and with rope, lower the boat to the ground. That idea was dropped and very shortly afterwards Ray and I were "inching" it down from the third floor. The boat was clumsy to carry and weighed over 100 pounds. It took over two hours with our combined strength to get it down and to the garage (Ray was now equipped with his "yacht" ready for next summer at the Belmar shore)

When I was thirteen, the year was 1938. One of the funniest stories happened this year and it involved the whole Heit family. We had two radios (no television). The first, a deluxe RCA radio with all kinds of dials and knobs, was located in the music room adjacent to the parlor. It was housed in a very large finely made cabinet. The second radio allowed in the house was in Ray's shop. Ray had special permission to have a radio in his shop while he worked on his various projects.

The event in mind, as I recall, took place on a Sunday evening in October. Allan the chemist was in his lab, Raymond was in his workshop listening to his radio, tuned to music on

WNEW radio station. He was working away with me helping whenever he said the word. Back to the music room, most of the other members of the family were huddled around the fancy radio listening to "The Witches Tales". Usually my mother and father allowed the two older girls and David to listen to this Sunday night "scary" program. After which, one of them was sure to have a nightmare of sorts. At the same time all this was going on in the Heit house, a relatively unknown writer of drama, Orson Wells, was putting on his first broadcast. It was a surrealistic presentation that was far scarier than any Witches Tales ever was, to both adults as well as children. To gain ultra realism, Orson Wells was able to convince the station executives to eliminate all commercials and instead, allow bogus news reports to interrupt the dialogue of his drama called "War of the Worlds". Also there was no introduction to War of the Worlds; it started with a staged news report interrupting the music of a dance band and announcing they would switch their broadcast to Princeton, New Jersey, where a newscaster was conducting an astonishing interview with a science professor at Princeton University, who came upon a mysterious canister that was lying in one of the nearby sport fields used by the school. All at once, the interview switches back to the dance band music and several minutes go by. Then the same interruption occurs again, and we are advised that something more grotesque is happening with the canister. We are then advised that the State Police and a National Guard unit were at the scene. The mood of the crowd has now undergone a change, from curiosity to fear of the unknown. Out of the canister came these monsters that start to expand themselves to frightening heights, and some of them have already started moving onto the major road going to New York. Take into account the dancing music program is being interrupted more and more frequently with these announcements. My brother Ray happened to come upon the program accidentally when he was casually rotating the dial to get a different program from the one he was tuned into. When he hears some of the interrupting news announcements, first he calls Allan who was in his lab, and was after all our family genius. Allan listened for a moment and then shouted, "it is a preposterous fraud, and scientific facts do not support such an absolute sham". I, being present during this exchange, listen to them and then turn my attention back to the program. Meanwhile, Ray does not pay any attention to Allan's bellicose impression, and rushes down the stairs to get our father. In a few moments my father arrives, listens a bit, then directs me to leave the shop. My father then locked the door, leaving him and Raymond in the workshop, concentrating on every syllable that came out of the radio. It did not take more than my father hearing "the monsters are approaching New York", and "that families should prepare for evacuation to sparsely populated areas". He takes immediate action by calling a family meeting with the Big Five and Mother. The decision was made to start packing blankets, canned goods, a can opener, and emergency water supply. Dad said to leave the Small Three alone until we packed the big Studabaker-President, the family car. By this time all the lights in the house were on and everyone was scurrying about. Ray said to me that he and I would hop on the Indian motorcycle and speed off on our own. Marilyn, my sister was on the phone tearfully saying good-bye to one of her friends, who mistook the noise of Ray's motorcycle starting up, as machine gun bullets and she went ballistic.

Dad also heard the sound of the motorcycle start up, he runs out of the house to the garage where Ray and I were about to get off into first gear. In a thunderous voice yells, "Get off that damn motorcycle and get into the car, if we are going to die, we will die together"! That did it; we were all on board the Studebaker except for Allan. Allan finally emerges from the house and calmly announces "I told you this was a fake…they just announced that the War of The Worlds was a fictitious program." With that said, we sheepishly unloaded the car and very quietly made our way back into the house. As a side note, I must say that I could not understand why the rest of the houses on the block had all their lights off and people were calmly walking up and down the street without the slightest sign of concern. Oh well, the Heit's have always seen things their way.

Shortly after my parents accepted my request to end the violin saga, physically I began a big change from the thin underweight violin prodigy. I was much more involved with "city sports" which like handball, was played against neighborhood apartment walls, while punch ball (modified baseball) and touch football were played in the street. At thirteen years of age, I noticed my weight at the end of the year had increased by fifty pounds without fat. I also noticed my appetite grew most abnormally, (if I missed a meal I was tempted to gnaw on the furniture). During the first year of high school my mother usually packed a lunch for me of, six hamburgers, placed on 12 slices of white bread with ketchup, (four hours later this cold and soggy mess was consumed along with a quart of milk, during the school lunch hour)! In fact my daily consumption of milk was five quarts! By the time I was sixteen, I was playing first string, tackle on the varsity football team, of New Utrecht High School. My nickname was "Iron Man Heit". The nickname was given to me because I played every minute of each game of my first season of football. After the football season was over, New Utrecht High School dropped football and I decided to move on to Erasmus Hall High School. Erasmus was one of the best athletic schools in New York City including an excellent football team. If I could get transferred, it could provide a good opportunity to possibly win a scholarship for college. Getting a scholarship was an ambition I had since playing football. I figured my folks would find it very difficult to send all the children to private colleges, so I thought football would help me get there.

Transferring to Erasmus was not as easy as I thought. I had no trouble with the Erasmus coach; he was set to assist me in any way and "get it done". However, there was another high school coach who called me at home and tried to force me to join their team instead of Erasmus's. Here I was at the age of sixteen being told by a coach, who is a member of the New York City school system, that if I did not visit his school and discuss admittance, he would "turn me in" to the proper authorities for excessive transfers. I called the Erasmus coach; he said, "Heit, you're coming to Erasmus. Don't worry about anything else." I went to Erasmus and easily made the left tackle position on the first string team. Erasmus Hall was anticipating a second unbeaten season. As the football season approached it is interesting that my name started to get around the sports columns in Brooklyn newspapers. I was not accustomed to such publicity, but it was a big help with my efforts to secure a college scholarship. It was not very long before we were playing football again and Erasmus indeed did have a spectacular second undefeated year.

Since this was my senior year, I did ask the coach to help me with college admission. I ended up with two possibilities. One was an offer from Colgate for full scholarship and the other was a letter, that unbeknownst to me, the coach sent to West Point. I was not told about it until two years later, at which time, I was already in the Army Air Corps as a flying cadet. Back to my senior year, the time in history is World War Two was well underway. In early January of 1943 I was still seventeen years old when I received my high school diploma. At about the same time, the Army Air Corps had a program for seventeen-year-old males, where by if they enlisted in the air corps cadet-training program then they would not be called to active duty until they became eighteen. I called Colgate's coach, Andy Kerr, and explained this program and told him I would be unable to accept the scholarship.

My eighteenth birthday was January 24, 1943. I discussed this whole situation with my father, he was quite negative, but I persisted. I told him the army air corps program was a fantastic opportunity for me to learn how to fly, for free! The "for free' outweighed any of my concern for flying combat missions. This was something I wanted to do ever since I took that flight with him and my brother Raymond in that old Biplane down at the jersey shore Spring Lake golf course many years ago. Also what about all the time spent with my interest in aviation: building, designing and flying model airplanes? My father was finally convinced. We arrived at the army recruiting station located in Manhattan's Grey Bar building on Lexington Avenue at about 3 p.m. and one week before my eighteenth birthday. (A seventeen year old had to be accompanied by a parent). The processing staff at the recruiting facility told my father it would be too late to start the enlistment process, which included a mental and physical exam. Beside this there would be several days required for processing and the next day the enlistment center was closed. My father was super; he demanded to see the officer in charge, whereupon he went charging into his office and confronted him with all the arguments I just made with my father when he showed initial reluctance to the whole idea! The officer was definitely impressed. So much so, he reversed the procedures by giving me my physical first, which was "a piece of cake". Afterwards, he took me into his office, sat me down, closed the door, and put the multiple-choice test before me. He waited until I was done, examined it, called my father back into his office and told me to raise my right hand. I was given the oath and sworn in. Congratulations followed and that was that. When dad and I left the commanding officers private office we

—The Line—Unsung But Not Outdone—

You have seen this picture before, but this time observe the underrated line more closely. Linemen Peck, Brooks, Saladino, Ginden, Massaria, Heit and Weiss, while End Andreson and Guard Henry Corbrin are missing.

> Stud, first string tackle, Erasmus High School. Two years undefeated New York City (home school for Sid Luckman, Gene Rossides – Columbia defeats West Point in 1948) and Stud Heit (2 years Co-Captain West Point "B" Squad)

found that we were the only people left in the whole recruitment facility. Everyone had gone for the day and the commanding officer was so impressed with my father, he stayed on to complete the task! The day was not over. That night was the graduation prom, so we had to speed home by taxi. I shaved, showered and decked myself out in the rented tux. A taxi was waiting to take a corsage and me to my girlfriend's house. There upon I rang her doorbell; her first question with a harsh face was "Why are you twenty minutes late?" I answered, "With the war going on, I was busy joining the army air corps". This was the end of Elliot Heit's life in Brooklyn, New York and the start of quite a fascinating sequel.

Chapter 2

World War II and Learning to Fly

The first step away from civilian life took place shortly following my eighteenth birthday. It was the day I was called to active duty. Along with a couple of hundred other recruits we were sent on a non air conditioned three day railroad coach trip from New York to Miami, Florida, where we spent about six weeks going through basic training. Believe it or not it was "a grueler", even though the training took place in Miami Beach. When this was complete, the Army sent us to various eastern colleges for six months exposure to college curriculum. The idea was to give each of us a "coat of paint" with academic life. This way we would be more like officer material rather than a bunch of youngsters starting military service at eighteen years of age. In my case, I was sent to the University of Pittsburgh, in Pittsburgh, Pennsylvania.

Geographically, the Allegheny, Monongahela and Ohio Rivers surround Pittsburgh. On my own, I went down to the Allegheny River, where I spotted a Piper Cub seaplane. I had a flash thought to take a few lessons before starting the air cadet-flying program. This came out of my own pocket from the army pay I received at the time. My first flying experience was quite unusual. First of all the aircraft owner and only instructor was a woman. Living then in "the stone age" of the male/female contest, I was not particularly impressed with the prospect of taking my very first flying lesson from an aviatrix. Secondly, the Allegheny River has at least eight bridges spanning the river from down town Pittsburgh to the suburbs on the north side of the river. Nevertheless, I went ahead with my plan. In a Piper Cub, due to the narrowness of the fuselage, you sit "tandem" style. The pilot is in the rear seat and the student sits in the forward seat. With a few basic instructions including a quiz on my knowledge of aerodynamics, we "cranked" it up and she taxied out to the middle of the river and waits patiently for some of the river craft to clear out of her take off path! I then suddenly said to myself, "How are we going to climb out of here after takeoff with all these bridges ahead and behind us?" Before I have a chance to think further, she finished checking the magnetos and shoves the throttle wide open. Seaplanes, because of the surface friction on water, require a longer run than a plane with wheels. Here we went, bouncing on the wakes created by several nearby craft and it seemed like forever before the Piper Cub gets "on the step" of its floats; this enables the plane to gather take off speed. In the meanwhile, she is talking to me through the Gosport tube, which pre-empted radio and is simply a hollow rubber tube attached to your helmet headset. Instead of listening to her, I am looking at the bottom of these bridges she is now flying under. All of the sudden the nose of the plane goes up at a sharp angle, right after passing one bridge and heading for another. By the time we are approaching the next bridge, we are about three hundred feet altitude. This clears the oncoming bridge by about seventy-five feet, which was too damn close for comfort. I am finally able to calm down a bit and I concentrate on her very noisy voice. She was wondering why I did not give her some kind of hand signal that showed I understood what she was saying: I did not respond. We finally settled down and she allowed me, with "Gosport" instruction, to handle the plane. Of course when we landed back on the Allegheny River, it was just the reverse of the take off. At least I knew what to expect with landing between bridges and river traffic. When we taxied back to the dock, I was relieved, but I can say as a close witness, she was a great pilot. I took two more lessons and became much more adapted to "dodge a bridge" flying. She thought I showed good flight reaction qualities and told me I would get though the cadet program successfully.

After, we completed our stint at the University of Pittsburgh; we were sent to Nashville, Tennessee's classification center. This would prove to be the first real hurdle. You either classify for pilot training, navigator training or lastly bombardier training. You are tested for coordination, depth perception, and other physical and mental tests. If you do not qualify for any of the three aforementioned programs, you are released from the cadet program with assignments in some other air corps capacity. The final alternative is that you may be transferred to a different branch of the army, i.e. infantry, armored, artillery, etc.

We finished classification in Nashville. I was classified for pilot training. All cadets who were chosen for pilot training were eagerly awaiting shipping orders for primary flight school, the first step toward earning our wings. It required three stages of training, primary, basic and advance, all of which took about eight months to complete. I was assigned to Lodewick Flying School located in Lakeland, Florida, for primary training.

Before going further with the training, a word about the overall war situation is needed. For a while the decision to "flatten Germany industrial complex by heavy bombardment" was having a very heavy toll on the Eighth Air Force stationed in England to wage such a campaign. We were losing substantial numbers of aircraft and flight crews. In fact, to a large extent, it was these losses that encouraged the air corps to start the air cadet enlistment program that initially captured my attention. By the time I actually arrived at the first phase of pilot training, the situation started to reverse. Our bombers were getting "the upper hand" and the losses were becoming more sustainable. This improvement also had an affect on the pilot training program. Quite a few of the newer enlistees who had not yet started the flight training phase, were diverted to other branches of service in the ground forces. Our flying class named 44J was still scheduled to graduate in December 1944. Despite this, we always had the possibility of having the same thing happen to us.

With the above background on the status of our training and the war, let us return to the Lodewick Flying School for my primary flight training. You cannot imagine the thrill I had at seeing this line up of beautiful silver painted Stearman PT-17 Trainers. We were one of the last classes to fly this classic craft. It was a biplane covered with fabric and had two open cockpits just like that first flight that my brother and I took from the Spring Lake, New Jersey, golf course, when I was seven and Raymond was twelve years old. I was spellbound by the sight of these planes at the Lodewick Flying School, and the anticipation that I would be flying one of them...for no charge! From my point of view, at eighteen, at that time, war did not seem to be too bad a deal. I could hardly wait to start to fly. We were assigned to civilian instructors. Mine was an Alaskan bush pilot and as big and muscular as a moose roving the frozen tundra of Alaska. The instructor sits in the forward cockpit and the student in the rear cockpit. Most of the communication is done with the Gosport that is located in each of our helmets, just like the Pittsburgh Piper Cub seaplane. When this huge bush pilot got into that front cockpit, if he did not have his hands on the controls, he would have his rolled up shirt sleeves and monstrously hairy arms hanging out of both sides of his cockpit. If I was doing ok, that is where his arms stayed; if I did not see his arms, that meant, he was on the controls and "the Moose" would start to growl at me through the Gosport. One day after a total of about six hours of instruction we flew to an auxiliary field, which is used for practice landings and takeoffs without hindrance from the usual air traffic at the base. On this one occasion at the auxiliary field, he taxied the plane to a position where one would be ready for take off. He then gets out of the front seat and says, "she is all yours; give me three take offs and landings"!!! Do you have any idea what it is like, for the first time in your life, you have no one else in the plane, just you and the plane. The Stearmen aircraft is waiting for you to advance the throttle to the full open. Suddenly, the plane is rolling down the dirt runway. You had "the stick" pulled back like you were taught, toward your stomach, and as you pickup speed, you release some of the pressure on the stick by moving it forward slightly. This allows the tailskid of the plane located at the bottom and to the rear of the fuselage, to come up so that you are in a position to become airborne, and that is exactly what happens! The plane and Elliot are together, alone, in the air (anyone who "solo's" an airplane will rank this first solo flight as perhaps, the most dramatic and thrilling moment imaginable). But wait, we have to land this wonderful machine and it has to be done to the satisfaction of my instructor "the Moose". Fortunately, he taught me well. After the takeoff I circled the field to prepare for the landing. Your first landing is when it is determined if your skills are sufficient to go ahead with the program. By the time I was making my landing approach, the Stearmen aircraft and myself were becoming fast friends. I gave the Moose three take offs and landings and I got approval with a heavy slap on the back, after I got out of the plane at home base. He said I did well and should have no problem in successfully completing the primary flight-training phase. He was right. We flew and flew, and it was all a very satisfying feeling to know I was fully engaged in the process to achieve my youthful ambition to fly. To complete the course we had to complete several cross-country flights, which were done by dead reckoning navigation, as we did not have any sophisticated radio equipment. We also had to learn to fly in formation, and we had to successfully pass the ground school courses for navigation and meteorology.

I am not gong to detail the experiences in basic and advance segments other than to say the training was done with much more sophisticated aircraft and flight equipment. We were also taught to fly at night and to fly "on instruments" with advanced radio equipment. I thought the primary part of the overall course with its profound impression on me was important for the reader to understand my compassion for aviation. When January 1944 came along and I was awarded my wings as a multi engine pilot, I was sent to Laredo Texas for transitional training. Training was done in the well-known four-engine bomber called the Liberator, (technically referred to as the B-24). It was used in Europe as well as the Pacific area. The Liberator was part of the evolution of bombers made famous in World War Two. It followed the better-known, B-17 Flying Fortress but it served our country well.

When I completed my B-24 training, I was made a copilot. Even though I was a little over nineteen, I was disappointed that they did not make me the aircraft commander. (The Liberator had a crew of ten, and I suppose that would be a "stretch" for a nineteen year old to fly a four engine bomber and at the same time command a crew of ten). After we finished B-24 Transition training, we were further dispersed to different USA air bases where pools were set up with other pilots, awaiting orders sending them to some other base for final crew organizing. When the crew was put together, then we were ready to receive our overseas assignment orders. In my case, upon completion, of B-24 training in Laredo, Texas I was ordered to report to Lemore Air Base, just 40 miles south of Fresno, California, in the heart of the San Joaquin Valley. Here, again, "rumors were ripe". The year is late 1944. We were part of "The Bubble" of new pilots who finished transition training and were then sent to pilot pools like Lemore Air base and "sit there" until they figured out what to do with us. The personnel on the base heard the higher commands were actually working on a point system for leaving the service and rejoining civilian life. When the spring of 1945 rolled into view, the war was practically over and the rumors just mentioned became a reality. As for myself, I noticed there was very little flying taking place at the base. In view of this, I went, to base operations and offered my help in any way I could be useful. They were very surprised at my comparative high degree of interest and further they had difficulty understanding why I did not want to just sit around like everyone else, "waiting to get out of uniform". They accepted my offer and I was made a utility pilot. I did not know what a utility pilot was and I am not sure they knew as well. (Incidentally, as another example of the "topsy-turvy" period, my secondary duty was a lifeguard at the officers club). Anyway, there they were on the tarmac, about fifteen beautiful and shiny metal planes doing nothing but baking in the heat of the San Joaquin valley with no one flying them, that is, no one until I came along. For me it was a dream come true. Just about anytime I wanted, I could "wrap on" a parachute and take one of the planes up (my uniform worn for these flights was shorts and a T-shirt). As long as I stayed in the general area, I could fly to my hearts content! I would fly up to Sequoia National Park in the Sierra Nevada range and then over to Big Bear Lake. Then if I felt like it, I would fly westward over to the famous Coalinga oil fields, site of the famous tea pot dome oil scandal which took place during the "roaring twenties".

At the time, I was a foolish nineteen-year-old pilot, who loved to buzz anything, especially at very at low altitudes. Just south of Fresno, there is a highway 41, which ran straight south to Kingsburg (about 40 miles distance). This road was a straight as an arrow and the whole length of the road was normally deserted except for the occasional auto coming down the road going either toward Fresno of the other way to Kingsburg. This highway stretch mentioned, was too good to resist a "Buzz Job". I would cruise along about 1500 feet of altitude, always looking to spot a car speeding along the road. I would then get ahead of it, about four miles. The trick was to bring my plane down as far as I dared, which was usually about thirty or forty feet above the ground of this straight road. To help me, further, my prior observations showed no presence of telephone poles or wires anywhere along the road. You can understand this heightened my temptation. Hear I am heading my plane thirty or so feet above the ground flying straight toward my unsuspecting driver in the oncoming car. It would take a bit of time before the driver realized that he was speeding toward what seemed be an airplane flying directly toward him, and the plane appeared to be flying down on the highway. Of course, when I was sure he was sure that his eyes were not deceiving him, I would pull back on the stick and go into a fast and steady climb. While doing this I could look out of the cockpit and there was the usual skid mark and waving of fist from the dismounted and disgruntled driver.

It was around the springtime of 1945, that I receive a very surprising call from my father. You may recall, while I was going through my high school football activity, I was hopeful for securing an athletic scholarship. This was a key element of my teen strategy. In this regard, my coach was successful in dealing with Colgate as a definite possibility, but due to enlisting in the army air cadet program, I was forced to turn it down. Also recall, that I was not aware that my coach had additionally contacted the football office at West Point. (While I was not aware of the West Point contact, I always had a strong desire to enter the academy). One of my early hero's was Carl Hinkle, All American football player from Vanderbilt, who went on to West Point were he was an outstanding football and La Crosse player. He was also selected as the first captain of his class of 1942. First Captain is the highest cadet rank one can achieve. First captain includes the responsibility to lead the entire corps of cadets.

I was in California when I received my father's phone call and had no idea what the phone call was about. He went on to say, a letter arrived from Andy Gustafson, one of the senior football coaches under Col. Earl Blaik, the head coach at West Point. The letter was addressed to me and it advised that congressman Donald O'Toole, of the nineteenth congressional district in Brooklyn, had a vacancy for an appointment to West Point. I could not believe that now, after more than two years passed since receiving my high school diploma, this promising letter arrives. My father then reminded me of my wild and hectic days in high school and said, "Elliot are you sure you will devote yourself seriously to the task?" I said with the strongest confidence, "I most certainly will". After my father spoke to me, Louis R. Heit, the man that he was, rolled up his sleeves and began an episode that reminded me of the way "he went at it", when he was able to push me through the New York enlistment center and get me into the army air cadet program two years ago. In this case, he calls up the congressman and gets an appointment to see him, but at no time does he indicate his purpose is to get that opening to West Point. Instead, he begs the congressman to give him some kind of job in the district (with no pay). Dad worked nights and weekends and did such an outstanding job, that he was promoted to District Captain. Now, my father secures another appointment with O'Toole, and he shows him the letter from the Army football office. Congressman O'Toole advised, "Louis, don't worry, your son will get the appointment". Sure enough, a few weeks later I received a telegram from our war department, advising me that I have been accepted, but as the first alternate! I reread four of five times and it still said "the first alternate". Just to explain my disappointment, when a member of congress assigns one of his appointments to a perspective candidate, he designates one candidate as the principle. The second possible candidate for the principle appointment is called the first alternate. The first alternate is only accepted if the principal fails a test, or if the corps has extra vacancies due to some unanticipated situation arising. If you are first alternate, the odds of getting into West Point are very slim. As it stood, that was my situation. When I explained all this to my father, he became enraged. He rushed to the congressman's office, and as the Congressional District Captain, he demands to be seen. He tells Mr. O'Toole, if his son Elliot does not receive the principal appointment, Louis R. Heit will go down to the editor's office of the Brooklyn Eagle and he will tell everything he knows about the skullduggery going on in the congressman's district. Mr. O'Toole explains that will not be necessary, the war in Europe was over in May of 1945, and the person holding the principal spot resigned his appointment. Almost immediately, I was advised that Elliot Eclipse Heit is now the principal.

    I am closer but it is still a far distance off before I arrive at West Point. For me there are many things still left to be conquered. Remember, I have been out of school for over two years; my brain needed exercise in a big way. Fortunately, I was still in the service, and as a member of the service on active duty, I was eligible to under take a West Point course at one of several excellent colleges under contract with the war department. Thus, I am told to report to Amherst College, located in the heart of the Berkshire Mountains, in Massachusetts.

Chapter 3

Amherst College and West Point

I arrived at Amherst in September of 1945 to start my prep program. Amherst has an exceptionally fine academic reputation. (If I were a civilian with my high school record, I doubt they would have accepted me.) The faculty was impeccable and they were able to revive my brain waves. Altogether, the army prep group for West Point at Amherst totaled about one hundred persons. (It is interesting to note, on July 1, 1946 when our class entered West Point it had a starting strength of 1200, of which 38% were veterans of World War Two). We had pilots with rank up to major, and we had noncommissioned personnel down to the rank of private. Many of our class served overseas, and were engaged in battle. We were for the most part, all of the same enthusiasm and determination to succeed at the military academy. Life long friendships began at Amherst, such as mine with a fellow by the name of Jack Murphy. (We will hear more about Jack later on). We were all housed on campus in the Morrow Hall dormitory. My roommate, like myself, was a pilot. His name was John Maddox, the son of General Maddox, head of the Chemical Warfare Department of the United States Army. John, the son, is thereupon called an "army brat". John and I got along very well. Since we were both pilots, still considered to be on active duty, we were able to go over to nearby Westover Air base and get "checked out" flying B-25's, Billy Mitchell bombers (this was the type of bomber that was used in the bombing of Tokyo, Japan during World War Two). We both loved flying at Westover, where Johnny would take off in one B-25 and I in another B-25. We would then fly "in formation" at very low altitudes "buzzing" all over the Berkshire mountains of Massachusetts).

Socially, there are two topnotch girl schools near Amherst College. One was Smith College and the other was Mount Holyoke. To complete the scene we chipped in twenty-five dollars each and bought a 1931 Model "A" two-door sedan with no roof! It would appear we were well equipped to enjoy our free time. (If we were graded on this aspect of life at Amherst, we both would have received "straight A's"). As for the studies, they were not as bad as I anticipated. I remember in particular, our history professor, who was outstanding. He was in his seventies, and he actually participated in the Verdun Peace Conference held in Paris, France following the cessation of World War One. He was absolutely vivid.

We had a fairly broad curriculum that would prepare most of us for the all-important validating exam that was required for all those without college background. (I believe any one with two years of college credit was excused). It was about a six-month course including the validating exam. I amazed myself by passing it without much difficulty. I was now ready to become a member of the class of 1950, which began on July first, 1946.

After completing our stay at Amherst, we received an unexpected graduation present from the war department. All successful Amherst prep graduates were duly ordered to report to Fort Benning, Georgia to undergo a special six-week basic infantry-training course! Me, a pilot, in infantry training! Yes, indeed, I along with the other pilots, as well as the officers that were in the ground forces during World War Two, were on our way. It was an interesting experience and I am certain it did some good for all of us. We still had a couple of months left before reporting to West Point. Jack Murphy and I decided to resign from the service with this in mind. He invited me to join him at his parent's country farm in New Jersey that was fairly close to his home in Staten Island, New York. (Staten Island is another borough like Brooklyn, in that, along with the Bronx, Queens and Manhattan altogether comprise what New York City consists of) Here is a quick background on Jack Murphy. He graduated from La Salle Military School and was commissioned at the age of eighteen as a Second Lieutenant in the infantry. (He was one of the youngest infantry officers in the army). At La Salle he was also made First Captain, and as much, was the leader of all cadets attending La Salle. Jack was also scrapper athlete at his prep school. He played sports with a vengeance as though he was going to war. This included football, which gets back to the invitation extended to me to join him at the farm. At the time we were discussing the matter, he told me his folks will not be coming out to the farm until after we report to West Point. We would have the farm to ourselves to jog, eat, exercise and get in shape for football at West Point. I agreed it would be a great thing to do. Well everyday we ran four of five miles and did all the football prep work we could think of.

On July 1, 1946, we reported in at Weehawken, N.J., which is across the Hudson River from New York City, where a special train carried all of us new cadets to West Point railroad station to mark the beginning of a most unique experience. It was an exceptionally hot day in July, and of course, the train was quite old and not air-conditioned, but excitement was running high, especially, since no one knew what could be expected upon arrival that morning. The West Point train station was located at the very bottom of a long hill. We were then ordered to leave the train, line up in four columns and, start in the high heat of the day, a long agonizing walk with baggage up the hill to central barracks. Central barracks is where it all starts. Upper classmen, it seemed by the hundreds, attacked us will all kinds of commands.

"Drop you bags." "Hammer your chin in," "suck up your ponderous gut", and so on.

The first indication of entering a new world was confirmed by the fact, there would be no more walking; everywhere we went for the next six weeks was "on the double" i.e. running. We were issued uniforms and assigned to barracks, or as called, divisions. A physical was taken including a photo profile, in the nude, of our posture (the photo showed us what we looked like and how far away we were from where we have to get to.) Despite all the exercise Murphy and I did at the farm, neither of us held back on eating. I "weighed in" at two hundred and five pounds! This was nothing more that "fat bait" for the upper class men to "chew on". They ran me ragged, with real gusto particularly after they learned I was previously a flight officer in the army air corps (I got the message quickly and adapted). In two weeks, I went from two hundred and five pounds to one hundred and seventy six. My trousers had to be taken in at the waist three times. One of my classmates who stood behind me "in ranks" was amazed to see the two seams of the back pockets of my trousers were getting so close to each other, it appeared I had one twenty inch pocket across the entire back of my trousers! Fortunately, the football team had separate team tables in the massive dinning hall that seated the entire corps of cadets for each meal. Freshmen cadets called Plebes are allowed to eat at these training tables. This was a sacred privilege for plebes. First of all, Plebes at team tables eat "falling out", which means you do not sit on the edge of your chair, four inches from falling off; nor are you eating a square meal at attention with eyes down on your plate. When the bread plate comes your way at the regular company table where you are eating a square meal, you take only one slice and divide it into four parts. Each part is then chewed and swallowed before another piece of bread enters your mouth (this type of eating goes on for one year at the end of which you become a second year cadet called a yearling).

Can you imagine a fellow like me doing this? In high school I ate twelve pieces of bread with six hamburgers between the slices for lunch, and then I come to this! When I was finally ordered to report to the football team table and I went absolutely berserk. As soon as I was assigned to a table I got out of my chair at the team table, and ran over to our table's serving table. I was grabbing food by the handful off this serving table. (The serving table is where the waiters deposit the food and a cadet server starts the distribution to the team table of eight cadets). I was stuffing the food into my huge mouth like a starving savage. This was a total no-no! My actions caught the attention of all the other athletes and they were in convulsions of laughter. But I also caught the attention of the officer of the day, who always dined on the upper deck of the dining hall where he could observe that proper order was maintained. He heard all the laughter coming from the athletic section and he caught sight of me, a plebe cadet, ravaging the food off the serving table. I was immediately remanded back to what was known as my company table. Once again, I was eating meager meals with one slice of bread torn into four pieces, etc. I spent a week with this punishment and was allowed to return to the team table where I was a quiet little mouse (for a while).

In Beast Barracks as this initial six weeks inauguration was called, we were allowed only one shower all day which took place shortly after dinner (can you imaging 1200 cadets sweltering all day long in the intense July heat and then all of our "sweaty, sweet smelling bodies" together in the immense dining hall...talk about zoo odors, we would have won first place. A little more detail about the shower is in order. Mind you, from the first sweat of early morning until after dinner, taking a shower was comparable in mind to getting a first row seat to the latest Broadway hit musical show. In reality here is what happens. In your room you prepare to be properly attired. This means, you take all you clothes off and you put on a soldiers rubberized fabric raincoat. Next, you put onto your bare feet, rubber overshoes as normally worn during a rainy day. Then you take a hand towel, put three folds to it and carefully place it upon your left forearm, which is at a ninety-degree angle to your body. Finally, with your right hand, you pick up a soap dish and place it in you "palm up" left hand, (which you will recall your left forearm was already perpendicular to you body with the towel neatly folded over the forearm). You are now ready to march, at attention, down to the basement, where the shower room is located. Upon arrival, in the basement locker room adjacent to the shower room, you remove the raincoat, hang it up, replace the towel and the soap dish on your left arm and stand in front of your locker, nude. There are fifty or so, other cadets, shoulder to shoulder, in front of their lockers, also nude, except for the rubber overshoes. Since all the cadets are in one room, nude, and shoulder-to-shoulder, covering the entire inside perimeter of this room, all it takes is one cadet to smirk and then all of us looking across the room burst into uncontrollable laughter. This ignites the upperclassmen and "they work us over", but good. After the "work over" you then assume the best possible position of attention.

In describing my first "Beast Barracks" shower, an unforgettable incident comes to mind. Before West Point and prior to being called into active duty with the army air corps flight-training program, I had a few months of waiting for the call. To put the time to some use, I started a trigonometry course at Brooklyn Academy, which was primarily a private "prep" school for West Point. I had no idea at that time I would ever be going to West Point as my mind was focused on the impending army air corps cadet program. The classroom procedures were styled exactly like West Point in order to acclimate the "preppers". Each person was given a problem card and the answer has to be written on the blackboard. There was a character in our group named George Maloney. I do not know what possessed him to have this habit, but he would always start singing out loud as he worked at the blackboard. His one an only song was "That Old Black Magic". He would be severely admonished by the professor, but the very next day, he would go at it again with "That Old Black Magic." Anyway, I received my notice for call to active duty, and said goodbye to "That Old Black Magic" who incidentally was prepping for entry into to West Point July 1, 1943. (Because of the war, West Point shortened the normal four year class to three years and that would have meant George Maloney would have graduated in June of 1946 – three weeks short of my entry to West Point)

Three years later, standing nude in front of my locker, there I was with my eyes straight ahead, waiting my turn for the long awaited first shower at West Point. I cannot believe it but I hear someone singing, "That Old Black Magic". It sounded quite like George Maloney, but it could not be; he was supposed to have graduated in June of 1946; it was now July of 1946. Back to the locker room scene, the upper class men were walking along and inspecting the line up of plebes in front to their lockers. The singing upper class man comes by my locker and suddenly stops, looks me in the eye and commands

"You; step out," and in the nude I follow him out of the locker room into the hallway. He commands me to "fall out" (fall out means be at ease). Then he says to me "What the hell are you doing here?"

I replied, "You ask what am I doing here; what are you doing here? You were supposed to have already graduated." George, then explains he had trouble with his math courses and he had to repeat a year on academic probation (this was very unusual, but George was very impressive in all other respects and the academic board allowed him to become a member of the class of 1947, subject to all grades being acceptable.) George became a very good friend of mine during plebe year. In fact, being of the same physical dimension I gave him all of my previous officer uniforms, which saved him quite a bit of money, and yes he did graduate as a member of the class of 1947.

Back to the action in the locker room. You are sucking up your gut, sticking your puny chest out, hammering your head in so you have four or five wrinkles in your chin and you are waiting for one of the upperclassmen to check your "sweating". Usually, the biggest "sweaters" go first. (My trick was before leaving my room to swallow four or five glasses of water, do twenty pushups then put on that rubberized raincoat and I was set to sweat). There is another upper class men in the five-stall shower room who has a stopwatch. When this upper class men had five qualified "sweaters" lined up at each of the five showers, the upper class man yelled out, "when I say go, you have sixty second to turn on the water, soap and rinse, turn off the water and get out!"

After showering, you return to your locker, put on your raincoat, over the body, which still has a lot of soap that missed the rinse, towel over left forearm, soap dish "palm up" in left hand and report to yet another upper class man. This time, you salute, and while holding the salute you say, "Sir, new cadet Elliot Heit reports that he is properly showered, has had his feet inspected and powdered, has had his bowel movement for the day, and is ready for bed as ordered."

If you say this correctly he will salute you back and you return to your room. All lights are out at 9 Pm. Five-forty five rolls around like you had a five-minute nap. Up you go for yet another day of beast barracks, which will continue as said before for another six weeks.

About midway during the beast barracks "adjustment", all the football prospects in our class were given a "try out" to evaluate their ability to play "A" squad football. "A" squad would be the equivalent of varsity college athletes. A word is in order about Army's football team structure. At the time of my entering West Point, Army had about the most powerful and successful team in its history. It ranked as one of the top teams in the country. Any football follower, would immediately recognize names like the touchdown twins Glenn Davis and Doc Blanchard, and Danny Folberg, Ug Fuson, etc. ; Most of these were named All American and held that honor all during their playing years at West Point. Additionally, the head coach was Earl "Red" Blaik, a legend in the annals of coaching. His assistant coaches were also exceptional, coaches like Andy Gustafson who coached the star studded Army backfield. He was followed by Vince Lombardi, who went on to the National Football league and became the immortal coach of the Green Bay Packers. Also to be mentioned are Sid Gilman, a line coach, who went on as head coach for the Los Angeles Rams and finally, one of my own favorites, Herman Hickman, All American guard and All American wrestler from University of Tennessee who later on became head coach at Yale University. This was the football factory I was about to meet for my "try out". Keeping in mind, I was in the army air corps for three years before West Point, which meant, I had not felt a football since I left high school four years ago. Despite this and despite the fact that Murphy and myself spent two months on his farm to shape up for football at West Point, I was literally slaughtered by these enormous mountains of muscle, and skill. On the day of my slaughter, Herman Hickman, a two hundred and ninety pound, squat and solid muscle, cigar-chewing rebel from Tennessee, calls out my name and set me up for a drill they called "two on one". I am the "one" and Danny Folberg with Ug Fuson are the "two". Their combined, in shape, weight was close to five hundred pounds against number "one", me, at one hundred and eighty. It was all over in about three minutes. I knew exactly how a cookie felt when the dough was pressed into the mold. That is the way I was pressed into the soil of the football field. Herman, the line coach was kind when he looked down on my "cookie" form stretched out on the ground and in his poetic way said, "Heit, remember - he who hits and flits today, lives to hit and flit another day" (Herman Hickman, which it is hard to imagine was the poet laureate of football; extremely intelligent and a lover of classic literature. After that exercise, I pulled myself up and walked off the field with feelings of deep disappointment. I look back at that experience as one of my failures in life. With all the success I had with football in high school this was very difficult to accept. While there were two other football squads called "B" and "C" teams, I had no desire to show up at either one. I gave football up until the beginning of the following year.

1st Row: Murphy JM, Heit, Monfore, Armstrong, Tate, Hoffman, Boyle, Hartinger, Lay, Cox CJ, Hammond LH. *2nd Row:* Diile, Dunbar, Johnson RF, Pazderka, Gradoville, Hoffmaster, Bryant CE, Dickenson, Rust, Bell CH, Rowan (Assistant Coach). *3rd Row:* Gorski, McCoy, Miller WB, St. Mary, Stannard, Reed IB, Storck, Denman, Shibata, Bryant GW (Assistant Coach). *4th Row:* Winfield, Streaidorf, Rupp, McGann, Ballard, Nance, Trompeter, Hastings, Hartnett, Pfeiffer (Manager). *5th Row:* Nutting, Stues, Gordon, Latterloh, Hinds SR, Michel, Anderson RD, Weber RL.

RABBLE'S TOUGHEST OPPONENT

B SQUAD

Seven victories, one defeat. That's the 1948 record for the team that daily plays the toughest outfit in the nation.

I cannot recall how it happened, but I do know on a number of occasions quite a few people suggested I go out for the "B" team. I missed football a great deal more than I had imagined and I started to realize it is the "love of the game" and not the newspaper articles and the hero worship that one plays the game for. It was a great decision I made to join the "B" team. While our primary mission was to scrimmage against the "A" squad, we also had our own schedule, which included other junior varsities from many of the eastern colleges like the University of Pennsylvania, Boston College, Etc. For the two years I was co-captain with Jack Murphy we were undefeated. Our "B" squad players were similar to the French Foreign Legion in that we were a rogue group of athletes who for the most part would have made " varsity" on a college team that was not quite the caliber of excellence existing in the Army team of those days. Our "B" squad coach, Colonel Joel "Dopey" Stephens was an excellent coach. To begin with he was a fantastic total person. Besides being a good coach, his warmth and understanding earned the respect of all Army football. Many of the "B" players moved up to the "A" team, but they never forgot "Dopey". As an illustration of the memory he left with all of us, a class mate and myself established a memorial fund whereby annually we award a plaque to the outstanding "B" squad player. The plaque is properly inscribed in honor of the Joel B. Stephens memorial. The fund was over subscribed by "A" and "B" players and now has sufficient funds to make the award in perpetuity. (For the record, the nickname "Dopey" was given by his pre-West Point college coach Col. Stephens was a "back up" quarterback with a lot of time on the bench and not so much time playing on the field. Toward the end of one season, the coach felt sorry for him and sent him in to play. The first thing "Dopey" does, he changes the play to his own designed play. This play does not do too well and the coach is furious. He grabs one of the cheerleaders shouting horn and he blasts, "you dopey blankety blank blank, get out of that huddle and get back to the bench". The name stuck but believe it or not it is said in a very respectful way.) Speaking of the coach's nickname, I was also given the nickname "Stud" over sixty years ago and, it is still used by all who know me except for my family. It became my name at Amherst, Beast barracks and then football. I mentioned previously, the "B" squaders were sort of a rogue group. One of the rogues was myself and another classmate Joe McCrane. Joe had a scholarship to Notre Dame, but decided to accept a West Point appointment (he was a marine private and during World War Two, served in Guadalcanal). We met for the first time while scrimmaging against the "A" squad monsters. Joe was playing quarterback and I was playing right guard. The ball is snapped to Joe and immediately half the "A" team came though my position. Underneath at the very bottom of this nine hundred pound pileup, are Joe McCrane and Stud Heit (my forever nickname). Keep in mind Joe and I have not met yet, I hear this strained, by the weight of the pile up, voice yell out "who left the door open and let these guys in"? I replied, "I did".

He then asked, "what's your name?" and I replied "Stud", his reply "Hey Stud can you do a better job at keeping that door shut; I don't have enough room in my fridge for all this meat". The whole pileup broke out in laughter, which coach Blaik was not too happy about, but this is the way Joe and I met. From there on began a friendship that took the both of us through four hilarious years at West Point, and many, many more years after graduation, and as always, we were always referred to as "StudandJoe" (as though it was one name).

Once beast barracks was completed, we are sworn into the honor code system and this ceremony also coincides with "joining the corps". In other words you made it successfully though beast barracks and it is time to tackle the academics and the life being a plebe for another ten and a half months (A plebe is the equivalent of a freshman in college).

Now that Beast Barracks has been completed, the academic year lies ahead. This plus the continuance of strict discipline, for especially the plebes, will go on from September until June of the following year. At that time, the plebes become yearlings, or second year cadets and are entitled to some "privileges" (not much, but you would be surprised by the improvement a plebe feels with even the slightest retraction). Before we go forward with more of the plebe year and the other three years of West Point life, a few comments should be made about the overall training that a cadet receives. The impression I am about to describe is my own and not necessarily those of the higher command.

At any particular time in the history of the academy, which was founded in 1802, the discipline imposed upon the corps of cadets undergoes constant review and revision in an earnest effort to comply with the military needs of the time, and to maintain the corps belief of the academy, which is duty honor and country. It is often said by graduates of any recent year that, "things" were a lot tougher when they went through the grind. And so it is, that I compare plebe year now with what my class went through, sixty years ago, and I heartily agree with the prior graduates attitude. At the same time, I will say this much for the present mode of life at the academy; the discipline and restrictions appear less difficult to adjust to. However, I would hate to be exposed to "getting through" the difficult academic challenges cadets have to accomplish these days. The curriculum was much simpler in the old days. (The word "simpler" is a comparative.) Many of us frequently were forced to put a blanket over our desks inside our barracks rooms, and with the aid of a gooseneck lamp, study in our "academic tent" for the next days classes, after taps was sounded. With the modern military in step with heavy emphasis on world technology and the ever-growing requirement for world soldier - diplomats, it is amazing that the total West Point program continues to produce such appropriate and outstanding graduates. Having said this and keeping this in mind, my cadet experiences are not completely similar to the present cadet program, other than the graduating results.

    It has been my own observation that people not familiar with the objectivity of West Point presume that most of what goes on in plebe year is pure hazing. It is understandable how the outsider thinks this way but it is not an accurate appraisal. Everything I learned in Beast Barracks, and there after, had application to something we had to inculcate in the way we dealt with problems, whether they were academic or of leadership nature. For example, let us take a quick look at the academic approach. In my day and age, the method of dealing with the academic program was designed to make it possible for even a "goat" to make the grade. (A "goat" was a term to describe persons of less mental endowment, but still equipped with the determination to overcome difficulties and succeed.) Our classes were usually about fifteen cadets. Eventually, when you entered the classroom, you received a three by five card with a problem, but all problems were almost verbatim from the same chapter of the textbook we were previously assigned to study. The teacher would then command, "Take boards". Everyone would go up to the blackboard, and with chalk write the answer to their problem on the board. You are allowed a certain amount of time and then commanded to "replace your chalk if you have not already done so." Each cadet takes a turn to describe their problem and explains his answer to the other cadets in the class. The teacher in charge grades each cadet <u>each day</u>, for their appearance, ability to analyze the problem, and properly and correctly recite his answer using a pointer at the blackboard. Now, the key that helps the goat get through his studies is two fold. First and foremost, was the system of assigning one chapter at a time. A cadet, in preparation could memorize important portions of the chapter and in most cases his three by five problem card would almost be a direct quote from the textbook. This is why "goats" usually spent lots of time in their quarters after taps under blanketed desks with the gooseneck lamp, memorizing important portions of the assigned chapter. The other factor that saved many goats is the daily grading system. Grades are then posted weekly in the archways where our quarters were located. If you needed help to bring up your score, you could get it from your roommate or seek help from the subject department, which can organize cadet tutors for assistance.

In my case I had two fantastic roommates, Burke Whitehurst Lee from Florida and Andy Jo Beyers from Texas. They were youngsters when they entered; my age of twenty-one sort of gave me a fatherly image. (If I were them I would not care too much for the roommate with the fatherly image). But despite my un-fatherly manner they were two very fine young men and we got along so well, that instead of changing room mates each year, we stayed together right though graduation. Both were much more academically in tune than me. So losing them was out of the question. In fact, I often used to say, I should have torn up my diploma in three parts and I would keep the smallest part for myself.

Every Sunday, it was compulsory to attend church services. The Jewish chapel squad was without their own chapel, so we used a memorial chapel in the West Point cemetery. (Some years later, a very substantial temple was erected mostly by private donations). While I did attend the Jewish services, my camaraderie with many Irish Catholic cadets also lead to a friendship with the then, Monsignor Moore, head of the West Point diocese under the jurisdiction of the Bishop. Whenever I had something that concerned me, I would find time to meet with Monsignor Moore for his advice. One situation, which is still very clear in my mind, was my constant dating of non-Jewish girls. While I never gave it any thought, it always came up when my parents came up to visit. The Monsignor would lecture me "Stud, do not give your marriage more difficulties than you need. The best chance for a happy marriage and, the wisest thing you can do is to marry in your own faith." While I continued to date non-Jewish girls, I did meet a Jewish girl about two months before graduation. We had four dates, got engaged, and then inaugurated our marriage with two hundred persons attending at the Ritz Carlton Hotel, in New York City. Aside from my immediate family, the only ones I knew well were my stand up wedding squad and West Point classmates, i.e. Jack Murphy, Joe McCrane, Gerry Kelly and one protestant, Richard Greenleaf Trefry the Third. An interesting postscript to this marriage was the bride went to high school with the brother of my close friend, Joe McCrane. It was Joe's mother, fearing "Stud's wayward social behavior", would lead to Joe getting serious with a non-Catholic. As for my marriage, it was an interesting challenge, but I always thought I was fairly easy to get along with, so I did not anticipate any difficulties. Besides which, I pleased my parents and kept the good friendship of Monsignor Moore of the West Point Catholic chapel. (There will be more about "my first" marriage a little bit further on).

One of the most impressive West Point traditions for me was marching on the plain. (The plain is like a huge carefully nurtured lawn, with a reviewing area and grandstand for VIP visitors.) What makes marching so unique, is the West Point army band lead by its magnificent sergeant major. When, they start their marching music, the blood in your veins takes an extra lap. I don't believe there is a marching cadet who does not feel the stir right down to the back edge of his heel as it comes down hard on the solid earth, with each step made on the plain. All of us are totally in step with what I always considered to be the best damn marching music in America. It is everything coming together; the excellently performed marches, the cross belts with the brass plates, our distinctive head dress, the glistening shined shoes, and with out a question, the perfect alignment of our marching regiments.

As a plebe our, daily schedule begins to become habit except for the fact that we do not leave the grounds of the academy for Christmas, weekends, Easter, etc. The only time away from West Point during all of plebe year is confined to special occasions when we march in certain New York City parades or the Army Navy game in Philadelphia. Even in those cases, we are only allowed a few hours of freedom before we regroup for the return to West Point. Additionally, anyone on an intercollegiate team can travel and catch a bit more of a break than the less fortunate. This was true with my "B" squad football experience. We always have two or three games away with other colleges (and always won).

All plebes must remain at the academy Christmas week but it is not so bad. The plebes are the only cadets on the grounds of the academy as all other cadets are allowed to be away. A temporary plebe cadet chain of command takes over, and we had several planned activities such as, the hops (dances with live music and all cadets attending in full dress uniforms.)

Besides Christmas it was a challenge to fill in Saturday nights. Believe it or not Joe McCrane and myself went to the gym Saturday nights and spend most of the time vigorously boxing each other with the gloves on in the ring! Vigorously was a kind word: we went at it pretty good. When it was over, it was our mutual opinion that it was a good way to spend Saturday nights during plebe year. The secret to success is, you had to be creative with any scarce free time you had and, you had to make sure whatever you did, did not create an honor violation. It is my opinion, having said this; the architects of the honor code deliberately left a sliver of freedom from violation for those cadets composed of an adventurous nature. The core of this sliver, starts with a "button board". A button board for each cadet is located in our quarters. If three cadets live in the room, each one has a button board that stands in a conspicuous spot. The board has all locations clearly identified and separately listed in a column. There is a button that slides up and down the column on a string next to the vertical list. i.e. library, gym, boodle shop, chapel, etc. When you leave the room you "mark" your board to where you are going. This allows the TAC officer of your company to do impromptu room checks. Anybody not present in the room must mark his card with where he is. If he is not where he marked his card, he is in violation of the honor code and is subject to dismissal from West Point. However, there is one line on the board that has no destination described. If you put your button on that line, and there is no impromptu inspection, theoretically, you could go to the moon and back, as long as you are back before reveille! One example of unmarked card mischief, for Joe McCrane and myself, was our decision to build a log cabin up in "the woody" hills about a half of a mile back from the football stadium. I cannot recall where we got the two axes (I believe it was from our janitors, who we were friendly with us. They were technically referred to as barracks police). We chopped the heck out of the trees and we were making progress with the cabin, but as the plebe year wore on, our enthusiasm waned. Despite this, it did "chew up a lot of energy and kept us busy".

Another episode and a lot more interesting than what Joe and I did, was a true story about a "brainy" cadet who spend hours at a time in the West Point library studying the maps that were drawn many years ago of the sewer system servicing the grounds of the academy. After he completed with the care his detailed examination of these sewer plans, he would use the system for some practical jokes played on cadets who had to "walk off" tours as punishment for misdeeds of one sort or another. The "walk off" always took place in the central barracks area. The cadets had to walk back and forth, with a rifle, white gloves and dress coat across the barracks area; do an about face and walk back again. These "walk off" tours would last a couple of hours or more depending on the infraction. The Mole, as he called himself, would enter the sewer system from a point outside the punishment area then proceed underground to that area running beneath central barracks where theses punished cadets were marching back and forth. The Mole would then position himself under a manhole or grating that was exactly beneath where a cadet was marching off his punishment. He would "bark" out in a loud voice from inside the sewer, "All right dumb smack lets see a better effort in your marching cadence and straighten up; put some effort into your step". The cadet with a shocked reaction would look out of the corners of his eyes to see where these barking orders were coming from, never realizing they were coming up from the mole in the sewer! Whenever the Mole entered his sewer system, his button on the honor code chart was always in the unmarked position (miraculously his was never absent from his room during an inspection). In fact he wrote a letter to the commandant of cadets a few years after graduation confessing to all the sins of the Mole.

When plebe year comes to an end, there is an impressive tradition. All the upper classmen "troop" the line of cadets in each company, and shake the hand of each plebe cadet. This is the signal that the plebe is "recognized" and can fallout. He is now officially a yearling (a second year man or equivalent to a sophomore college). We then had a month off! We could go anywhere we wanted. I took advantage of signing up for a job as a counselor at a boy's camp. It was a poor decision that lasted only two weeks and I quit. Joe McCrane then invited me to his family's bungalow on the beach of Bay Head, New Jersey. His family allowed us to have the bungalow to ourselves and we had a great time. I left Joe a little early so I could spend some time with my folks before returning to West Point for the second month of the summer. This was spent at Camp Buckner, a part of the huge landmass belonging to West Point. It was here that we had a mix of military training and some further relaxation with all kind of summer sports. Also during the month at Buckner, all football players had to report for daily practice and we went at it pretty hard. By the time we arrived back at our regular quarters, we were in football shape and ready for another year of academics.

Reveille was, as always, five forty five with the drum and bugle corps "doing their thing" in the loudest manner possible. (This goes on every day for four years). Classes began at eight AM. At three PM and until five PM, football players reported for practice. (In the fall late practice under the lights was not unusual). The practice field was adjacent to the marching plain and has a rather deep drainage ditch all around the field perimeter. I mention this detail, as once in a while during an occasional slow day Jack Murphy and I would "hit the ditch" and bury our selves in the autumn leaves. After a brief respite, we would reappear and continue with practice. There were a few times, our "B" squad coach would yell out "Anybody seen Stud and Jack, I swear I saw them only a few moments ago?"

As a "B" squad player, out primary mission was to scrimmage against the "A" team. (We additionally had our own play schedule with other junior varsity colleges such as Boston College, University of Pennsylvania, Plattsburgh, etc.) Occasionally we played against varsity teams of small colleges. Whenever we scrimmaged against our "A" team, we had to use the plays of the team Army was going to play that upcoming Saturday. This drill included wearing the enemy colors, be it Notre Dame, Michigan, Penn State etc. As mentioned before we were the rogue team of sport at the academy. To add to our "roguishness", all our equipment, such as shoulder pads, hip pads, pants, jerseys, 'T' shirts, athletic supporters were leftovers, used for many years. Our helmets were beat up leather instead of the modern plastic ones (none of our helmets ever had a nose/face guard. Our cleats were the worst of all. The shoes were worn our so badly, the middle of the sole between the front and the rear cleats touched the ground. Despite all this, we loved the game and all of us were deeply attached to our coach, Col. Joel "Dopey" Stephens. We were "his boys" and he coached us very well. With our own schedule we were undefeated for two years.

One year comes to mind. We were playing the varsity team of a small town college in Plattsburgh, New York, (way up in New York State, near the Canadian boarder). Our reputation of being the West Point monsters preceded us. Believe it or not, we were still graciously received and the team hosted us for dinner in a somewhat grubby tavern. When the opposing team ordered a second round of beers, their strategy suddenly dawned on us. They figured, sheltered West Point cadets who were not allowed to go out, even for an occasional beer would be perfect targets for a few "extra" beers the night before the game. The only thing wrong with their strategy was the fact that thirty eight percent in our class were World War Two veterans, who easily could handle a couple of beers. For the most part, they were relatively children, still "wet behind the ears". The Saturday game was a slaughter and, " a lopsided" victory for Army. Some of the Plattsburg team played with hangovers and some were just plain out of shape. We, the rogue team, took it all in stride, thanked them for their hospitality, and went on our way back to our "rock bound highland home" with yet another victory.

When football season was over it was time to start planning in detail our first Christmas holiday week. Actually, we began strategic discussions for Christmas while we were up at Camp Buckner in August. Planning time away from West Point has an energy all of its own. Cadets will cover every minutia of detail and more, to be included in the trip. From our point of view the planning stage is almost as much fun as being away (not really). Our target for Christmas, 1947, was Lake Placid, New York, 280 Miles and 11 inches, from New York City (the 11 inches is because we love detail). Joe McCrane's father was a Dodge/Plymouth dealer from Teaneck New Jersey and he had a 1940 Dodge Business Coupe we could borrow for our expedition. Do you remember what a business coupe was? It had two seats in the front and a shelf in the back to hold the drivers business papers. Our crew consisted of Joe McCrane, the driver, Gerry

Kelley, Jack Murphy, one other non-Irishman, Bob Willerford and myself. We were all athletically built guys, and two of this load had to lie curled up on the back shelf, plus three husky fellows on the two front seats. Complicating matters was the manual stick shift, which came up about two feet from the middle of the front floor, making it almost impossible to shift, and poking the extra person on the front seat each time the driver shifted. About seven hours later, five terribly tired West Point cadets arrived at the Mount Marcy Hotel in downtown Lake Placid. We finally managed to get out of the car and tried to stand up but the long squeezed ride did some temporary damage to our cadet posture. At check in, the manager could not do enough for us. The hotel was on a small hill and our two rooms were lakeside rooms about two blocks from Lake Placid. Our view from the third floor was perfect. We were all looking out on the beautiful but frozen lake, when I spotted a piper cub airplane on skis tied up on the lake and near to the hotel. Additionally, while we where waiting for our room assignment at reception, we picked up some of the usual flyers promoting "things to do" and noticed we could rent a dog sled. Putting this together with the ski plane sounded like a great way to get the next day started. In the mean time Gerry Kelley suggested we secure a supply of beer, which we did almost immediately. Gerry also said he wanted to buy a "growler". I never heard of such a thing, but he described it as a container that we could pour our beer into, and the growler could then accompany us wherever we went. Everyone agreed we should have a growler. We bought something similar to what Gerry had in mind, and at the same time, made arrangements for me to get checked our in the Piper ski plane to be used the next day. Lastly arrangements were make to charter the dog sled. The proprietor of the dog sled asked if we had noticed there was no snow on the street! Our quick reply was we intended to use it on the frozen lake and somehow we would manage the short distance to the lake without the aid of snow. (By the way, although there was not much snow around Lake Placid, it was bitter cold). All arrangements having been made, we returned to our rooms and stored the beer cans between the storm window and the regular windows. It was an excellent means of refrigeration, but it has a significant effect on the lighting of the room. (We took care of that problem each time we filled the growler).

That night for dinner we took the growler into this very quaint and attractive dinning room. The matre'd was advised of our reservation, and had a round table for five nicely set in the middle of the dinning room, with a table cloth and a centerpiece of flowers. We asked the waiter for our table, if it were possible to remove the flowers and replace it with the growler. He was nice enough to check this with the higher authority and permission was granted. After dinner we were showing signs of fatigue from the Dodge business coupe therefore we chose to go to bed early in preparation for tomorrow and our active day on the lake.

The following morning we were dressed in cadet cavalry trousers and warmly outfitted with sweaters, jackets, gloves and ski caps. After breakfast, we picked up the dog sled appropriately pulled by eight huskies. But with Joe McCrane sitting in the sled and me handling "the mushing", the dogs could not budge the sled on the "no snow" street. Joe removed himself and I kept off the runners, which allowed the dogs to proceed to the frozen Lake Placid. Once on the lake, Joe resumed his position on the sled and I did the same on the runners. The rest of the crew followed us to where the ski plane was tied up. The Piper Cub seats the pilot and one passenger in tandem. For those of you not up to date with aviation history, the cub is like a kite with a motor and propeller. The plane is covered with fabric and the fuselage is barely wide enough to accommodate a normal person. Our hulks were further encumbered with the heavy clothing worn, (we could have used a giant shoe horn for "loading up"). Our plan was for me to take up each one of the expedition for a ride around the area surrounding Lake Placid. Keep in mind; it was bitter cold and no cabin heat other than a contraption that ineffectively transferred some heat from the air-cooled engine. The plane's owner spent about fifteen minutes cranking the propeller by hand. Suddenly, after a few engine "coughs", it catches on and after warming the engine up, Jack Murphy and I taxi out for take off. (I never flew off skis, but none of the passengers ever asked me). Skis are not like wheels, that is, there are no brakes. This means all stopping procedures have to be lengthened considerably to take this into account. Be that as it may, we "put the coal" to the sixty-five-horse power engine and in a fairly short run, we are airborne. Lake Placid is located in the Northern end of the Allegheny Mountains, the scenery beneath us, was magnificent with the miles and miles of pine forest dotted with other lakes similar to Lake Placid. We returned to our lake and landed uneventfully. I taxi back for the next passenger and this goes on until Joe McCrane is the only one left. I was returning with Bob Willerford, from his flight with me, when I see below on the lake there is someone in the middle of the lake with a dogsled and the "musher" is flagging me frantically. I cannot figure out the problem, but I put the cub down on the ice near the dog sled. As I taxi up to the scene, I see it is Joe McCrane. I open the door flap and yelled, "What in God's name is going on?" His ridiculous reply was, he was pretending he was awaiting "the serum" I was supposed to have for his fictitious sick friend in some remote cabin somewhere! What a mind Joe had (wait until later on in the book, it gets much worse). Bob Willerford gets out, Joe gets in and I take "the serum" deliverer on his tour of the area.

The next day we rented a toboggan big enough for all five of us and instead of us using it on the toboggan run, we went up to the ski area where they had enough snow left from previous storms to keep them open. Toboggans are okay on runs set aside for them, because the rums are designed to accommodate the fact that you cannot steer a toboggan. Never the less, there we were the five of us plus the growler on the toboggan, and we got moving at a pretty good clip and, straight as an arrow down one of the advanced ski slopes. Fortunately, the slope was straight and not too crowded with the five of us rattling down the hill. Furthermore, we were able to yell out sufficiently in advance to clear the way, and avoid disaster.

When at last we returned to the hotel, we got the definite impression that the hotel staff and guests were not all together pleased with our bizarre sporting events. The finger pointing and huddled conversations were sufficient for us to realize the hotel removed the welcome mat. We packed up and left early the next morning. A hint that our leaving suited the management was they did not penalize us for leaving two days before the guarantee for the rooms were up. It was just as well that we left, no sooner were we on the road heading for New York City, than a blizzard took place. Getting out of those mountains and back to the city was quite a chore especially with the sardine can Dodge two seater.

During our years at the academy, there were many other situations like Lake Placid, they all had similarities. Especially for the requirement that some type of soft adventure was in the plan to "hype" things up a bit. A typical story was the occasion of President Harry Truman's inauguration parade in 1948 following Truman's successful campaign against Alf Landon. The Corps of Cadets were ordered to proceed to Washington by special train direct from West Point. We were in full dress uniforms and I am not sure of the time we departed for Washington but it had to be in the wee hours of the morning, because we arrived at the Washington rail center around eight o'clock in the morning (the rail center or yard is not the same as the railroad station. It is where trains get hooked up prior to assignment and was located about six or seven miles from downtown D.C.) We had until 11 AM to wait for the busses that would bring us to the starting point for the parade. The reason for supplying this detail is because Joe McCrane and myself were starving, and we knew to serve breakfast on the train full of cadets would take a lot of waiting and would not be the kind of food to satisfy us. We figured we had about two and a half hours with a thirty-minute "cushion" to jump off the train, hail a cab, have a hearty breakfast at some "spiffy" hotel and get back in time to "form up" for the busses to take us to the inauguration parade. The taxi took us to the Mayflower Hotel, which at the time met our requirements for spiffiness. They were serving breakfast in this very ornate dining room. We cornered the matre'd, explained our plight, including the inaugural parade and our hunger. It worked; we had two waiters attending our famished needs. Decked in full dress and with our parade hats, we entered the dining room and gained recognition from all the other breakfast guests. We receive splendid service with a monstrous breakfast of large orange juice, sirloin steak, eggs, potatoes and coffee. The bill was seventy dollars plus tip. This was 1948! We gobbled everything there was on the table, paid the bill, grabbed our parade hats, and we were out of there in less than thirty minutes. The matre'd had the doorman holding a cab for us and back to the rail yard we went at break neck speed. We found our train and our car; got on board, let out a burp, and rejoined the flock with a satisfied smile on our faces.

A word should be mentioned about the way West Point has been brought to the attention of the reader of this book by me. Perhaps I over emphasize some of our frivolous conduct. Most everything we did was done to lighten the burden a bit here and there for ourselves, and those many other cadets who got to know us. This kind of conduct was "built in" with people like Joe McCrane and myself. I guess in both of our cases it traces back before we entered the academy when we experienced prematurely, a number of unexpected situations in our service during World War Two. We found our natural sense of humor gave us the edge in most cases, and was also contagious with others, in their respective units who got to know us. At West Point, Joe and I, fully accepted the challenge of Beast Barracks and the academics, and we successfully emerged from it all. In thinking back to all the hard work involved, we both felt blessed that our sense of humor was of immense help to us. We truly were the clowns of the class. We were constantly putting on "skits" of one sort or another. A quorum for us could be as small as a couple of cadets. During the years following plebe year, quite often a cadet company would hold a dinner for their classmate's parents and friends at the Thayer Hotel, located on the academy grounds. There were many occasions where Joe and I were invited to attend these functions on the condition that we would perform. One of the popular performances they liked, was the singing of World War One songs such as, "Keep Your Head Down Fritzi Boy" and "A Rose That Grows In No Mans Land", etc. We were able to borrow two World War One campaign hats from the West Point museum for costumes, and on we went. With all our pranks and comedy, it was never done to be critical of West Point. Joe and I always felt deeply honored just to be the smallest part of this great institution.

In our junior year or as Second Class men, there were some noticeable changes taking place. For one thing, the dialectic society, which originated at West Point in 1824, gave me the directorship for producing the 100th Nite Show for our graduating year. I insisted Joe McCrane join me as co-director, which was agreed to. (In fact, for the 100th Nite production itself, we added our "mafia" Gerry Kelley, Richard Trefry, and the class humorist Bob Peltz)

Let me explain about the 100th Nite tradition. West Point in the winter season from November until February is literally draped in the gloom of winter weather. Snow and rain pounding on the gray masonry is so depressing, they labeled November through February, Gloom period. By the time February rolls around a little twinkle of sunshine starts to climb up the barrack walls of the gray buildings facing east and we all suddenly realize there are only 100 days until graduation for first class men. To celebrate the end of the Gloom Period the graduating class must put together a 100th Nite Show, to which the whole corps attends.

As a preliminary "warm up", for our show in 1950, the class of 1949 was already casting for their 100th Nite Show and they made an exceptional request to have me, a member of the 1950 class, sing an original piece of music written for their show by Sammy Kahn, a very famous lyricist for many hit Broadway shows and personally for Frank Sinatra as well. He came up from New York City, and auditioned me. I passed and sang the song for 1949's 100th Nite Show.

At the time this is going on, Jack Murphy left the "B" squad rogue team and started his climb to become the first captain of our class and the leader of the entire corps of cadets. Handsome, articulate, a natural born leader without a flicker of fear, he was a magnificent example of what West Point is all about. (Incidentally, he stayed on playing lacrosse and earned his varsity "A" letter). We missed him on the "B" squad football, but the team carried on admirably for my last season of football ever.

Through my participation in army athletics, I met so many wonderful people on and off the gridiron. One of the standout personalities was Marty Mahr. He came over to the United States as an immigrant from Ireland, just before our country entered World War One, and had an Irish brogue as thick as can be. He had difficulty finding employment, but managed to enlist in the U.S. Army. When the war was over he remained in service and ended up at West Point as part of the army cadre that is assigned to the academy for maintenance duties. He happened to get involved with assisting the boxing instructor. Ultimately, Marty became the boxing instructor as an enlisted soldier and not only does a spectacular job at it, but he won the hearts of just about every cadet, who had no choice but to learn how to box from him at West Point. When I met him in 1948, he

The Dialectic Society

OF THE
UNITED STATES CORPS OF CADETS

PRESENTS

"All's Well That Ends"

THE FIFTY-FOURTH ANNUAL

Hundredth Night Show

Co-Directors
ELLIOT HEIT and JOSEPH McCRANE

Board of Directors
HEIT, McCRANE, PELTZ, and CROWE

Creative Directors
HEIT, McCRANE, PELTZ, TREFRY, KELLEY

Friday and Saturday, March 10th and 11th, 1950

POST THEATRE

TO THE HUNDREDTH NIGHT SHOW..
WITH ALL GOOD WISHES FROM THE BUMSTEADS AND

CHIC YOUNG

One of West Point's cherished traditions

JOE . . .

. . . STUD

The Co-Directors for the fifty-fourth year of West Point's
Hundredth Nigh Show

was already retired and because of his outstanding performance as the boxing instructor at West Point for so many years, they allowed him to keep his quarters for an extended period of time. When I met him, he was on in years, but he had a certain magic image and he was such a living legend at the academy; I felt privileged to make his acquaintance. Whenever I could spare the time, I would walk by his tiny house and invariably he would be rocking away on the porch dressed in his West Point Athletic sweater and puffing on an oversized calabash pipe. His brogue was still as thick as the trunk of the large maple tree on his front lawn, but I could understand him very well. The accent was a part of Marty Mahr that made him the unforgettable character he was. (Warner Brothers, were so impressed with his story they made a feature film staring Tyrone Power as Marty and Maureen O'Hara as his wife)

On January 20, 1950 my father wrote a letter to me. A pertinent part is quoted to the reader, "Note the 1950 underlined on the date of this letter. This is your year. All the glory, all the fame, that follows with your four year stint at West Point is yours and it was really and truly a great accomplishment indeed." I say amen. It was hard to believe, that on June 5, 1950, I would finally receive my diploma. By that time I was already engaged to Joan Engelhardt, and the wedding was scheduled for July ninth. The Academy granted me permission to rejoin the Air Force and I would report toward the end of July to Randolph Air Force base, the historic home of the air corps, in San Antonio, Texas. There I would undertake a pilot training refresher course.

With my marriage, the honeymoon, and travel to Texas, the schedule was very busy. Having said this about my schedule, I have to describe to you one other anecdote, which was the final sequel to life at West Point with Joe McCrane. At some time prior to setting the wedding date, Joe and I were still eating our meals at the team table. In so doing we developed a friendship with the waiter who brought the food from the kitchen to the serving table set up for each team table. This particular waiter always got a "big kick" from our antics that usually took place at breakfast everyday. One day we asked the waiter to join in the fun. Joe and I would pretend he was our own private waiter. We taught him how to fold a small face towel over one arm and come from the kitchen to where we were seated with a small tray that held our juice and a jug of coffee. We renamed him "Jeeves" and Jeeves would serve us in this grand style. He would also describe the menu for the meal. Of course, all our tablemates enjoyed the wake up humor with gusto. He did this without any suggestion or pressure. He, himself thoroughly enjoyed our cavorting. He was so good at what he did that Joe and I asked him if he could get some time off immediately following graduation. We further explained that if he could, we would invite him to be our chauffeur and cook for the ten days down at Joe's beachfront cottage in Bayhead, New Jersey. We also told him that we would pay for his services. I thought he was going to jump out of his shoes with the overwhelming desire he had to accept this offer. Unfortunately, my wedding and honeymoon interfered. (Joe never forgave me for that.)

Chapter 4

Post West Point and Return to Flying

One very unfortunate event took place on June 25, 1950, just twenty days after graduation. This particular date affected our class more than any other graduating class. The academy starting with our class significantly changed the postgraduate training procedures. Normally, upon graduation, you are sent to branch school for troop leadership training. During this six months course of intensive reality, it is not longer theory; the graduate receives had core platoon combat training in tactics used by his particular branch whether it is infantry, tanks, artillery, engineers, etc. In the case of our class of 1950, the military, who had no idea we would be at war, and long before June 25, decided to send graduates directly to troop assignments as platoon leaders instead of branch training. The theory, apparently was to give our class actual leadership assignments for a short period, then with more objectivity, bring them back for more formal training. As a result, many of our class received their chosen assignments to places like the far eastern command and Fort Lewis in our state of Washington. When the war started all these men were called back from their honeymoons, and were sent directly to their assigned units. These units were then placed immediately into battle positions in Korea. Twenty-eight members of the class were killed during the Korean War. These untimely deaths and the rest that served in Korea, distinguished themselves as uniquely worthy graduates of what West Point is all about; "Duty, Honor and Country", (the former Look Magazine had an extensive feature article called "The Tragedy of the West Point Class of 1950").

Jack Murphy was no exception. As the leader of our class he proved to be outstanding in battle and won the Distinguished Service Cross among others for his courage and bravery. Before he left the states for Korea, Jack must have recently seen John

Wayne in a World War Two movie. At one point in the earliest phase of the Korean conflict Murphy's unit was surrounded and an enemy group attacked him, personally. Jack bayonets two, then picks up a machine gun and fires from his hip. The attack is repelled and the next morning, they counted twenty-two dead enemy soldiers. His service in Korea was also brought to the attention of the President of Korea and every year after the armistice was signed, Jack was personally invited by the President to come to Korea to celebrate the occasion.

As for myself, I was in the midst of my refresher training, with another member of my class, Russ Leggett, who also was a pilot in World War Two. While we knew each other quite well at the academy, and before that at Amherst prep course, we really did not become "buddies" until the pilot refresher program. At West Point he was a "starman" which means a B plus academic grade average for all four years. Extremely intelligent, although somewhat reticent, we early on decided to stay together after we both selected multiengine training at Lubbock, Texas rather than single engine. Our wives got alone especially well and it made life in the non-metropolitan town of Lubbock, up in the northern hunk of the Texas panhandle very easy to take.

B-25 Billy Mitchell Bombers, which I formerly flew at Westover air base during the Amherst prep period, was our advanced trainer. This made my Lubbock training a "walk in the woods". It was during our time at Lubbock, Russ and I were told, because of our prior pilot experience, we could have our choice of assignment! We decided to stay together for that choice and we asked for assignment to a B-26 outfit that would be preparing for action in Korea. The B-26 is a much more sophisticated and more recently produced bomber than the B-25 Billy Mitchell trainer. Our entire refresher course was only six weeks, so there was still plenty of war going on in Korea when we completed it. Further more, we knew our Korea forces were making good use of the B-26 for interdiction attacks. (Low level strafing and bombing of enemy positions). Russ and I shook hands on this and our wishes were made known, and approved. The B-26 was a fantastic light bomber. Originally built for service toward the end of World War Two. They did not get much combat service before the war ended. After the war, some were "moth balled', some assigned to National Guard units, and some assigned to regular air force units. When Korea happened, these planes were "plugged in" immediately. Russ and I were assigned to the 85th bombardment group based in Langley Field, Virginia. Off we went to Langley and our new residence in near by Newport News. Russ and I were immediately assigned to transitional training. There was only one pilot in these planes, which meant the transitional phase of learning to fly with an instructor was skipped; after a short course in ground training, you took the B-26 up for your first flight solo. What a beautiful craft to fly. Two huge propeller driven engines that if I recall correctly, had over two thousand horsepower each! It could easily do close to three hundred miles per hour; it would take those B-25's we were flying during our refresher course in Lubbock, Texas and make them look like the Wright Brothers at Kitty Hawk. We practiced day and night and this included strafing runs with our fix-mounted machine guns, skip bombing on the water, and a host of other combat maneuvers. Russ and I were like two kids that were locked up in a candy shop; we loved every minute of it. All of a sudden, our training comes to a complete stop and the planes are removed from Langley Field for assignment elsewhere! We could not believe this was happening. It took a couple of days before the announcement was made that the 85th bombardment group was chosen for a top-secret mission involving the atomic bomb!!

This turn of events has a major affect on my military career. You will recollect, that we received a choice of assignment when we completed our pilot training refresher course in Lubbock, Texas. We chose to be assigned to a B-26 unit following completion of that course. Russ and I knew the B-26 had only one-pilot instead of the normal complement of two pilots, where one is the commander and the other is a copilot. By being an aircraft commander, there is a distinct advantage for quick recognition and promotion. Additionally, we were very fond of the B-26 as a formidable weapon to go to war with. When the secret mission was announced at Langley field, simultaneously, they told us the B-26 would be replaced with a four engine jet bomber called the B-45 Tornado. Relatively few of these planes were produced and only toward the end of World War Two. None of them were involved in the war and when hostilities ended, they were "mothballed" until the Korea conflict started. The planes became active in Korea flying very high altitude photoreconnaissance missions. They had a crew of four: a pilot, a co-pilot, a bombardier/navigator, and a tail gunner. As they arrived in Langley Field, Virginia for the secret mission it coincided with the arrival of, fresh from Korean combat, a large batch of new pilots. This obviously meant we would lose our position as aircraft commanders and thus become somewhat insignificant co-pilots. This was sad news for Russ and I. I told Russ he should work on transferring to Wright Field, Ohio, which was the home of most military aviation research. With his brain, such an assignment would be a natural for him. But Russ was stubborn about continuing to fly, even if it meant sitting in the "idiot seat", as we referred to the co-pilot position. Instead of the pilot and co-pilot sitting side-by-side, in the B-45 they sat in tandem with the pilot in the front seat and the co-pilot twiddling his thumbs in the rear seat position. The co-pilot seat had very few of the control systems and little of the instrumentation, thus the nickname, "idiot seat". All of this was definitely not in keeping with our choice of assignment as given to us when we completed our pilot training in Lubbock, Texas. The situation angered me sufficiently to ask for a day off so I could drive up to Washington, D.C., and discuss the matter with the career management office for the Air Force. This proved to be disappointing. In the mean while, at Langley Field, our wives were ordered to report to the base for a series of talks on how to conduct themselves with respect to the secrecy. All flight crewmembers were sent to Barksdale, Louisiana for B-45 maintenance training. This was followed by a visit to Albuquerque, New Mexico to get better acquainted with the bomb.

Following my disappointed career management visit to Washington, I would keep myself as busy as possible, by volunteering for any kind of assignment that came up. The first exercise that developed was a ten-day survival course in the Rocky Mountains. Without food and water, I took a crew of six men and lived off the environment, while walking thirty miles over terrain similar to the Russian Ural Mountains (the whole scenario was a "dry run" of being shot down in Russian territory and "walking out"). Next project was a survival course above the artic circle (I got as far as Billings, Montana and it had to be cancelled as all transport aircraft were required for logistical support of the Korean action). Following my return to Langley, I found I was selected to attend a nine-week course at the Air Command and Staff school, located at Maxwell Field, Alabama.

When I returned from Maxwell Field, I asked our commanding officer for a private conference. He agreed and I explained my frustration and disappointment that after going through flight school twice, and spending four years at West Point, I was still not properly assigned to apply my command training. He understood, to a point. At least he told me that he would get me checked out as a B-45 aircraft commander. He did that and was quite satisfied with my performance. However, time still rolled by without any upgrade of assignment.

In the meanwhile, Russ was going about his business as a B-45 co-pilot in his usual stoic manner. I remember with pain, the date was December twelfth, 1951 and Russel's B-45 crashed into the Chesapeake Bay, one mile from touching down on the runway! Everyone on board was killed. I immediately drove to his house to inform his wife, and the next day, I rode in the baggage car with his coffin and took him home to Catasauqua, Pennsylvania. This was a major shock to me, especially since we were such close friends and the whole accident was such a waste of life and devastation to his family. To worsen the incident further, at the time of the accident his son Lawrence was just a little baby, only several months old (he grew up and became a colonel in the Marine Corps). Though he did not know his father, his mother made sure he knew as much about him as she did. Charlotte returned to her hometown in Pennsylvania where she spent the rest of her life.

Speaking of babies, prior to Russel's fatal accident, my wife gave birth on August 30, 1951, to a lovely baby girl who we named Robin. She was a beautiful cherub. To complete the scene, we had a wonderful collie dog, who naturally felt protective of Robin. Whenever we took our baby in her carriage for a walk, he was close by to fend off anybody nearing Robin's carriage. My wife Joan was also very close to Russel's wife Charlotte; when I took Russ home on the train, Joan packed Robin up and drove from Virginia to her parent's home in New Jersey. She left Robin with he mother and father and then continued to Pennsylvania for the funeral.

After that was over, we eventually went back to Langley Field, but I sensed Joan, who was never gung-ho about the service life, was beginning to show more concern than ever before. A few days after returning to Langley Air Base, I asked my squadron commander one more time, would it be possible for me to transfer to a B26 national guard unit that was just placed on active duty and assigned to Langley Field for updating their training pending further assignment overseas. He granted permission to do this and once more I become an aircraft commander.

In the meanwhile, my former unit soon after I joined the National Guard unit flew the B-45 Atomic bombers from Langley field to a secluded air base in England called Sculthorpe, where they set up operations to carry out the secret mission. It did not take more than two weeks after my transfer when headquarters of the guard unit received communication from Sculthorpe, England concerning me. It requested me by name and as a B-45 aircraft commander, to report immediately to Sculthorpe, England for duty with the secret mission group. While our wives could go, my wife definitely did not want to do this. Aside from the fact that she had no interest in going to England, she was pregnant with our second child to be. I had no choice but to proceed to England without her. I had a suspicion that when I arrived at Sculthorpe, I would be right back in "the idiot seat".

Before leaving Virginia, I had a few days to wrap everything up in our rental home, and to then drive my wife to New Jersey. Joan wanted very much to remain with her family, rather than "tough it out" alone in Virginia. Once I got back to Virginia, I went to the operations officer of my new unit to see if I could have a B-26 for a half day. I explained my desire to fly one of these machines for the last time before rejoining the B-45 Atomic Bombers in England. He granted my request. I went to the flight line to pre-flight the aircraft assigned to me. While carrying out the inspection, a line mechanic ambles up to me and said, "Hey lieutenant, do you have space for me to go along?" I said, "Sure, bring your comic books and go to the nose of the plane. From there you can see just how the bombardier flying a real mission can look below for his targets on the ground." Up he goes into the bombardier's compartment. Little does he know he was about to get the ride of his life! Earlier in this book, I mentioned my temptation several times for "buzzing at low altitudes", on this particular day, it was a fixation about to take place. We took off and flew up to Newburgh, New York, which was about five hundred miles from my Virginia airbase. Flying over the city, I executed a maneuver call "a wing over", (this maneuver practically turns the bomber on its back and this makes it easy to go into a steep angle of decent) so I could get down quickly to the surface level of the Hudson River. I was about forty feet above the water with almost full throttle, giving us a speed of close to three hundred miles an hour.

We were flying due south directly, toward West Point, which juts into the Hudson and rises above the river about one hundred and fifty feet. My scheme was to fly a straight line toward West Point, then pull up at a safe distance from the shore line of the school, buzz over the marching plain, go flashing by the administration building, and immediately get back down on the river. I would then fly under the Bear Mountain bridge that was about ten miles south of West Point and continue flying further south toward New York City area, at a respectable altitude. (I figured my speed was such that no one would have time or thought to record my aircraft number). I had about two minutes before getting to West Point, when this dazed, frightened face crawled back from the bombardier compartment to the cockpit and yells, "lieutenant, lieutenant, are we going to crash?" I replied, "no, but I am going to give you a very close look at those buildings ahead of us." When I pulled up to fly over the marching plain, I adjusted the pitch of the propellers of the two, two thousand horsepower engines. This makes a thunderous noise that added to the feat. We were out of there before anyone had a chance to get to a window. (I was sort of a modern mole; the only difference with the original mole story previously described in this book was, he was below in the sewer system, and I was, thank God, well above the sewers). My passenger breathed a big sigh of relief, but I warned him, it was not yet over. I did a job buzzing over my folk's house in Pelham Manor, just outside of New York City. Then I flew over Englewood, New Jersey, picked out my in-laws house and gave then a "close shave". From there, it was directly back to Virginia with no other antics. We landed, my unwitting hitchhiker wobbled out of the plane with his unread comic books and not even a thanks! As for me, that flight was a perfect tonic to rid my frustrations and say goodbye to an old friend…the B-26. Incidentally my wife had called her parents that day to say hello. Her father got on the phone and told her about some crazy pilot who flew so low over the house that my mother-in-law hid under her bed fearing an air raid! I acknowledged nothing, but it was one of my better days (weirdly enough, there was never any report submitted by anyone on that day's event).

The last thing I did before boarding a flight to England was to take my collie dog to my grandfather's farm in Connecticut, where he told me, that "Fio" would be treated with the best of care. I really hated to leave that dog behind, but I had no other better options. With a farewell to my wife and child I was off to another chapter in the life of one of eight.

Chapter 5

Flying Atomic Bombers in England & Return to Civilian Life

My military flight to England from the United States landed at an Air Force base a bit north of London. I had to get to the town of Fakenham. The towns name appeared to sound like two words in one, i.e. FAKEN and HAM. I sought assistance at the air base. They reviewed my papers, and I was told to proceed to London's Victoria Station, where I could get the proper train to "FAKEN-HAM". At Victoria Station every time I asked somebody where do I go to get a ticket to FAKEN-HAM, they all looked at me with puzzlement and said, "Sorry chap, never heard of FAKEN-HAM." I finally went to the ticket agent and showed him my orders. "Sir, he replied, you mean a ticket to FAKENEM"

I finally was taught that you do not pronounce the H in Fakenham; instead it is correctly pronounced Fakenem. I was beginning to wonder what this town would look like and more importantly what kind of pirates lair is nearby at Sculthorpe Air Force Base.

Being in such a remote area was for security purposes, no doubt but never-the-less, I had to think about buying a car to "get around a bit" as they say in England. I took into consideration, I was almost a bachelor; I also has the thirst for soft adventure; and there were many other non-essential reasons - - all of which lead me to purchase the car of my dreams...the MG 1953 TD! I walked five miles to the town of Kings Lynn, and found out they indeed had an MG dealer. I walked into this attractive shop with all these wonderful machines on display. A salesman approached me. He was impeccably dressed, complete with flower in the lapel, a silk foulard tie, and topped with "a smashing" fine English accent.

"Sir, can I be of assistance?"

"Yes, I would like to buy that red, MG, Sports car over there in the corner."

"Sir, you don't buy an M.G. … You marry it!"

I was amazed at his diction and his statement. He gave the history of the MG from page one; the more he spoke the more I was ready to part with the U.S. $1,575 total cost! (In those days, our dollar was much stronger than the pound; in fact the U.K. was in the midst of a very deep recession following "the Blitz" and the whole war scene.) If I had kept my MG, today as an antique car, it would be worth about forty thousand dollars. His final farewell statement as I picked up my gorgeous car was,

"Sir, remember the name of this car is MG TD. Do you know what TD stands for?"

I replied, "I guess it is the model number"

"Sir, I beg to correct you; TD means TOP DOWN sir, and regardless of the weather it is always TOP DOWN."

And that is the way I drove my sports car. He was "spot on", every MG I observed on the road had the top down despite the weather. It was amazing to see these country people dressed to the teeth in rain gear, riding down the roads TD!

On my first drive to London, I went to Burberry's clothing store and bought a Burberry cap for my car attire. I also had a car cover made for my MG by the same tailor who later made some civilian clothing for me! Finally, due to the extreme dampness, I removed my hubcaps every night, and kept them in my quarters under wraps until the next outing, to avoid rusting. I did marry that car!

Traveling the English countryside with my MG Sports car. TD of course.

The weather in England continued to be dreary. In fact, toward the end of November a terrible storm came off of the North Sea and hammered the east coast of England doing all kinds of damage and flooding in the lowlands. It was one of the worst storms on record. If one looked at a map of England, they would see an area on the coast within fairly close proximity to Sculthorpe, our air base, called the Wash. It indents the coastline as though it were a giant bay. The Wash comes to an end about forty miles from the English Channel and any storms emanating from the North Sea hit the Wash with a "lot of muscle". Such was the case with this horrific storm. At the end of the Wash lies the town of Hunstanton which when first established was built behind a dike that most of the time kept the sea water from flooding the town. During the late night of one of the worst nights of the storm, the power of wind and tide bored down on the Wash with such strength, the dike finally caved in with twenty feet of water flooding the entire town in a matter of minutes! Back at our Sculthorpe base, we were all asleep when suddenly the combat alarm goes off, and we all thought the nuclear bomb against the one million Russian forces poised at the border of East Germany was about to happen. We were in full combat dress when an announcement was made to leave our parachutes and small arms in our barracks and rush to the headquarters building. At headquarters, there were about twelve trucks ready to deliver us to Hunstanton to give the Brits "a much needed hand".

When we arrived in Hunstanton it was an unbelievable sight. The town was flooded with twenty feet of water in a matter of minutes after the dike broke. Dead livestock and all kinds of animal life were floating throughout Hunstanton. The high water levels were flooding homes and store buildings to the second floor. Mind you this was taking place at one AM in the morning. All of us went to work doing the best we could to help clearing the animal carcasses and removing the floating debris. The one thing that immediately caught our attention was the Brits themselves. Keep in mind; the war was over only seven years ago. These people immediately put themselves into action. Out came their uniforms worn during the blitz as volunteers, they organized quickly and they were underway by the time we arrived fro Sculthorpe. Blankets were being distributed. Hot soup and bread was distributed from a well-stocked chow line, (no wonder the Germans could not overcome England). All the towns' people and our Air Force unit worked until well after daylight, but the most impressive sight was to see these determined people helping each other cope with their misfortune. It was unforgettable.

As expected my assignment at Sculthorpe was in the idiot seat as co-pilot (co-pilot was a misnomer; a cadaver could do the job just as well). Flying as the co-pilot status allowed me lots of time to ponder over what has happened to me since graduation. Things started off very well. It looked like; all was falling into place until the secret mission came along. Then progress came to "a screeching halt". While at Sculthorpe, I flew as co-pilot on six or seven missions, but this contributed little or nothing to my progress. Despite my efforts, I found my future stalled to a point where I made my decision to resign my commission effective at the end of three years of service, which would take place June 1, 1953. I discussed this with my commanding officer that always held respect for me; he was a complete gentleman. I was taken off flying status and I was assigned as safety officer of the squadron. I stayed with this job until I returned to the United States for my separation from the service.

In the time span, before leaving England, I had to figure out a lot of things. Keep in mind; I have been in the military service since I was eighteen years old. Now I am about to leave the service, what will I do? Can you imagine I never had a civilian job! I never considered my years in uniform as a job; it was my career and suddenly, it would all become history.

I was twenty-eight when I left England and the military. My wardrobe was almost all uniforms and very little "civvies" besides some athletic outfits. Thus, I had to take care of refurbishing my clothing. For this I went to the same small tailor shop in the town of Kings Lynn that made the auto cover for the MG. The tailor started to work on a custom-made grey flannel suit, a Harris Tweed jacket with beige twill trousers. I was so oblivious to what kind of clothing to order; I confess the gray flannel suite came to mind when I saw Gregory Peck in the movie, "The Man in the Gray Flannel Suit". The Harris Tweed jacket and calvery twill trousers came from a musical comedy play I went to see in London and the lead actor was so attired. The material he showed me was elegant and I told him to go to work. I must have had at least ten fittings. To me, since I had grown accustomed to English style, the clothing he was working on looked top notch, but he was very slow and meticulous. When he was almost finished, I could not wait any longer, so I paid him and asked that my suits, upon completion, be shipped home to me in the States via surface freight.

Besides ordering my civilian clothes, I had to face the fact that my wife Joan would need a replacement for the Chevrolet we presently owned. I did not believe she would be happy "sharing" my M.G., so I bought her a tiny English car called a

Morris Minor. It had two doors, manual shift and an engine about the size of a small "Singer sewing machine".

When I arrived home from England, my wife was just about to give birth to our second child. She was born on July 5, 1953 and we named her Karen Beth Heit. A point of interest; two days before my wife went to the hospital, she was as usual driving my newly arrived M.G. (instead of the Morris Minor that I had bought for her). The MG's steering wheel fitted somewhat snugly against her pregnant stomach. A car in front of her stopped short and Joan slammed on her brakes. This lurched her forward pushing her stomach against the wheel with enough force "to break her water". That started the birthing cycle and my new daughter's eventual arrival into the Heit clan.

Chapter 6

Climbing the Corporate Ladder in New York

Temporarily we lived in the home of my wife's parents in Englewood, New Jersey. It was pleasant and a fairly large English Tudor. Joan's mother and father were very nice people. Her mother was quite attractive, but was relatively quiet and was Lutheran. My Father-in-law was truly something else. He came from a very orthodox Jewish family, who threw him out of their house when they discovered he was seriously dating a Christian girl. Once that happened he had to find a way to stay alive. Sidney Engelhardt was a tough guy from a rough neighborhood, in Jersey City, New Jersey. He used to box for sport and for a while did it professionally, in order to be able to buy something to eat. Then he dropped boxing, or it dropped him after a few "long counts", and Sidney became a cab driver. He was pretty good at driving and he knew his way around the city. As he was always "a good talker", I am sure he made out very well with tips. There were four other brothers, two of whom were running a small bus line in New Jersey. The route was from Jersey City to nearby Weehawken, where the bus passengers could catch a ferry across the Hudson River to New York. Most of the people worked in New York, so the bus service was very convenient for them. Sidney helped his oldest brother, who was the owner of the Jersey City bus line, but it was not long before Sidney and two of his other brothers decided they would try the bus business on their own. One thing led to another and it was not too long that the Orange and Black bus line became a large size commuter service that utilized the Lincoln Tunnel to drop passengers off directly in New York City. This made it possible for the Orange and Black to eliminate the inconvenience of an additional ferry ride for their customers. As the communities along their bus route system expanded, so did their bus line. I believe they were operating a hundred buses and expanding by acquiring additional bus lines. One of the companies they acquired was a relatively small one called Gray Line New York Tours. Sidney, who was the main "power plug" of the Orange and Black, put his son Kenneth in charge of Gray Line. The Gray Line of New York is a member of the Gray Line Association, which is a worldwide franchised sightseeing enterprise, with the Engelhardt's holding the franchise for New York City. I provide you with this scenario in order that you have some idea of the environment I returned to from England. Most every night while I lived in the Engelhardt residence, Sidney would take me aside after dinner and we would sit in the den for hours and hours on end, with Sidney doing all the talking, but I truly mean all the talking. Actually, he was fascinating to listen to and I did not mind doing all the listening. These séances, usually lasted three or four hours and went until one or two o'clock in the morning! One night, he gave me a minute or two to reply to his question, "Do you have any thing in mind about what you want to do?" I replied, "Yes, I am thinking about getting involved with a real estate company." He responded, " I have just the company, J.I. Kislak. They are a powerhouse in the real estate business and I know the President very well." That took care of my immediate problem of employment. Mr. Kislak met with me, and assigned me to the manager of one of his offices in Englewood. I was to prospect all the up market homes in Englewood to determine if they would like to sell their homes by listing with the J.I. Kislak Company. Financially, my remuneration would be sixty-five dollars a week and this would be against draw. I did not know what he meant "against draw", but did not want to appear stupid, so I said that it would be fine. I knocked on the doors of countless homes. Some people just slammed the door in my face, yet others would invite me in. Their first question after closing the door was "how much is it worth"? Not knowing the back door from the front door, I would explain that I have a list of specific questions to ask them; afterwards I would then return to the office where we will work out the figures. Invariably, they would ask me to leave, as they did not have the time to bother. This went on with seven to eight homes a day for two weeks. In the mean while Kenneth, my brother-in-law was "having his hands full" running Gray Line New York Tours. He was understaffed and he kept making the suggestion to his father, "what about putting Elliot to better use; let him come to Gray Line with me. I need the help, and I think he would catch on quickly, beside which, this way he can help the family business, rather than pushing doorbells." Rather than pushing doorbells, rang a bell in Sidney's mind. That night during our usual séance, he asked me, "How much do they pay you at the Kislak Company?" I advised, sixty-five dollars a week. Sidney says, "I'll double that to one hundred and thirty a week, if you go to work at Gray Line." I said it would be great, but I had to first explain the circumstances to Mr.. Kislak. Sidney agreed and asked that after I finished with Kislak we should meet at his office to further discuss working at Gray Line. I forgot to tell Sidney that my sixty five dollars a week was "against draw" which I subsequently discovered, meant that Kislak was paying me weekly against any commissions I may have earned from homes that I listed and were sold. In my mind that meant that I owed Kislak one hundred and thirty dollars, as I was not responsible for one single house being sold. When I finished meeting with Mr.. Kislak, I went to my father-in-law's office. Sidney asked me what happened at the real estate company. I told him what I explained to Mr.. Kislak, and before leaving gave him a check for one hundred and thirty dollars that represented the two weeks he paid me. I further explained that I did not make any commission for him "to draw against". I thought it was the right thing to do. When Sidney heard this I thought he was going to have a stroke. "You did what!! How much was the shoe leather you wore out? How about your walking five miles a day and the abuse you had to take from the homeowners? Boy, you certainly have a lot to learn and you better start learning fast from the first day you walk into the Gray Line office!"

That first day came very quickly. Gray Line offices and tour dispatching area were located in New York City's midtown area; specifically, on Fifteenth Street between Broadway and Eight Avenues in the Capital Greyhound Bus Terminal. Even though we were in the Greyhound terminal, Gray Line was an independent and private company. I met the staff which consisted of Eddy Blaine, who was kind of a combination salesman and assistant operations manager, Virginia Savage, the administrator and Kenny's secretary, one bookkeeper, and general manager, Ken Engelhardt and now Elliot Heit walks into the picture. I spent four days just looking around the office trying to figure out who does what and also what I do. I knew right from the start; Eddy Blaine did not like me and wondered to myself, "what in God's name is a West Point graduate doing in this kind of "earthy" business"? Finally, some action takes place when

Ken asked me to come into his small private office. He closes the door and says,

"What the hell are you doing here? Let me tell you a few things about the sightseeing business in New York City. It's a dog eat dog business. Even though we are the prima donna of the five companies all doing the same thing in New York, the competition is downright cut throat and only the vicious survive. Eighty five percent of our business comes from cigar stands and bell captains in the midtown hotels and all the other sightseeing companies are "hot on the tail" of this hotel business paying as much as 40% compared to our 15 to 20% we pay to top producers. I want you to get your carcass out of this office and make theses cigar stands and bell captains your best friends."

"Ken, I'd be delighted to do this, but what will I talk about; I don't know the business?"

"Listen Elliot, I don't care if you go out there and paint your rear end purple to get their attention. You have a helluva personality; you don't have to talk business right off the bat. You have more interesting experience than the whole lot put together. Talk about yourself. They will listen and you listen too. They will teach you the business better than any school could ever do. Now get out of here and start painting your rear end".

That's just about what I did and it worked. First of all, in comparison with the sleazy people from the other companies that were calling on the agents, I looked like a shining knight in armor. I did learn a lot from meeting these unscrupulous sales people who could spot an "out of town tourist" fifty feet across the lobby floor of a hotel. That poor tourist innocently approaching the newsstand for a candy bar or pack of cigarettes, did not realize they are D.O.A. (dead on arrival) at the newsstand. Before they know it, they have two free tickets to the Ed Sullivan TV show and two tickets on the all day Gray Line Tour Number Six for $19.90. (The agent receives $3.98 commission from Gray Line and almost $8.00 from our competition). If you have any idea of how many candy bars or cigarettes they would have to sell to keep $8.00, then you would understand why they "hawk" sightseeing tours. I remember one agent, Mr.. Kaufman at the Taft Hotel who has a newsstand no bigger than three feet deep, including the counter and about eight feet long. He did not pay rent and lived in the hotel for almost nothing. The hotel manager believed that Mr. Kaufman provided a valuable service for hotel guests and deserved every break he could give this good soul. If the manager had any idea how much Mr. Kaufman was "racking in" he would have had a heart attack. This "good soul" behind the newsstand counter, where he never had a chair to sit down because he wanted always to be "on the ready" to attack his sightseeing targets, sold a total of $500,000 worth of tours!! Think about it, 20% would mean that poor Mr.. Kaufman earned $100,000 and remember he did not pay rent on the newsstand!

Of the one hundred or so agents selling sightseeing tours in New York City hotels, about fifteen were in the same league as Mr. Kaufman, although Kaufman was "on top of the pile". I like Mr. Kaufman, had my targets. Day and night I did attack my targets, the agents. The result was slow in coming, but it was beginning to show. Everyday I would carry a satchel weighing about twenty pounds full of our brochures for our agents. I also had my billing pad so that I could collect the cash from each agent for all tours sold at the conclusion of my visit; no checks were accepted. I usually had to refill my satchel with brochures three to four times a day.

The retail sightseeing business only lasted about two and a half months in the summer, and then you would have to create other business to keep the buses busy. This was the wholesale part, and it consisted of special sightseeing groups that were mostly high school seniors coming to New York as a graduation gift, from all over the country for an educational tour of the big city. Also, conventions and special tour operators from other parts of the U.S.A., all of which included Gray Line in their programs, and finally the bus charter business that mostly originated from all five boroughs of New York City. As time went on I became more and more involved with the sales development of the company. I earned good recognition with both wholesale and retail areas. It was not long before Ken made me sales manager, and then subsequently Vice President of sales.

The sales development was an area that made me feel like a duck in water, i.e. that was where I belonged. To pursue this further I became a member of the American Society of Travel Agents referred to as ASTA. ASTA was one of the most significant travel organizations in the world and still remains as such. During the fifties they had two divisions of membership. The main division was the travel agents, and the other was referred to as the allied division. The latter division included all companies other than travel agents that were associated with tourism. The list included airlines, steamship lines, hotels, bus companies, rental cars, etc. Walt Johnson who was senior vice President of Marketing for American Airlines became chairman of the allied section of ASTA. He selected me as a member of his board of directors. Annually, ASTA has a convention that alternately is held either in the United States or abroad. In 1958, it was abroad, and the country was Cuba! They expected 4,000 people would attend. Walt Johnson commissioned me to go to Havana 10 days prior to the meeting to help supervise the set up. At that point in my travel career, I have not been out of the country since my military days. It was indeed an honor, after only five years in the tour business, to serve on Walt Johnson's board.

A few weeks before my scheduled departure, things in Cuba started to flare up with Fidel Castro. So much so, ASTA was actually considering cancellation of the event. However, the State department sent a message to our chairman underlying the importance that the meeting continue to be held in Cuba. As they put it, this would be in the best interest of the United States. We obviously went ahead with the plans and I would shortly depart for Cuba.

A few days before that, Joe McCrane, my close friend from West Point, calls me up and tells me, he is in New York and suggests we have dinner at his friends restaurant call The House of Chan. This place is a landmark spot in the city, located at Fifty-first Street and Seventh Avenue. While dining there, Sou Chan, the owner, comes to our table. I was in the midst of telling Joe about my upcoming Cuba trip. Sou Chan then tells me he has a bank account in Havana. Castro has restricted bank clients from taking any money out of Cuba. He asked me for assistance by requesting I take out as much money as I needed from his account for spending while I was in Cuba. Since, at the time the currency of both countries has the same value, I could pay him back in U.S. dollars upon my return. I told him that that would be fine. Sou said he would have a letter of introduction ready by the time we finished dinner and he would also call Mr.

Yoh, the general manager of the Bank of China in Havana to advise of my forthcoming visit.

I arrived in Cuba, went to the Riviera Hotel, checked in and called Raymond Yoh. We had a very pleasant conversation, but he told me Castro put a "tighter lid" on bank accounts by only allowing withdrawals to account holders appearing in person. (With the political situation in Cuba worsening by the day, that appearance at the bank would not happen). After I ended my call, I spent a few minutes thinking about calling Mr. Yoh back, and as a courtesy, invite him over to my hotel for cocktails. I reasoned, the activity for the convention was not in full swing yet and I could cover what ever has to be done within the time before the convention began. I call Mr. Yoh back, he eagerly accepted. Our meeting marked the beginning of one of the most interesting visits to Cuba that I could ever expect.

Raymond Yoh as general manager of the Bank of China knew just about everybody who was anybody in the structured society of the country. His bank was owned directly by China. It is also of interest to know that the Chinese have been a vital part of the populations of many of the Caribbean islands. (This was an aftermath of the period when the early coal burning ships "employed" Chinese laborers at very low cost. These crewmen would "jump ship" whenever they could. It was most often that these opportunities occurred during a port of call at any one of the Caribbean ports.) In the ensuing years the Chinese showed their mettle. Chinese by nature are very industrious, whether it is Singapore, Malaysia or the Caribbean, and such was the case in particular, with Raymond Yoh, in Havana Cuba.

During the day or night any of my free time was spent either with him personally or with business associates. One of them, Ramon Del Collado was the owner of Trocodero Rum Distillery and was, at that time, one of the leaders in that industry. When Ramon was seventeen his mother gave him at thirty six foot power boat completely fitted out for off shore sport fishing. He became very friendly with the well-known author Ernest Hemmingway who was also a top sport fisherman, while Ramon was the captain of Cuba's tuna fishing team. During my time in Cuba, Ramon invited me two or three times during the convention to have lunch on board his boat, after which we would fish for an hour or so, in the Gulf Stream that ran less than a mile past Havana Harbor. The Gulf Stream at that point was and still is home to the giant blue fin tuna with weights up to six or seven hundred pounds. To bring you back to the reality of what was going on, one day an armed cutter pulled us over and boarded our craft. They carefully inspected the craft for some indication that we may be escaping to the States.

It might appear that I should have spent more time at the ASTA luncheon and meetings. As an Allied member, our end of the travel business was not allowed to attend the meetings involving travel agents activities where they were discussing policy business. We, of course, attended all other social gatherings as well as our Allied division meetings.

In the meanwhile, Raymond Yoh and I became very good friends. He enjoyed playing tennis and so did I. In Cuba, most people prefer to play at night when it is somewhat cooler. We would get through by about eleven P.M. and go to dinner at midnight!

For the last formality of the convention, ASTA held a concluding event outdoors that featured an address by Fidel Castro. Max Allen, President of ASTA, introduced him. Just before Castro began one of his well-known type of addresses, we suddenly heard overhead the sound of several low flying military aircraft and we all thought the opposition was about to bomb all of us including Castro. That was not the case. In place of bombs, the planes dropped thousands and thousands of propaganda leaflets featuring the wonders the people could expect when Castro puts his form of government fully in place. It was an interesting way to close the 1958 ASTA convention, to say the least.

No sooner did I leave Cuba, I heard the authorities arrested Del Collado, closed his rum distillery, and sometime later was mysteriously assassinated. Despite my best efforts to stay in touch with Mr. Yoh, I was not successful. Castro closed the Bank of China and I heard he gave Mr. Yoh an air ticket for him and his family to Miami. He also gave him five dollars to start a new life in the United States!

A weird incident took place, very soon after returning to New York. A call from a major TV studio inquired if I might be interested in participating in the program "To Tell The Truth". They found out through the company that handled our public relations that I just returned from Cuba at about the same time the first American to be kidnapped was taken by Castro's revolutionary forces. This fellow, who was returned safely, was employed by the Fremont Mining Company on the east end of Cuba known as the Oriente Province.

I do not know how many people these days still recall this TV program "To Tell The Truth"; it was one of the most popular shows at the time. The format featured a celebrity panel and three individuals to be questioned by the panel for a limited period. Of the three to be questioned, two are liars and one is the true person. I was game to participate; if for nothing else it would give our Gray Line Company a little publicity. The studio interviewed me, and shortly thereafter I was on. It so happened that the actual person who was kidnapped was not a very impressionable individual, so the panel in the interest of the limited time, focused on myself and the "other liar". Most of the questions had to do with the knowledge of the Spanish language and engineering, (since the Fremont Mining Company was basically engineering; my West Point engineering courses as well as Spanish as my elected language course came in very handy and I was making an excellent liar of myself). The panel had by this time centered their attention on me. Perhaps you remember the name of one of the panelists, Kitty Carlisle. The time for questioning is almost up and Kitty asked me "Number three, what was the date you were kidnapped?" I was absolutely flabbergasted! I blurted out "I don't remember". Can you imagine a person being kidnapped and not remembering the date and every other minute detail? The panel immediately abandoned me and went to work on the two others, but time was up. Aside from disgracing myself there was one consolation. The panel never guessed the right person; as a result, we won the maximum prize of $1,000.00 (divided three ways).

When I finally arrived home, of course the whole family and I am sure a great many of my friends, across the country had watched my performance. Sidney Engelhardt knew how to press the right button when he said to me, "Elliot, I'll tell you what impressed me the most about your TV performance .... you looked neat"

When I finally arrived back at the office, I attacked the usual pile of mail and messages. By this time, I had a secretary, Kitty Walsh who was so top notch she should have received a Legion of Merit award. (Gray Line was also beginning to grow and we were fast becoming one the biggest Gray Line franchises in the system). Back to the pile of messages, one particularly caught my attention. It was from Mr. Ernest Strasser, manager of the New York office belonging to a Swiss tour operator called Hotel Plan.

Before going on, allow me to define what is meant by what we call the state of touristic development from abroad to the United States. One must separate this kind of activity from what is normally understood to be international tourism. Keep in mind I am describing tourists' who live outside of the United States and desire to visit the USA. In 1958 this type of tourist development hardly existed. To give you some idea of the size of the market, the first specific measurement became available in 1961. At that time from the entire world only 600,000 internationally domiciled tourists visited the Untied States (and the 600,000 included Canadian visitors as well). With extensive market development these visitors have now reached over 50,000,000!

Referring back to Mr. Strasser of Hotel Plan, Switzerland, when I finished my call with him I realized I had just taken my first step into entering the birth of an entirely new unique market.

Mr. Strasser told me, that Hotel Plan has an agreement with a Swiss franchised system of independently owned grocery stores called MIGROS, to organize a visit to New York. The group would be 350 persons and I had to submit an all-inclusive quote (hotels, transfers, sightseeing, etc.). What I am trying to get across to, you the reader, is that our in-bound travel industry, throughout the U.S. was in the first stages of infancy, and I was bearing witness to its beginning. I work very hard on the MIGROS project giving personal attention to supervising every facet of the program. The tour operator, Hotel Plan was completely satisfied to the point that they continued to do business with Gray Line for many years. They also assisted me several times during the course of my international travel to Switzerland for developing additional activity for what we called "Visit USA" programs.

One of Eight

Not too much later during the same year of 1958 Gray Line received a cable from the P&O Steamship Line in England that they would have one of their cruise ships, The Canberra, pay a port visit to New York. They required arrangements to have sufficient buses at shipside to accommodate 1200 passengers, for a tour of New York City. This request was so large that Ken and I thought it wise to bring it up at a meeting with the big boss Sid Engelhardt. Please keep aware that none of us received any international proposals for service until 1958 because our Gray Line company never considered the business potential from abroad; all of a sudden in one year, we had the Hotel Plan's MIGROS Group, and now in the same year, the P&O Steamship company's 1200 passengers. The meeting with Sidney was funny. Paramount in Sid's mind were two things; one, "Who the hell is the P&O Steamship company, I've been on a lot of cruises and I never came across that name. Don't do anything until I check with Dun & Bradstreet". Secondly, "Ken, you and Elliot must make damn sure, the ship does not leave port until the bill is paid and payment must be in cash." Sid received the report from Dun & Bradstreet. The report had a brief paragraph on the history of the P&O steamship lines. If I recall correctly, they were an English company that started service about a hundred years ago, the full name is the Peninsula and Oriental Steamship Company. This was one of the largest fleet of steamships in the world!! The next paragraph in the D&B report was a single sentence describing the estimated net worth, which amounted to many, many billions. To be fair to Sid, none of us were accustomed to doing business with accounts in another country.

Once more, the service when off like clockwork, and as Sid Engelhardt instructed us, on the last day of their stay in port, Ken and I were counting the 1,200 collected tickets in the purser's office of the ship. This took the better part of the morning, and frankly I could never understand why they did not throw us out. The only hitch in our plan was the actual payment. The P&O staff could not pay C.O.D. because the tour was an optional service and they would have to get paid by the cruise passenger upon return to England, when each passenger must settle their account before they disembark. We reluctantly accepted their signed statement guaranteeing the amount due and left the ship to confront Sid Engelhardt with the results of our collection effort. To this day I do not understand why Sid was so easy on our failure to collect the payment before the Canberra left port. My hunch is it had something do with the estimated value of the P&O described in the D&B report. It was not very long before our bank account was properly credited, (by the way, I kept the P&O account for over twenty years despite the fact that I was no longer connected with Gray Line New York tours after 1969).

Things were starting to happen in rather rapid succession with the development of the inbound USA market. The next item will illustrate the progression of events. Once again in late 1958, I came across an article in the travel section of the Sunday New York Times. It was an interview with the President of SAS Airlines (which stands for Scandinavian Airlines). Mr. Warren Cramer, the President was describing his plan to create a task before of USA companies that would join SAS in a common venture "to Hit" the travel agents from all Scandinavian countries. He also specified his team would consist of a USA domestic airline, Hilton Hotels, Greyhound Bus Company, a rental car company and a few other services. Each company invited would have their senior member attend and make a presentation, that all together would demonstrate the strong interest in the new market and what specifics they would offer. It was the first time a project like this was to be undertaken. On Monday following my reading of the Times article, I was on the phone with SAS, pleading for a word with their President, whom I never met or heard of. I kept leaving messages that I was vice President of Gray Line New York Tours and his article in the Times won my close attention. It did not take too long to get the President on the phone. I "laid it" right on the line, "Mr. Cramer, how can you possibly consider such a task force without the representation from the Gray Line sightseeing organization which provides a network of companies throughout the most recognized cities and national parks in the United States? Your task force as it now stands, gets the tourist from Scandinavia to the United States, the Hilton Hotels will sleep them, but who of your proposed team has the responsibility to fulfill the initial desire of these tourists from Scandinavia to *see* the United States? The Gray Line stands ready to fulfill this function." Mr. Cramer replies, " Mr. Heit, you are quite correct; can you join us". I was shocked, but elated. I told him that it would be more fitting to have our general manger participate. Furthermore, I will personally bring this to his attention and then call you back. Ken was initially reluctant to be away from our business for ten days and he was not sure this project would amount to much. That last half of the preceding sentence was exactly why I wanted him to go instead of me. I did not need to be sold on the growing potential of "Visit USA", but he needed this opportunity to "feel the future". Ken finally decided to go, and in early 1959, off they went to make their presentations in Denmark, Norway and Sweden. While this was the very first kind of promotion and certainly there were mistakes made, overall, Ken and the other members of the task force began to realize "Visit USA" was about to enter reality.

In the following year of 1960 there were plans being drawn up for an extravaganza "Visit USA" promotion for 1961 sponsored by Greyhound bus lines, Pan American World Airways (at the zenith of their operations), and the Gray Line Sightseeing Association. The overall plan was to have a star studded group fly over to England, Greyhound would ship over to England a brand new double-decker scenic cruiser, and Pan Am would do the flying, take care of all ground arrangements, hotels, public relations, government clearance for the bus, and routings to cover seven countries with specific promotional events taking place in nineteen cities (all to be done in five weeks). For the first time a meaningful title was adopted, "Visit The USA", (Visit The USA became the battle cry of the travel industry worldwide for many years and this particular project was the launch vehicle for a long enduring promotion. The Gray Line Association, which was the management core, at that time of well over 100 individually, owned franchises such as Gray Line of New York, was also included in the leadership team. The association selected me to represent them for this unique Visit USA project. Pan Am assigned one of their senior sales reps and the Greyhound Bus Lines did the same. The three of us formed the spearhead of this all-important undertaking. There were also fourteen others that would be traveling with us throughout Europe for five weeks. These included one of the administrative assistants to President Kennedy, senior staff from each of the federal government departments such as immigration, national parks, and customs. Of course we also had "Miss Visit USA", a genuine Texas cowboy who wore his traditional garb at all times. He was incidentally an All American basketball player. In addition we had a three piece jazz combo all of whom studied at the Julliard School of Music, two very efficient and very attractive Pan Am stewardesses which were hand picked and changed as we entered each new country, and lastly two Greyhound drivers.

While it would appear to be a "sideshow" on the road, they were all good people and we became welded together quite effectively to accomplish the mission to the total satisfaction of Pan Am, Greyhound and Gray Line. It was truly the start of something big and I was grateful to be a part of it.

As I look back on the program "Visit The USA", there were so many wonderful happenings, but one was a very unusual episode that occurred in Switzerland. From the time of our arrival in Switzerland we were severely forewarned to forget any attempt to drive our colossus over the Swiss Alps into Italy. They were down right insistent we put our bus on a railroad flat car and we all get on a train to Italy. By this time in the schedule of the overall trip, we were so successful that we felt invincible. We did demur to the extent of accepting a suggestion that we make a survey trip to the Brenner Pass. The three of us from Pam Am, Greyhound and Gray Line made arrangements for a driver and a jeep to drive us up to the top of the Brenner Pass.

In the process of going up the Swiss side of the Brenner Pass, our survey did not disclose any turns in the road that our giant bus would find too difficult to make. Mind you, we did not go all the way to the top, but from what we saw on the Swiss side of the mountain as far as we went, it was unanimously agreed that we could "do the Brenner Pass" with our Greyhound Scenic Cruiser. One of the pressing matters that forced our decision to take on the Brenner Pass was we had to be in Rome as per schedule, because we had a private audience scheduled with the Pope. We arrived back in Zurich, Switzerland to prepare for departure the next day. The next day was upon us and off we went. Every thing going up to the top of the pass was just as we predicted. It was slow going up the winding road to the top, but our coach with our expert Greyhound drivers were dong a great job (two drivers were assigned by Greyhound just in case a back up was required). As we slowly approached the top of the Brenner Pass, it was decided it would be an excellent photo stop and we could stretch our legs. When we got off the bus, the drivers and the three project leaders walked over to the part of the rest area facing the Italian side of the Brenner Pass and we were shocked by what we saw below of the road leading into Italy. It was so convoluted with twisting hairpin turns; it looked from a distance like somebody squeezed a giant tube of toothpaste against a blackboard. (Some one later told us there were thirty-eight hairpin turns on the Italian side of the Brenner Pass).

After our brief rest at the top of the pass, everyone was on board and we started with some anxiety, down to the first hairpin turn. The driver at the wheel was a total professional. He realized quickly the huge bus could not make it around the turn in one movement, instead, he would back up a bit then go forward and steer further around the curve each time. He followed this for four curves. To get as far as we went took almost two hours. On the fourth curve, he was trying to repeat his success thus far, but on one of the back and forth series of movements, the rear end of the bus which protrudes about eight feet behind the rear wheels became stuck on the high end of the embankment that was built into the road around each of the hairpin curves. These embankments prevent vehicles from losing control on the curves and going over the edge of the road and into the canyon. (The canyons run very deep, especially at the top and middle of the pass). You have to appreciate our predicament. The bus was now completely spread across the curve we were caught on and we covered both sides of the two-lane traffic, thus preventing any vehicles from Italy trying to enter Switzerland and vice versa. The Brenner Pass is one of only four passes crossing the Alps and our mighty Greyhound bus had for all practical purposes closed one: the Brenner Pass!! The poor driver tried several times to get some traction on the wheels, but with the rear end stuck on the embankment, the rear wheel did not have enough of the weight of the bus for traction. When the driver pressed the accelerator the rear wheels would only spin around but the bus did not budge. Can you imagine what was happening? The Brenner Pass had only two lanes, and these two lanes were all there was to the width of the road, in other words, there were no shoulders on the road. The only thing separating vehicles from toppling off the road into the canyon was a small wall bordering between the road and the abyss. (This wall was about eighteen inches high and about the same in width!) I mention this detail because the wall enters the episode a little further on.

With the road traffic now backed up several miles in both directions, the next on scene where the Italian police, referred to as Carabinieri in Italy. They had to walk up from a considerable distance and they were in their full Latin mood of anger. The immediate solution was to unload the bus and get the growing crowd to help push the bus into the canyon! We were trying to get them to not do this, but their blood pressure was high as we could tell by the veins sticking so far out of their necks and faces. It made them impossible to deal with. The situation was at a stand still (things were going so badly, our spearhead leaders were considering tearing off the bus signs, which were on each side of the bus that read VISIT USA.). Just them a Swiss Army officer approached our disaster area. He introduces himself and with amazing calm he examines our plight. With typical Swiss self-control, we are told he can help us! To do this, he explains that his army truck was fairly close to our site and that there was ten Swiss soldiers on the truck along with several large house jacks and some large boards, which they needed for a camp construction project they had been assigned to. He was sure the house jacks could lift the rear wheels of the bus and then he would slide the big boards under the wheels. After the jacks were removed the rear wheels rested on the boards and the rear end of the bus was clear of the road. The Swiss Army officer then told the driver to carefully follow his signals. The driver was very careful! The bus moved along the boards and managed to cover part of the curve, then the soldiers, under the watchful direction of their officer had to repeat the exercise once more before they could clear the one curve. As soon as the bus cleared, the left lane of the road finally opened. The Carabinieri commanded us not to move the bus until the bottleneck of traffic was partially cleared. This phase of our difficulties took about five hours, and we still had thirty-four more hairpin turns to go! The Swiss Army officer told us he would help the drivers navigate another two turns and if it went well he would take leave of us. What he explained to the driver; he must stay as far as possible to the outside of the curve rather than the usual tendency for a driver to "cut across" a curve. To make sure the driver fully understood, he placed himself on that small one foot wide wall and walked very slowly, backwards, motioning with his hands to the driver, thereby guiding the bus so that the wheels almost touched against the little wall while the Swiss officer was atop of the wall and walking backwards! It worked very well and I must say it was one of the bravest deeds I have ever seen. The officer was satisfied we could navigate the remaining turns, but before he and his soldiers left us every single member of our group congratulated him. We also wrote down all details of his address. Soon after we returned to the United States, Pan Am sent him and his wife a first class ticket to New York City;

Greyhound gave him an unlimited pass for one month of travel anywhere in the United States, and the Gray Line Sightseeing Association gave him a thirty day free pass for as many cities as he could visit.

In the meanwhile, we went about our business of navigating the rest of the dangerous hairpin curves. Just about the time we thought every thing was under control we lost the power steering. This made it necessary for each man on board to take a turn in assisting the driver to turn the steering wheel. The power steering outage delayed even further our arrival in the small mountain village in Italy called Lugano. When our limping Greyhound coach entered the village it was close to midnight. Everyone was exhausted and especially the men assisting with the steering around the curves. As we got to the center of the town we saw all the lights were on. It appeared that the village was wide-awake and it seemed like the whole town surrounded the bus and yelled in Italian all kinds of greetings. When we unloaded they carried us forward like heroes who just completed a daring mission! Well they were right. We were deposited in the restaurant and bar of a small inn. The concertinas started with music, the cognac was poured, every body was dancing and suddenly not one of us felt the least bit tired anymore despite the harrowing experience and very long day.

The next day we realized it would be impossible to make it to Rome in time for our private audience with the Pope. We contacted the Pan Am office in Rome and advised them. They were then able to salvage the rest of the Rome program. This was deeply disappointing for all of us and it represented the only event of many events that was not completed as planned.

On our way to breakfast we saw a newspaper of the day, featuring on the front page a prominent article and a large photo of a Greyhound scenic cruiser. The headline read:

HANNIBAL THE II GETS STOPPED
AT THE TOP OF THE ALPS.

The article described our adventure in detail but it was done with a good touch of humor.

The Visit USA program was the single most successful of all similar types of projects to date and as well as most all others that were subsequently offered. Not only did we have a very effective slogan VISIT USA that was used by the travel industry for years but also we left an enduring mark on all the general public attending the many the travel agent receptions we offered. The public was further made aware of our presence by conspicuous parking of the scenic cruiser in city and village squares with advance publicity Pam Am arranged for on radio, television and newspapers. Our full crew was always on hand for these occasions, including the American jazz played by our three-piece jazz band. Hundreds of people at each stop were allowed to walk aboard HANNIBAL THE II, to see first hand this singular giant size bus that was used to cover over 100,000 route miles of Greyhound's bus system. For the thousands of people in the nineteen cities visited, this was indeed a spectacular event. Simultaneously, the travel product these people learned about was entirely unique. Pan Am, Greyhound and Gray Line combined strategies that focused on value for the money (the average European world traveler at the time had the image that the USA would be a wonderful place to visit, but Hollywood's exaggerated way of depicting the rich life was a detriment to making such a visit) Thus our combined strategy concentrated on what was reasonable and required to VISIT THE USA. With this in mind, Greyhound led off with their famous see America ticket. For $99.00 you could travel anywhere in the United States for 99 days!! Pan Am followed suite by introducing their special round trip coach fare for $999.00. (Now if you do not think that was a bargain in 1961 then you should know the regular coach fare was $1,500.00 for the same trip! It also shows you how much competition to date has affected airfares to Europe, because now you can travel round trip with some airlines for under $500.00.) Then there was the Gray Line Association offer for 30 days of sights at a cost of $99.00. You can see we had the product and we were able to get the attention of the market place. There was no question – VISIT THE USA was on the march and it was a profound pleasure for me to be involved.

The monster Greyhound "double-decker" scenic cruiser, Hannibal the II

While not of great significance, during the sixties, I had an indirect involvement with Nakita Khrushchev, Prime Minister of the Union of Soviet Socialist Russia. He was planning to make a major address at the United Nations in New York. Since this event coincided with the Russian airline, Aeroflot, launching for the first time, service from Moscow to New York, Mr. Khrushchev decided such a precedent setting event would be a good way to "piggy back" attention to his own historic trip to New York and Washington. Pan Am World Airways was once again selected as the host airline and would be responsible for all ground arrangements for the Prime Minister's entourage as well as a very large Aeroflot staff with many senior Aeroflot executives in attendance. In as much as I was involved with other similar types of Pan Am functions they invited me to plan and operate the ground transportation for the complete project. Pan Am placed a lot of their reputation "on the line", and to assure everything would go accordingly to plan, they assigned a Russian speaking Pan Am regional manager to work side by side with me. His name was Jim Edwards. Very Tall, handsome blonde who in addition to his Pan Am employment, was a big game professional hunter as a 'side line". He was well educated and had the manners of a nobleman; he could have had a career as an actor in Hollywood. The both of us studied together for several days, to learn the details of the operation. The program including a Washington visit was about seven days and during that time we never lost sight of each other. He was a most interesting character, but on the last day of our assignment, his response to my following question "floored me",

"Jim, now that this is over and done with, what are your plans?"
"Elliot, I'm going to hand in my Pan Am badge, and I am going to open a wild tiger farm in the Himalayan Mountains!"

I repeated my question, and he gave me the same answer. I was too dumb founded to respond properly, so I wished him the best of luck, and I felt pretty sure we would never meet again.

Would you believe, about fourteen yeas later, my wife and I were in India on business, when we were offered a trip to the country of Nepal. Nepal is a small country "sandwiched" between India and the China boarders and nestled in the highest part of the Himalayan Mountains (the home of Mt. Everest, the highest peak in the world). Katmandu is the capital and it is over-run with many diplomats representing countries from all over the world. Why this is a fact I do not know. Perhaps it provided the only "available" window on the then secretive and closed society of China.

One day in Katmandu, my wife and I were walking back to our hotel after a sightseeing visit to the palace of the Royal family. The path took us through the center of Katmandu. As we looked hither and yon, my eyes caught a store sign that read:

PAN AM WORLD AIRWAYS / TIGER TOPS

I turned to Carol and asked her to look at the sign, and further, did she remember the name of the Pan Am fellow who worked with me on the Khrushchev project about fourteen years ago? Her reply was no, and I said we must go into that shop and check it out.

"Pardon me madam, is the owner of this shop, a tall, lean and good looking gentleman? If so, what is his name?" She replied, that his name was Mr. Jim Edwards! I could not believe, here we are thousands of miles from anywhere, in a midget size country and as close as you can get to the top of the world, (without climbing Everest) and Jim Edwards reappears in Katmandu after fourteen years. Unfortunately he was not in his office, but I left word to have him call my hotel. He did and we met for cocktails and some fascinating chatter. Jim did exactly what he told me he would do when the Khrushchev visit was completed. But his style was a bit more involved. He was able to make friends with the Prince of the Royal family of Nepal. After explaining the idea of Tiger Tops, the prince insisted that he wanted to be a partner and would allocate enough area in Nepal National Park for the site. Incidentally, when our Tiger Top friend arrived at our hotel, he had another partner with him who was part of an exiled white Russian Family. White Russians were forced into exile during the communist revolution in Russia during World War One. They were the capitalists of the society, at that time, and usually had close ties to the Romanov Royals of Russia; because of this many were executed and many were exiled or escaped to Siberia. Jim was insistent that Carol and I visit Tiger Tops for a few days. Unfortunately, we had a special flight scheduled by our friends in Bombay, India for the next day that would fly us at close range to Mt. Everest. I could not change our plans, which would disappoint the Bombay group, so Jim went into detail of what Tiger Tops is all about. To begin with the company is a raving success and receives people from allover the world. To briefly describe what it is; you live in a tent set up about fifteen feet above the ground in sturdy trees. You live in the "tree tent" for two or three days. In the mean while, they "bait" the nearby tigers that roam the site, who attack the bait and the cameras in the treetops record the event.

We had a wonderful visit with him. Upon my return to the states, I learned that Tiger Tops is quite familiar to travel agents most anywhere, so it can be said that Jim Edwards did, indeed, open a wild tiger farm he said he would fourteen years ago.

Another story that took place in 1964 involved the Verazano Bridge connecting Staten Island to Brooklyn, which was about to opened in November of that year. It was, and still is, one of the longest and most beautiful bridges in the United States. It was located at the very mouth of New York's lower harbor and very close to the Atlantic Ocean. It was truly a grand entrance gate to New York City. Jack Murphy was a close friend and West Point classmate and now a member of the US congress. He called me up a few weeks before the ceremony to open the bridge, and advised me that he, as the congressman representing Staten Island part of Brooklyn, and lower Manhattan invited President Lyndon Johnson to fly up from Washington as the honored guest to inaugurate the bridge opening. Jack then asked me to find a sky writer and instruct him to fly over the Staten Island side of the bridge. He wanted the sky writer to put up in the biggest letters possible LBJ-JMM, (the President initials and Jacks initials). I said ok, I would take care of it. I did not have any idea where to start. After a bit of thinking, I realized skywriters must be licensed by the federal aviation agency. I was correct, and after consulting with them, they came up with one skywriter located in Colts Neck, New Jersey, (about a twenty minute flight to the bridge site). I called this incident the live version of the comic hero, Smiling Jack. I started to explain my task at hand but when I told Smiling Jack my friend invited the President of the United States, he immediately hung up the phone. I called him back and managed to get the whole plan across, without him hanging up on me again. As if to dare me, he says, it will cost $2,000.00 cash and a deposit to $1,000.00 has to be received before he goes near his two-winged Waco relic from bygone days. I reported back to Jack Murphy and he accepted the skywriter's deal. The way this was plan was going to work, the President and his entourage would arrive at eleven in the morning at Floyd Bennet Naval Air Station in Brooklyn, New York and the limousines would make their way along a prescribed route to the Verazano Bridge. We established a point along the way, when the President was twenty minutes from the south end of the bridge, one of Jack's staff would call me. I then would call Smiling Jack, our pilot and he would crank up his old Waco and put LBJ-JMM in big letters over the south end of the bridge. The night before, I am so nervous, I do not believe I slept more than a couple of hours. During one of those hours the alarm goes off, I jump out of bed, it was 7 AM. I ran to the window, looked out, and there was a fierce wind that was bending the tops of many trees. I felt relief and joy, I ran to the phone and called Smiling Jack to cancel. Smiling Jack did not like the news very well; he said he believed that he could put those initials up in the sky about two hundred feet under the clouds, which would leave LGB-JMM about eight hundred feet above the ground.

"Listen to me Smilin' Jack, with this gale force wind, by the time you get the last letter up in the sky, the first one will be floating somewhere over Africa. The project is cancelled."

We gave him five hundred dollars for his trouble, and that was that. I then called Jack Murphy in Washington and explained the situation. Jack, who never gives up, suggested the skywriter create one of those cloth signs with the initials and then he could tow it over the bridge. I told Jack to put the whole project "back into the drawer" and lock it up for good. Frankly I was relieved, but Jack was very disappointed. The preceding incident shows you what kind of unique situations you can get caught in if enough people know you fly small planes.

Here's one for "the book" involving my small plane flying experiences. My brother-in-law and myself were after one particular account whose national headquarters were located in Dallas, Texas. We both were having a tough time convincing the sales manager for the company to use the Gray Line of New York for his various tour programs that included New York City. I told Ken to let me fly my plane, thirty-six hundred miles round trip to Dallas just to prove our determination to get his business. Ken thought my idea was a little excessive but agreed to it. I phoned Ed Smith in Dallas to request a meeting and advising him of my plan to fly to Dallas. He agreed to see me, and off I went. We had a cordial meeting and I left feeling something good would come of it. After all that, day after day went by with no news, until about two weeks passed and finally a phone call from Ed Smith. Ed started off with a question, "Elliot, would you do me a favor?"

"Sure Ed, just name it and it's yours." (Ken was standing at my side while I was talking to Ed and I gave him a big wink that indicated we were about to "crack the account"). Ed continued, "Well, Elliot that is great. My situation is, one of my brothers died a few days ago and in examining his will, it was his final wish to be cremated and have his ashes scattered over the Atlantic Ocean. None of the family knew what to do, and then your trip to see me flashed in my mind as the solution. Would you fly your plane out over the Atlantic Ocean and scatter my brothers ashes?"

I was stunned, but I gave him a stuttered yes. He then told me another brother who lives near the airport I fly from will call and meet me with the remains. Before the big day arrives, I am thinking about how I can accomplish the task. One idea was to take a plastic bag, the kind you usually get from the cleaners, and seal up the end where the hanger protrudes. Next I would empty the remains into the plastic bag. When the plane arrives at the designated spot, I would slow the plane down, open the window, put the plastic bag containing Ed's brothers ashes outside the window, while holding on to the fishing line attached to the plastic bag. Finally, I would have a broomstick with a nail on the end so I could punch holes in the bag. This would allow the ashes to be released over the Atlantic, as per Ed Smiths brother's last wishes.

Instead of any of the above process, what actually happened on that day did not involve a plastic bag or a broomstick. Ed Smiths surviving brother shows up at Teterboro Airport, dutifully carrying the urn. I asked him if I could take a peek, and was permitted. In the can, it looked like a bunch of black and white chips. I told his brother I did not think we would have any problem. Ed's brother further tells me he has never flown in a small plane and that he was quite nervous about the whole project. I tried to comfort him, but it did not do much good. I got him in the plane and buckled his safety belt then handed him the can with the ashes. I was hoping this would distract him from being so afraid. Off we go, flying south, following the Hudson River, then lower Manhattan, the Statue of Liberty, the Verazano Bridge, Ambrose light ship, and at last, the Atlantic Ocean. I identified the Ambrose light ship as the checkpoint for the beginning of the Atlantic and then slowed the plane down to quite close to stalling speed of sixty-five miles per hour. I turned to him and asked for the urn. He was trembling but managed to hand it to me. I opened the window; I opened the can and threw the contents out the window. Guess what happened? Almost all of the ashes flew back in! Ed's brother's face and hair were covered with the ashes of his deceased brother, and I assumed I was in the same condition. Some of the ashes went down into the flight controls and every time I made a flight adjustment you would hear the crunching of the chips. Chips and ashes were everywhere, including dancing on top of the instrument panel. We were a mess and so was the plane. I tried to comfort him, and said that I was sure I got at least eighty percent of the ashes outside, but with the ashes and chips all over the instrument panel and crunching in the controls, I am pretty sure he thought that eighty percent was inside the plane and only twenty percent made it outside to the Atlantic Ocean. Hardly a word was said between the two of us all the way back to the airport. He did offer to help clean up the inside of the plane, but I told him not to worry, as the ground staff would take care of it. As soon as he left, I went to work as best as I could to clean his brother's ashes out of the plane. A ground crew person came by; he took a look, and asked what had happened. I told him that I had had some fertilizer in an open bag in the back seat and the window suddenly opened. I finished cleaning, and headed for home. I kept my car window opened and I was furiously spitting the taste of Ed Smiths brother's ashes from my mouth. When I got home I rang the doorbell. Joan my wife answered the door and said, "You look like you got hit by someone with a leftover Halloween sock filled with flour."

I told her I would explain after I took a shower, shampoo and emptied a bottle of Lavoris mouthwash. This story was told at least a hundred times over the world and listeners had tears of laughter. Incidentally and understandably we did not get Ed Smiths business.

In the sixties, I became an active member of the West Point Society of New York. While we had a relatively large membership with over two hundred "grads" we never seemed to have enough funds to enlarge our activities. I suggested we give the Pennsylvania Railroad some competition with their annual promotion to provide transportation from New York, with special trains, to and from, the Army Navy football games held in Soldiers Field Stadium, Philadelphia. I told the board we could do the same with busses for less and still have money left over to accrue for activities of the society. (Up to this point the railroad never contributed anything to the West Point Society of New York). The board approved my recommendation and we began the service. Each year, it grew larger and larger. It reached a point where we were sending at least a thousand fans to the game, and the coffers of the society were beginning to grow nicely. Each year we did this, the service became more involved with coffee and buns becoming part of the fare.

One year about two weeks before the Army and Navy game, I received a very unusual phone call. The gentleman on the phone introduced himself as General Mark Clark (a four star general, who commanded the invasion of Italy during World War Two). He was interested in going to the Army and Navy game by bus. I found this quite strange and my immediate suspicion was, Joe McCrane my close friend was playing yet another trick on me as he was known to do many times. Sometimes, Joe would call me pretending to be David Ben-Gurion, Prime Minister of Israel, or some other V.I.P. Because of this possibility, I took the precaution to tell the assumed General Clark that he should meet me at the terminal information booth at seven AM, so that I could personally see to all the details. By suggesting this meeting, I was trying to figure out if the General Clark that was on the phone was actually the General or if it was Joe McCrane. By the way, General Clark was six feet five inches tall and even if he is in civilian clothes, I would be able to recognize him immediately. The day of the meeting, I am standing by the information booth at six forty-five waiting for the seven AM test. At precisely seven

A.M., into the terminal came this very tall person, alone, and he approached the information booth. I still could not understand why General Clark chose the bus to go the game. If the first Army Headquarters in New York knew that he was in town, he would have been "limousined" to Philadelphia with a motorcycle escort. Anyway, I introduced myself as the vice President of the West Point Society of New York, and told the general it would be a pleasure to offer the service as our guest. He politely said that was not necessary and then asked how much was the bus fare. I advised it was eight dollars, and then he handed me a ten-dollar bill. I gave him the tickets and his two dollars change. He thanked me and boarded the bus to the Army Navy game. It was just as simple as that.

During the sixties, I undertook a unique way of promoting our Gray Line Company in the southeast area of the USA. It involved using my experience as a pilot to call upon trade contacts in a way similar to my unsuccessful flight to Texas. In the southeast most of the specialized group travel business was promoted and organized by the railroads like Atlantic Coast Line, Seaboard Airline Railroad and the Southern Railroad. The reason the group operators chose the railroad rather than airline was price. The railroads were, at the time, losing out to the airlines, and they already had large numbers of existing passenger cars with lots of unused space available for special excursion group fares. To make this type of promotional trip practical, I explained to my brother-in-law, that I would approach the general managers of important New York City Hotels with heavy tourist traffic; I would be willing to take their director of sales with me, providing the hotel management, in each instance, shared the expense of the plane. Piloting a plane for a business visit not only would provide a positive impression on trade contacts, but it would open potential business for those hotels that agree to partner the expense. I was never turned down. Each year I would do this and it helped Gray Line considerably with the hotels who joined us as well as with accounts we visited.

For these unusual flights, there was always a considerable variety to my "co-pilots". Some looked upon this like it was a scary adventure that they wished their boss chose someone else; others couldn't wait until we started. Many times, while I was busy with my charts navigating our course, I turned over the controls to my "co-pilot" who was thrilled to actually fly a plane for the first time in their life. I will never forget the sales director from the Statler Hilton Hotel. This particular hotel was doing a large amount of business from Japan. At this time the Japanese were just beginning to develop their appetite for travel to the United States. To assure good relations with Japanese tour operators, the director of sales for the Statler Hilton was in fact Japanese, his name was Takiguchi. When I picked him up at his hotel we drove to the airport where he expected to see a big twin-engine aircraft with all amenities on board. Instead, there was this lonely looking small single engine plane with tight seating even for the two of us. He said to me in broken English, "We go four thousand miles in this small bird? Why not my boss tell this to me?"

I told him not to worry, lots of times we will have a tail wind which will give us a ground speed as much as one hundred and seventy miles per hour which is much faster than the cars on the road below us. Realizing that he had no choice, he buckled up and we took off on our adventure. In no time at all, he was fully on board and I could tell he was anxious to learn how to fly. He was amazing the way he picked up piloting. He was able to make banking turns, change altitude and make it possible for me to comfortably navigate. I started to consider that maybe Takiguchi was a pilot in World War Two, about twenty years ago! I did politely ask him about this, and he laughed. He never flew before, but it was something he read a lot about and dreamed of doing someday. We became quite good friends on the trip and I depended on his assistance.

One funny incident took place while we were walking along the street in Birmingham, Alabama. He called my attention to many people while passing us by were staring at him. I told him, in Birmingham at the time, they probably have never seen an Asian person, small in height, with slanting eyes and a different complexion. I told Taki it reminded me of a story of an Orthodox Jewish businessman from New York whose plane was forced to land in Birmingham due to engine trouble. The airline provided the passengers with bus service to the city while the plane was repaired and inspected. The Orthodox Jewish man, complete with full beard, black suit and large brimmed black hat was walking down the streets of Birmingham, just like we were doing. This fellow from New York noticed that everyone was "giving him the eye". After walking a couple of blocks he noticed that some of the onlookers were actually following him. He abruptly stops, turns around and says in a heavy Yiddish accent, "Vaht's the matter with you people; you never see a Yankee before?" Taki laughed and we went on to the airport to continue our flight program.

My next happening of the sixties had a major effect on my future and that of Gray Line in New York. It was the New York Worlds Fair in 1964 and 1965. The last World Fair in New York was held in 1939, and then the war took place, followed by getting our country's economy back into a peace mode. By 1964 the country was ready for a fair and New York City could not have been a better location. Part of our Gray Line planning had to do with an idea I had; run buses with pick-up service from midtown hotels to the World Fair to be held in Flushing, Queens, which was about fifteen miles from Manhattan. With most of the good New York tourist hotels located in mid-town I was convinced that tourists would use such a service. These visitors from all over the US and Canada as well as those originating from other countries would not know the first thing to do about using the subway or a city bus to get to the fair and they would be delighted with the "door to door" service. If we had a pick up service operating from the front doors of each established mid-town hotel to go to the fair and return; we could "clean up". My brother-in-law was not overly anxious and neither was anyone else, including Ken's father, Sidney Engelhardt (there were quite a few deals, where by the time we got through with discussions, the opportunity to decide was lost). I was engaged in such a discussion with Sidney and he finally made a move I could work with. He said he would start the door to door Worlds Fair service, if I could get at least three of the biggest travel companies in the country to put the door to door service in any of the Worlds Fair packages that they were working on for their clients. "Sidney, fair enough I will get back to you ASAP". I then contacted American Express, Thomas Cook, Greyhound Highway Tours (a very large travel division within Greyhound), and several other very big tour operations that in normal years brought thousands of their clients to New York. I did not get three to agree; I secured four or five and with no difficulty, and thus the planning for the service began in earnest. Everyone involved was cautious about how many busses to assign; on the first day of the opening for the fair, we started with four buses (about 200 seats). These buses were assigned to specific routes for hotel pickups. On that first day of the World Fair we carried over four thousand persons! All of the sudden, we did not have enough buses or drivers. The company attorney flew to Miami and was offering $10,000 for a summers work to bus drivers of the Miami Transit Company. Quite a number accepted the offer, left Miami Transit, and in less than two days they were behind the wheel driving our buses in New York City (for most, it was the first time they have ever been to new York). We were carrying on some days over 5,000 passengers. Not only was the bus to the World's Fair successful but also our regular tours were going crazy with tourists. Ken and I, most of the time, worked seven days a week and sometimes quite a few of the family chipped in to do whatever they could to help.

Between Ken and myself we received countless service requests coming from the heads of all kinds of companies who brought into New York City thousands upon thousands of people. One incident of this type came from one of the largest incentive travel companies in the country. The President calls me and says, "Elliot, I have a group from Carrier Air Conditioning Company who wants the whole works; Worlds Fair, Circle Line boats around Manhattan, and your sightseeing tours. They will be in New York for four days and should be about 5,000 persons! This President is calling me by my first name like he was part of my family; I never met him nor heard of him, but we suddenly became very well acquainted. We did the business and it was successful. I handled all arrangements except hotels. Can you imagine this fellow took over the entire capacity of the big hotels like the New York Hilton, The Americana, and about half a dozen of somewhat smaller ones? We were literally over run with activity. Every imaginable convention seem to have made New York their meeting site. Organizations like the Boy Scouts of America had 100,000 scouts gather for their jamboree at Valley Forge, Pennsylvania but not until they spent several days in New York. (The Boy Scouts selected me as their bus coordinator for the transportation from New York to Valley Forge). It seemed there were opportunities that came with each day of the fair. Some times they happened just because we were part of the swirl caused by our involvement with the Worlds Fair.

As an example, take our service to the World's Fair; we offered for those who did not have admission tickets, the convenience to buy admission tickets from us. We bought a pretty substantial supply before the fair and we were already running low on inventory. Toward the middle of 1964, there was no assurance the fair would run for another year, so the fair officials reduced the 1964 admission price of advanced tickets substantially. I bought 25,000 tickets for half price, but was severely criticized for my hasty action. As it turned out the World's Fair officials did decide to operate in the following year, and they raised the admission price one dollar! We kept 10,000 tickets to finish out 1964, which cost less than what we paid in the first place. We also sold 15,000 tickets to other tour operators who needed them for the second year of the fair and we netted $30,000 profit! The big money was coming into the company and we were becoming well recognized by our industry as one of the best up-and-coming sight seeing companies in the Gray Line Association.

An unusual incident developed in the January of the second year of the fair. Allow me to give you a little background to this story. Through my West Point classmate, Joe McCrane, I became a member of the board for Shannon Airlines, domiciled in Shannon Ireland. I was invited to join because Joe mentioned to the other directors that I was a commercially trained pilot and had extensive experience in the travel industry. It cost me $7,000 to do this, but that meant nothing when compared to the experiences about to happen. We operated three-leased ancient propeller driven aircraft. Our pilots were left over flying crews dismissed from KLM to cut their operating costs. Our franchise by the Irish Free State permitted us to operate charters world wide from Shannon, Ireland and we could carry passengers or freight. About a few weeks after I met the other board members, George Foley, our Shannon attorney at law, contacted me. He received word from Ireland; an Irish trade mission will be on a worldwide trip that will return to Ireland via the Untied States. This would include a stop over in New York where they would visit the World's Fair and I would be responsible for all services to and from the fair as well as VIP treatment at all exhibits that I would arrange to visit. The finale of the visit would be a black-tie private dinner at the posh 21 Restaurant. The trade mission itself was composed of various ministers from the Irish government and these ministers are most important to the future success of Shannon Airlines. Well, that was what the Shannon

Board wanted, but I really had no idea of where to start and then what to do.

It is possible, that some readers of this book have visited the New York World's Fair in 1964 or 1965. If you did, you had to wait on endless lines for two or more hours to gain admission to some of the more fascinating exhibits. How do I get the eight or nine ministers into these selected pavilions? My first attempt was to contact our General Motors sales people. My thinking was we purchased many General Motor buses for our various services; this should give us some leverage to get access to their great exhibit at the fair. They assured me that matter would be properly handled. Next, I called the Irish pavilion and I told them a hometown team of government ministers was coming to visit the fair and I thought it appropriate that they spent some time at the Irish pavilion. They were overwhelmed and insisted the visit to their pavilion would not be complete without an authentic Irish lunch as their guests. Then I set up the transportation from New York City via helicopter to land right on top of the fair's heliport building. Return transportation would be via hydrofoil, and of course; I went along to make sure everything "clicked". It did mostly, but I did think there was one spot that I was definitely heading into real trouble. Our group was coming out of the General Motors building. I was walking along with a few of the ministers. We took a break sitting down on some benches along the way, when Mr. O'Malley, Minister of Education turns to me and says in his best Irish brough, "Elliot, that General Motors exhibit was tops. Do you think you might get our group into the General Electric exhibit?" (For the readers benefit, this exhibit was even more popular than the GM visit we just completed). I really did not know what to do, but I made an attempt based on my knowledge to date that all the pavilions had a VIP door and this was carefully guarded. I excused myself from the group, ran over to the General Electric exhibit, which strangely enough was a completely round building (incidentally, with a line of people about half a mile long waiting to get in, my confidence was at a low ebb). I circled around to the outside of the building and sure enough there was the VIP door, and the guard as well. I ran up to him and said in my most plaintiff voice, "Sir, you have to help me. I am here today with eight ministers from Dublin, Ireland, and they have expressed a keen desire to see the General Electric exhibit."

I did not have the least idea of how he would respond to my plea, that is, until he replied in an Irish accent. His accent was so thick you could barely understand what he was saying. I did get the important part where he said, "Stop wasting time sonny, get those good souls over here and we'll get them in!"

I did just that. But now comes the biggest surprise of all. The General Electric exhibit was the most unique of all in the fair. Just imagine the inside of the round building is a round theater of seats divided in four sections each section separated by a wall. In the center of the circular theater is the stage which it self is circular and it too is divided into four different stages that are also "walled off" from each other. The whole circular stage then rotates until the four stages are lined up with the four different seat sections. Then, four shows go on simultaneously and end at the same time of fifteen minutes each. At the end of the fifteen minutes the stage rotates again and the next show is presented to the audience. (The audience does not move; they stay in their seats and see all four rotating shows).

With this explanation made, my eight ministers are rushed over to the VIP entrance and as they enter the circular theater the guard is practically kissing each of his countrymen. The audience lights dim and the first of the four shows they will see, begins, but hold on, the section we are seated in had only the eight ministers from Dublin and not one other person from that half mile line outside occupied the other two hundred empty seats! Our ministers had their own private theater for all of the four rotating shows!! After we left the General Electric building they huddled around me and their spokesman said, "Elliot me boy, we've been all over the world on this trip. We never received such VIP treatment!" Their surprise was nothing compared to my own.

One of my intriguing stories in the sixties again involved Shannon Airlines. You will recall my mention of investment in Shannon Airlines. Early in 1965, the Shannon Airlines board contacted me. This time they asked if I could "break away" from my work at Gray Line for five weeks, and go to Ireland. They wanted an evaluation of the competence of staff in both administration and market development. Since the assignment would take place mostly in February when my regular business was slow, my brother-in-law Ken was agreeable. I arrived in Shannon Airport on the west coast of Ireland in late January.

As an aside, you rarely see a picture of the Emerald Isle taken in the winter. Ireland is always shown with its countryside coated in a wash of green; with the bursting of spring flowers and other horticultural phenomenon taking place. Whereas in January and February you only have rain, rain and some more rain, compounded with penetrating cold. This bleak weather engulfs Ireland because of the nearness of the Gulf Stream and further is the fact that Ireland is almost at the same northern latitude as Iceland. When I arrived finally at Shannon Airport, the door to my TWA aircraft opened and I descended to the tarmac, which lead to the arrivals building. By the time I entered the building I was chilled to the bone and this condition lasted until I re-boarded for my flight home.

My next surprise took place when the non-heated cab drops me off at the Limerick Hotel, in the town of Limerick. As you enter this cold and grey stone mausoleum, etched in a stone close to the entrance is the engraving,

Established 1665

After checking in I received my more or less four-pound key to my room. I walked up to the third floor of the elevator-less hotel. By this time, darkness has come upon Ireland (due to the latitude of Ireland, in January and February darkness sets in before 3 pm).

As I enter the dark room and begin to search for a light switch, it came to my immediate attention; there was no heat in the room! I called the front desk and they advised that it was perfectly normal for a building of this age not to have centralized heating or air-conditioning. After a hot bath, for which I was very thankful for, I did calisthenics and twenty pushups, to get my blood flowing and warmed up, then I turned off the light off and jumped into bed. As I pulled the covers over myself, I felt something close to me that felt like a dead fish! I grabbed "the something" and threw it against the wall. Suddenly, I was covered with hot water, and all my bedclothes were soaked through. A flick of the bed lamp revealed "my fish" was a rubberized hot water bottle that the hotel provides free of charge, to warm up the bed before you sleep! (I spent the remainder of the night asleep on the sofa covered by my lined raincoat.) That fist night in Ireland ranked at the top of my list of bad bed experiences. I actually became better adjusted with each passing day, especially when I learned not to expect too much.

The next day finally arrived and after a pretty good breakfast I was picked up by Shannon airlines office staff and taken to Shannon Airport where our offices were located. Alan Fellows was the general manager and for the rest of my stay in Ireland he attached himself to me like Velcro, for fear I might be his guillotine. (Actually, I was impressed with Alan, although not impressed with the overall operation.) While on the subject of management, and before getting into the knitty-gritty, a word must be said about Shannon Airlines President, Kermit Roosevelt. I do not know exactly how he came on to the scene to be President, except from day one of our incorporation as Shannon Airlines; he was already in the chair. By family, he was the grandson of the former President of the United States, namely Theodore Roosevelt. Oddly enough, he worked at the US Central Intelligence Agency and was their key figure in ousting of Mossadegh, Prime Minister of Iran and replacing him with the Shah of Iran of the Royal House of Pahlavi. Surprisingly most of the work received by Shannon Airlines originated from the Middle East. An Example of this was the contract from the Saudi Arabian government to fly the Hadji from Jetta to Mecca for the annual Muslim pilgrimage. Why was Shannon, the neophyte airline, suddenly landing this kind of lucrative contract?? Read on and you will get the answer to this question.

Shannon Airlines was also a member of the Irish bourse, which allowed us to bid on projects that were submitted to the bourse for cargo or passenger lifts. These types of orders were insufficient for economic survival, so we had to lean on our own ingenuity. There were some ideas, that in no way, would make is possible for any one of our three planes to ever get off the ground but there was one plan Shannon Air brought up that was a knockout concept, (before explaining this further, it was my initial observation that the creative juices for our small insignificant airline were no different than the boiling brains of airline management of the early thirties airline history, when the entrepreneurs of those days devised the most bizarre schemes just to get any revenue for survival).

Here is our "knockout" concept. To begin with you do not have to be brilliant to realize that Ireland is known world wide for Irish lamb. In 1964, believe it or not, there was very little "fresh" meat made available to the rest of Europe, particularly in Italy. The problem was, it was too expensive to fly meat, and so it was frozen and shipped frozen via surface means. With that background our Shannon "boys" further pointed out that Fiat, whose main head quarters was located in Milan also had an assembly plant at Shannon Airport in Ireland. I said to the Shannon staff, "So what, what does Fiat have to do with Lamb and our airline"?

Our first fleet aircraft for Shannon Airlines was an aging Douglas DC-4. Shortly after, we added two more aircraft, also of early vintage.

In response, they told me, they could get the butchers of Milan to act in concert, to become the first major Italian city to have fresh lamb flown in by Shannon Airlines. There could be daily flights with fresh lamb going from Shannon to Milan. My query then was, "How can you compete, price wise, with the surface transportation?" Their reply was, "That is where the Fiat assembly plant become the last piece of the puzzle."

Alan Fellows, our operations manager, contacted Fiat in Milan and set up "a back haul" service for the plane. This means the plane would land in Milan with the fresh Irish lamb; the plane would get "hosed down" and pick up the Fiat parts needed for the assembly plant in Shannon. Here is "the kicker"; we would carry the lamb one way to Italy, and the same plane returns to Ireland with the Fiat auto parts. We quoted the butchers and Fiat one-way charter rates with no charge for what we normally call the "dead head" return. It is normal to charge a rate for the "dead head" return (also known as the empty return). This made our one-way rate for the Irish lamb to Europe to be very competitive with the round trip rate the surface shipper quotes for frozen meat. In other words, the lamb and the auto parts were separate flights using the same plane with only a one-way charge for each shipper.

The wholesale butchers of Milan were invited to Shannon to witness, how Shannon will operate this innovative procedure to ship, for the first time fresh meat to the Milan, Italy market. The DC-4 aircraft we would use was thoroughly inspected and cleaned; all the seats were removed. The DC-4 was a four engine propeller aircraft of some vintage, but in good working condition. Our ground crew went to great lengths to make everything perfect. They even spread heavy-duty butcher paper throughout the floor of the planes interior! As for the Shannon staff, each one of us was dressed with brand-new full-length white butchers coat. The five wholesale butches from Milan all arrived at Shannon Airport, on the same flight and our rented limousine whisked them to our airport operation office. As they were being briefed, eight trucks or, or as called in Ireland, lorries, lined up behind each other alongside the plane. Each lorry was filled with freshly killed Irish lamb pistolaes (each pistolae weighed about sixty pounds and I would guess there were about thirty in each lorry). As the Milan butchers left the briefing room and headed to the plane our Shannon staff in our clean white full length butcher coats joined them, to be prepared for any questions from the butchers). Earlier in the day, I had asked one of the staff, "What kind of refrigeration does the plane have?"

He gives me an odd look and says, "none".
"How do you expect to keep the lamb at the proper temperature?"
"That's why we have taken the cargo door off. If the temperature is too warm the pilot pours a little power on and climbs to an altitude where the temperature is correct for proper storage of the pistolaes!"

As we approached the plane, there seemed to be a bit of commotion going on by the aircraft's cargo door. We immediately saw what the problem was, as well as the solution. The problem was the backend of each lorry was about six feet below the floor level of the plane. One of our ground crew commandeered a forklift truck and lined it up against the backend of the lorry. Another ground crew member then pushes the pistolaes out of the lorry and on to a large square shaped board on the forklift. Then forklift raises the board to the level of the floor of the plane. At this point, another ground crew member takes the pistolaes off the forklift onto the plane, and yet another ground crew person is inside the cabin of the plane evenly distributing the lamb. Abruptly, all of the white coated Shannon staff including myself, get the big picture and we jump into action, pushing, lifting and stacking the pistolaes from the lorry's to the aircraft cabin for the flight. If it was not for the fact we were going to miss our take off time by a wide margin, I would say that scene of unloading the lorries and loading the plane with the ground crew and the white coat brigade, throwing around these sixty pound hunks of lamb was an absolutely hilarious scene and it would have made a fantastic bit in a comedy movie. (You should have seen those white butcher coats; they were dripping with blood.) What made it funnier, all this time, the butchers from Milan were not lifting a finger; they just stood in amazement watching us. They eventually drifted off while we worked continuously into the night. We finally unloaded the eight lorries into the plane, and I am telling you something; when we were done, there was very little difference between the Shannon management in the bloody butcher coats and any of the pistolaes, we were both quite bloody and beat up. Finally our flight crew was ready to board the craft and it appeared the cargo was properly secured and the weight evenly distributed. As previously explained, our pilots were ex KLM pilots made redundant during a purge by KLM to reduce operating costs. They were not too bad, but neither were they, the best. The plane roars down the runway with its' heavy load and gradually takes to the air. The white coat brigade in our bloody butchers coats go to the flight crew locker room to take much needed showers and change clothing, and then we are off to the communications shack to check on the progress. A crackle comes over the radio. The crew reports they have an hour and a half to go before arriving in Milan. That would mean they would be landing at about one in the morning. They would then have to unload the plane and load the Milan trucks, which would take another two hours. Then off to the Milan market place and most certainly they would have arrived in time for the five AM start of business. It all sounds pretty good, doesn't it?

WRONG. Another message from our flight crackles over the radio, "Milan is socked in with dense fog and the airport is closed. We have been diverted to Genoa, Italy". (Fog in Milan during the winter months is practically a nightly occurrence, but this was going to put us in the graveyard). The Milan trucks were immediately ordered to "push the pedals to the metal" and race though the mountains and down to Genoa, unload the cargo from the plane to the trucks, and then speed as best as they could back over the mountains and into the Milan market. Needless to say we missed the five am Milan market, and in fact, did not arrive in Milan until 4PM with a lot of useless Irish lamb. When you figure out just the non-flying part for the lorries in Ireland and Italy, air tickets, the cost of the spoiled lamb and amenities for the visiting Milan butchers, labor costs of all kinds, and don't forget the ruined butcher coats, it all added up to a financial disaster.

Unfortunately, there were a few more bad deals. After this experience and another week with Shannon Airlines it showed me there was very little chance for Shannon to succeed. It was time to go home. About a year later the airline went bankrupt to the tune of $300,000, which was a lot of money in 1965, but what worried me more so, was how much was I going to have to contribute? This question became a very strange situation; a situation that always surrounded Shannon Airlines. I never had a knock on my door with the delivery of a registered letter starting off with, "Your share is...".

About ten years later, I was attending a travel conference and met a fellow who used to sell aircraft spare parts. I just thought I would mention if he ever heard of Shannon. He said yes he had heard of them, but he was never able to get the account. I told him how lucky he was; he probably would have never been paid. He advised that I was completely wrong. He further stated, just about every one in the business knew Shannon Airlines were financially supported by the Central Intelligence Agency!!

The whole decade of the sixties was "chocker blocked" with many different scenarios that had a major affect on my commercial and private life. Let us begin with the private life. In a simple statement of reality, Joan Heit and myself were never really meant to be. We stuck it out as long as possible based on the old fashioned idea that the children's stability depended on, "Elliot and Joan the unit". With my deepening involvement in a very active commercial life and Joan's very deep involvement with her family, we were growing apart. Despite efforts to "plaster it over", for the benefit of the children, our marriage came up short. I tried to focus on the children, by being a very proactive father with whatever little spare time I had. Unfortunately, my attempt most always, lacked my partner's presence. As an athlete since high school days, it was easy to become a fair tennis player, and a pretty good skier. I taught my youngest daughter Karen how to ski and just the two of us, would go on many ski weekends. I will never forget one incident. Karen at fourteen was quite developed physically. She and I were checking into a quaint family inn, up at Mt. Snow, Vermont. It was noticeable that other guests in the hotel were treating us somewhat oddly. I could not understand what was going on, until a middle-aged bachelor asked, "How do you do it at your age?" I replied, "Do what?" When he said, with a shrug and a wink, " You know".

I nearly came to blows with him! I found out the other guests had viewed us in the same way as the dirty old man and his teenage girlfriend. As time passed in the "not so" quaint inn, the people accepted that we were father and daughter.

At another time, I told my wife I was going to fly the kids down to Florida. I thought the flight would be interesting and then Karen and Robin could also visit their grandparents, who spent a good part of the year in Miami Beach. Joan was completely against this project, but we went anyway. Even though Robin and Karen were in a plane piloted by their father, the long trip of two days was still a bore. Karen chose to return by commercial flight. Robin, my oldest, stuck it out with me, and returned back to New Jersey with another two day flight, and that finished any further flying interest. It was almost as though Robin and Karen were aware of the impending situation.

One of the dramatic steps taken by me was moving out of the master bedroom and into the maid's room, (do not worry; the maid was long gone before the move). I think it has a reverse affect on Joan because she thanked me for being so considerate!

We were definitely approaching a "crisis crunch". As an example of this increasing separation from Joan, three times per week I was up at six AM, and would leave the house in my tennis outfit. Before leaving the house I would throw a suit, shoes, plus some sundries into the car and drive to New York. I used to park on Central Park West around Seventieth Street and run to the Central Park Tennis Club. There I would meet Lore Moser who was the general manager of a chic restaurant in the park called Tavern On The Green. This status gave her membership in the tennis club and I was her guest quite frequently. This was a total platonic relationship. It was quite enjoyable; I got my exercise as her tennis was good and I was still able to arrive at my office by nine o'clock. It was a great way to get away from the silence at home and to start my day. The tennis in the park continued on until the very last day of my marriage. On that conspicuous day, there I was with my car, "packed to the hilt" with all my clothing. Once again, but for the last time, I left the house dressed in my tennis togs, for my morning match with Lore of the Tavern On The Green. Of course I kissed the kids goodbye, and assured them we would be seeing a lot of each other. I shook Joan's hand, and shoved off for my seven thirty match.

On that day, I do not think God liked my style very much; I will tell you why. When I finished playing tennis that morning, I took my usual shower, dressed and rushed out to my car, which as I had mentioned was a convertible. I went to unlock the door, but it was already ajar. Looking inside the car and then the trunk, revealed that every stitch of clothing, shoes etc, were gone!! I was robbed of everything I had except the clothes on my back. I thought that God did not understand me, I was a very moral person, and my early morning tennis match, was strictly for the tennis and to get the day started. I must say, the robbery was a heck of a going way present from my Teaneck, New Jersey family. It took me a while to find an apartment in New York; in the meantime I stayed at the McBurney YMCA. My brother-in-law thought I was crazy.

To give you a peek at my marital future, there was a small story that took place a couple of weeks or so before I drove off from Teaneck for the last time. While Joan and I were at odds with each other, the situation was kept secret from everyone. Bob Peltz and his wife invited Joan and I to a very elegant dinner party held in their posh Park Avenue apartment. (Bob was previously mentioned as one of my classmates from West Point, and a close friend). Upon arrival, we rang the doorbell; the maid, who escorted us to the living room where cocktails and hors d'oeurvres were being served, opened the door. After two rounds of this we adjourned to the dinning room and we were seated according to a planned arrangement. From were I was seated I noticed that there were two vacant chairs at the far end of the table. At that moment the door chimes sounded, possible signaling the late arrival of the missing couple. Once again, the maid carried out her duties, to greet and properly escort the guests to dinner. Then there appeared the most beautiful woman I have ever seen, but she was by herself. She was shown to one of the two vacant chairs. She was introduced as Carol Goldworm; and she explained her apologies for her late arrival and that her husband, who owned an exclusive dress factory in Milan, Italy, was unable to get out of Milan due to the fog that besets that area quite frequently. Back to Carol, when she entered the apartment, her slender form was attired in a dress that seemed to be made of a material that gave off a silver sheen. When she talked, she had a bubbling manner that made you want to listen even if you did not understand a word she said. When we were first introduced, our eyes met for a moment, then for the rest of dinner I would occasionally lift my eyes toward her chair and enjoy a few peeks at this charming chatterbox. My wife seated across the table from me, may have noticed my bad conduct, but the glances were worth it. I know it sounds ridiculous for me to say this, but I thought to myself, "I do not know whether I will ever see this person again; If and when I do, it will mark the beginning of a romance that will lead to a marriage, no matter how long it takes."

About a year passed by, and once again, Bob Peltz hands me another invitation, but this time it was at his beautiful summer home in Westhampton, Long Island, the playground for the wealthy adult community of New York. At least it seemed so to me as the homes were quite large and elaborately decorated and most of the parents had sent their kids away to summer camps. My car at this time was one of the early Camaro models; a neat little racing green two seat convertible and towed behind it, on a trailer, was my fourteen-foot sunfish sailboat. In my suitcase, I had my dinner attire, and sport clothes. Separately my tennis racquet and the sailboat were also "on the ready."

While in Westhampton, I went to the Aspatuck Tennis Club, where well-known tennis personality Bobby Riggs was at that time the "tennis pro". You might remember Bobby Riggs from his big "duel of the sexes" match with Billy Jean King. He linked me up with John Scali as a tennis partner. (John Scalli was the US delegate to the United Nations). Oh, also his tennis was superb. I was playing quite off that day, and just could not get into the swing, so to speak. I was diplomatically asked to leave the courts. I sat on a bench on the sidelines, and from the caliber of playing observed, they were certainly correct to ask me to leave the courts. While watching the match, a woman sat down and made herself comfortable on the bench, where I was sitting. When I turned to look, to my surprise, IT WAS HER! It was the same beautiful girl that was the solo dinner guest at the Peltz's party held in their apartment in New York. I could not believe this was happening.

"Do you like tennis?
Carol replied, "No, and I find it boring to watch"
"Listen, I have a sailboat, what say we steal off for a quick sail on the bay?'
"That sounds more like it, I'm game."

(Now, you have to understand, when someone in Westhampton invites you for a sail; at a minimum, it is a forty foot boat)

I then accompanied Carol to my two seat Camaro roadster, which had the fourteen-foot sunfish in tow. She looked a bit surprised, but when I opened the door for her, she hopped right in and we were off to Hampton Bay. We sailed the bay then beached the sunfish on one of the many small islands. We looked for shells and walked and talked a bit. After a while we decided it was time to return to the club so I put her on the sailboat and prepared to launch from the beach. As I leaned over to see if she was properly situated in the small cockpit of the sunfish, I just could not resist planting a small kiss on her lips. It could have caused an explosion, but nothing was said and that was the end of a perfect weekend.

It was not very long after the Westhampton visit that I received a phone call at my office from Carol. She asked if I would like to see her again. Again, I could not believe that this was happening, but it was. I called her back and we made an appointment to meet at the Spring Close Inn, in Westhampton. I explained to Ken my brother-in-law what was going on and he was totally sympathetic even though my wife was his sister. The Spring Close Inn is top notch for Long Island duck and for our lunch they certainly lived up to the Inn's reputation. Frankly, I could have had a peanut butter and jelly sandwich and our lunch would have still been one of the best in a long, long time. After a wonderful meeting at the Inn, I returned to New York and Carol went to her house in Westhampton. As time went by, our relationship was taking on a serious direction. For me, my situation was quite clear. When I moved out of the Teaneck home, that was already, according to New Jersey divorce law, the first step. The law states the husband must abandon the wife regardless of fault and we must stay separated for two years before the divorce takes effect.

The Legal action between Joan and myself was completely amicable with both sides realizing the futility and waste of life. In Carol's case, it was a bit more complicated, although, there were humorous anecdotes along the way toward her divorce. He husband was not a bad person. He was Jewish and Carol, Episcopalian. While he was the creative element in a very successful family business, Bob's mother and sister dominated his attention. This caused Carol to feel isolated despite the fact that they lived affluently. A perfect example of this was her solo arrival and our first meeting at the dinner party held at the apartment of my classmate, Bob Peltz. The circumstances of her isolation and my years of marital difficulty sort of created a destiny right then and there for the two of us. There was never a desire to have a tryst; neither of us was put together that way. It was the realization that here we were two people who accidentally discovered each other and felt the blessing of knowing we were meant to be. Incidentally that was thirty years ago; our wedding was March 15, 1974. In Carol's case, she was "the heavy", i.e. she wanted the divorce.

Well, at last we made it to the wedding date. The event took place at Carol's apartment, 1175 Park Avenue. It was a beautiful residence. Carol had the living room adorned with all kinds of fresh flowers and she also arranged for a well-established caterer called the Silver Pallet. We were more than sufficiently stocked with French champagne, to be enjoyed by seventy guests. The marriage vows were performed by Vito Titone, a Supreme Court judge for the state of New York, supplied by Jack Murphy, congressman from Staten Island, and best friend.

For the wedding ceremony, I insisted Carol's children, Susan age nine and Robert age six, must participate to show new family unity. Robert held his mothers hand and Susan held mine, and the judge barely held his position (from one too may trips to the champagne table). Carol's mother, Alice was there, but she was definitely not in favor of the wedding or her daughters divorce from Bob Goldworm. To prove this, she wore a black dress, a black hat and shoes to match! Everybody else was in a great mood, especially the bride and groom. Of course Joe McCrane and Jack Murphy were present. There were a few other West Point graduates in attendance, Tom Messereau and Ted Halligan. They both had graduated a few years before me, but we had become friends during school, as they were both excellent football players. Tom served on General McArthur's staff during the occupation of Japan, and later opened a very successful restaurant in Englewood Cliffs, New Jersey called the Opera. (Tom's wife was the daughter of Gene Leone of the famous Leone's restaurant of New York City). Ted Halligan's wife Irene was Dave Garroway's executive director during his early television history in the most popular morning show. Subsequently, she became Mayor Giuliani's director of public relations.

By the time the festivities were over, it was quite late. One of the last to leave was Carol's mother. I took her down stairs and placed her, in a pre-paid cab back to Long Island. From the time she entered the apartment for the wedding, until the time she left, she did not utter a word. Strange as it may seem, we eventually became very close, and she advised me, in later years, that she loved me as much as her own son.

Sometime after we met I bought Carol's daughter a birthday present, a small dog called a Shepoo. A Shepoo was a controlled mix breed of a Shitzu and a Miniature Poodle. I have yet to meet either of the two children, so I left to Carol the job of arranging the pick up. Susan, Carol's daughter and her mother went to the pet shop to lay claim to this tiny ball of fur. They named it Penny, and she was deeply loved by all of us for nineteen years. The reason for introducing Penny at this point is the fact wherever Carol and the kids went Penny was part of the party. This included skiing!

One winter before we were married, Carol decided to take the children skiing up to Sugarbush, Vermont. I was in Chicago on business. I called Carol and she told me about her skiing plans. It would take place on a weekend and I decided to fly to Vermont from Chicago and meet up with Carol and the children who as mentioned before never met me. (Carol was separated, but she was nervous about the children meeting a strange man during the separation period prior to her divorce.) I told her not to worry. I would be arriving from Chicago to Burlington, Vermont, where upon I would rent a car for the short trip to Sugarbush. I stayed in the bunk bed annex of the hotel and pretended I had been hired as a ski instructor. To complete the scene, I wore a ski mask to prevent any kind of identity problem. When we finally got together, with my ski mask in place, I introduced myself to Robert and Susan, as Sidney the ski instructor. We spent the entire day teaching Susan, Robert, and Carol the traditional snowplow. The kids were making good progress, but Carol had a tough time. The hit of the day was my taking "snow dog" Penny up to the top of the beginner's slope and holding her in my outstretched arms and my body in a crouched position, as though Penny was skiing. The kids were hilarious and so excited to see their dog almost skiing down the slope; it gave then great encouragement to improve their own skiing (and so did Carol). After an early dinner Robert and Susan had brushed their teeth and were ready for bed. They were looking forward to the next day of lesson two with Sidney the ski instructor.

Carol and I had dinner with Doug and Eddy, two friends of ours. After dinner I went to Carol's room to have a nightcap before going back to my bunk bed in the annex. Keep in mind, I do not usually wear my ski mask to dinner, so while we are having the night cap suddenly, we heard a patter of feet and a knock on the door and Sidney the ski instructor is about to be discovered. As Carol goes to the door, she tells me to hide under the bed. I do this effectively, but much to my dismay, the children tell their mother, their room is cold and very dark and they did not like it. So into their mother's bed they go and I spent the entire night looking up at the mattress springs! The kids were right; it was cold, and much colder without a blanket on the floor. (The New England Inn keepers like to turn down their heat at night for conservation reasons, and of course, the proprietor of the inn was somewhat unaware of my plight).

In the morning Robert and Susan went back to their room to prepare for breakfast, and it was then I got out from under the bed. I felt like I was mugged, and I was also coming down with a bad cold. Worse yet, I looked outside the window and it appeared that during the night we picked up about twelve or thirteen inches of snow, and it was continuing to snow even harder. The television revealed we were having a blizzard and we were notified that all airports in the vicinity were closed. Compounding the problem was my need to be back in Chicago by Monday for a meeting chaired by the President of Greyhound Corporation! The snowstorm continued unabated throughout Sunday. The ski slopes were closed. My ski mask disguise would no longer work, so the children were able to meet Sidney face to face. When I went outside to look at the damage the storm was causing, I saw that my rental car was getting buried. I asked my friend Doug Jacobsen if he would help shovel some of the snow off my car so that as soon as the storm subsided, I could get to Burlington airport and "sweat out" a flight to Chicago. I explained my upcoming meeting and why it was urgent that I returned to Chicago ASAP. He took one look at me and said, "If you don't get something for that cold you have, the only place you will be going to is the hospital."

With that exclamation Doug starts to dig my car out and his wife mixes up a very hot brew for me called a Moscow Mule. I was desperate, so I gobbled a large mug of this concoction without questioning its ingredients. (Later on I found out it was composed of vodka and onion soup). By the time I overcame the alcohol content, my friend Doug gave up digging, but as sick as I was, I had to finish getting the car free of the snow. The storm finally subsided. I said goodbye and managed successfully to get to the airport despite treacherous road conditions.

The Chicago bound plane was fortunately grounded in Burlington, when the storm began and the crew was also grounded. They were as anxious as I was to get back to Chicago, their operational hub. The plane only had about ten passengers on board; that was enough for the pilot to close the door and take off. The runways had been plowed and we were on our way. Even with all my efforts, our arrival in Chicago was already well past the Monday meeting time with the President of Greyhound. Tuesday morning, I rushed to his office and he was in a rage (it almost looked like Doug's wife already got to him with one of her Moscow Mules). He did not give a hoot about the blizzard, digging the car out, etc. I was not there in Chicago on Monday as planned and thus another notation was made in his little black book that he carried with him at all times in his jacket pocket.

Chapter 7

Traveling the World as a Corporate Vice President for Greyhound

In 1967 there were two scenes that are worth reporting. One was very serious and one was very funny. Let us go to the serious one first which started in 1967, but required almost two years to be resolved. In the spring of 1967, I received a personal phone call from the Executive Vice President of the Greyhound Corporation inviting me to participate in a meeting to take place in the May Flower hotel, Washington, DC. I was told to tell no one about this meeting. I agreed to do this and flew to Washington the next week. I was directed to a suite at the Mayflower hotel and as I entered, there were about five senior executives from the Greyhound Corporation. They told me about their plan to open a new sightseeing company in Washington to be called White House, and they would like to offer me the position of being the President. I told them I was honored, but I turned it down. I explained, for one thing, I do not think they could afford me; I also explained that some day the Greyhound Corporation may want to acquire the Gray Line of New York, so why remove a major part of the company's management. They responded to my concern for proper salary by saying this would not be a problem. In so far as Gray Line New York, they brought up the possibility to my father-in-law several times but he never took it seriously. I explained that is because you did not present it properly. "Why should he sell one of his shining stars, and then weaken his other transportation interest that are all interconnected with the Gray Line? Offer him a package." My statement "sunk in" and they immediately called the President of Greyhound and conveyed my thoughts. The meeting was over and I flew home. My wife tells me her father called and he was in some kind of rage about something I said to the executives of Greyhound. I called her father, Sid, and "right off the bat", he asked where did I get the idea that the Engelhardt's would sell Gray Line New York to the Greyhound Corporation? I said, "from you. You were always complaining about the union problems and all the different costs that surrounded the business. You often said you would like to get out, and apparently to me, here was your chance." He then cooled down enough to tell me Gerry Troutman; the chairman of the board called him and will be in Washington next week. Mr. Troutman wants the both of us to be there for further discussion on the matter. (It took almost a year and a half, but finally, it was agreed to go to contract). Ken, my brother-in-law and general manager for Gray Line was not very happy about the prospect. In a way I did not blame him. After all, he was an important part of the family business and his security foundation was being undermined. As it turned out, Ken made out the best of all the family with his share of the sale proceeds, a five year contract at good salary level, and several significant finder fees received when he subsequently became involved in the sale of the company on two occasions some years later.) As for me, I was very pleased as it represented an opportunity to get out on my own (I also received a five year contract and a share of the sale proceeds which I shared with my separated wife).

All of the forgoing was finalized in the fall of 1969. When the ink just about dried, I received yet another call from Greyhound. This time it was Herb DeGraff, Senior Vice President of Marketing of the Greyhound Corporation (It is important to point out that the Greyhound Corporation is not the bus line; it was the parent company and it owned the bus line as well as about one hundred and thirty other companies such as Dial Soap, Armour Meat, etc, etc, and now even the Gray Line New York Tours). Herb, who I have known for years in his prior activity as a consultant for the Gray Line Association asked me to come to the Greyhound Corporation headquarters in Chicago, and join his staff as Vice President of Sales and Planning. At that time the corporation was the forty-third largest company in the United States. I was flabbergasted by the offer. I conferred with Carol, who was practically my fiancé and she had only one word to say, "Go." I spoke to Ken my brother-in-law and he thought it was an opportunity I should accept, even though my presence at Gray Line New York would be missed. I called Herb DeGraff and said I would accept the offer only if he arranged for my nineteen foot, full keel, Cape Dory sailboat that weighed three thousand pounds, to be shipped at company expense along with all my household goods. The boat was in storage in Three Mile Harbor, way out on Long Island, about eighty miles from New York. In comparison, my household goods, without the boat, would literally fit into two or three shopping bags. Herb said the boat would be taken care of, and I agreed to go to Chicago.

Before going to Chicago I said there were two stories in 1967 that are prominent in my memoirs. One was the Chicago move to occupy "my new seat", in corporate America. The other very funny story, once again brings Joe McCrane back into the picture. At the time, Joe, was like myself, also involved in several business activities with his wife's father who owned Hialeah Racetrack in Miami, Florida, and Garden State Racetrack in New Jersey. Additionally he had Joe build the Cherry Hill Inn, a three hundred-room beautiful hotel in South Jersey near the racetrack. This was a terrific success; Joe managed the Inn and was also connected to the Garden State track.

He called me in January of 1967 to explain the Hialeah Race Track in Florida just bought a brand new thirty eight foot Chris Craft sports fishing boat, complete with a captain and we could take it out for a week of fishing and cruising the Gulf stream. He also suggested we fly down in my air club's Cessna Sky Lane. I checked and the plane was available. We set the date for a week after his phone call. About two days later, Joe asked me how far a flight is it? I replied, about twelve hundred miles. He ponders this information for a moment, and then says, "At two hundred miles a sandwich, we will need twelve sandwiches each!!" Experience has taught me to take everything that Joe says and divide it in half; I did just that but it was still a dozen sandwiches, and then he goes on to make sure I go to the Stage Deli, and ask for Ben to prepare this order as Ben was the owner of perhaps the best known deli in New York City that frequently hosts many of the famous Broadway show people. I told Joe I would take care of that detail. I did not tell Joe, I also went to an Army & Navy store, where I bought two sets of World War Two leather flying helmets and goggles. I made sure Joe's helmet was undersized so that it would add to his comic look. I picked up all the stuff and brought it home, so that I would be ready the next morning to go directly to Teterboro Airport and fly to North Philadelphia Airport to pick up Joe at 10 AM. Incidentally, Joe called me back after giving me the deli order. I should make sure to have enough pickles and buy lots of Dr. Brown's Celery Tonic and Cream soda's, (and this guy is an Irishman).

That night it rained a bit, followed by a big drop in temperature making it one of January's coldest and iciest days. As a result, the runways at Teterboro were slick with ice, causing a risk of skidding during takeoff. Thankfully there was little wind and not a cloud in the sky. Take off was okay with no sideways skidding. I arrived at North Philadelphia Airport on time and there was big Joe in all kinds of sweaters, fleece leather flying jacket and big mittens. His first question, "Where are the sandwiches and soda?" I opened the cargo compartment and two very large shopping bags labeled with "Ben's Deli, the Best Kosher Sandwiches in New York City".

Joe inspected the two bags and then threw his luggage into the backseat and gave the look of approval. We took off with another icy runway, but again we were lucky the wind this time was coming straight at us. If it were coming at an angle, it might have made us skid off the runway. Up we went and then at five thousand feet, we leveled off and initially followed the New Jersey Turnpike south to the state of Delaware. Our first refueling stop would be in Raleigh, North Carolina, about five hundred miles from our starting point. When we settled down, I explained to Joe, he would do a little of the actual flying of the plane while I checked out our map position and corrected our heading if the wind was drifting us off course. Unfortunately, we were flying against a rather strong head wind.

This brought Joe to question, "Hey Stud, I'm looking down at the turnpike and I see cars going in the same direction that we are, except they are passing us!" His next question, "What time are we going to arrive at Miami Airport in Florida?"

"If everything goes right about four pm."

"That's not bad, when we get to Raleigh, I'll call Hialeah Racetrack and tell them to make a dinner reservation for seven o'clock tonight."

"Joe, we are not flying a rocket ship; I mean we will be arriving at Miami Airport TOMORROW at four pm."

He was shocked, "Two days to fly to Miami is about what it takes when you drive a car?'

"That is true Joe, but isn't this fun?"

...and so we grind on to Raleigh, North Carolina. I purposely picked out an airfield that was a left over WW II training base that was turned over to the city of Raleigh for a municipal airport. I chose this airport deliberately, because there would e very little air traffic. I explained to Joe that this airport is perfect for us to put on a little show. With that said, I gave him his bag containing the undersized helmet and goggles. He knew immediately his role and I took out my helmet and goggles to complete the scene. Mind you we are flying completely enclosed in a cabin with the helmets they used to wear in the old stunt planes with open cockpits. We circled the field and received clearance to land. As we finished the end of the landing a jeep drives up to our plane with a big sign "Follow me". The jeep turns around on the active runway to take us down to the other end. By the way, there is not one other plane at this airport, nor in the air coming in for a landing. I turn to Joe, "Joe, act one is about to start."

We stopped on the runway put our goggles down over our eyes and we went to the luggage compartment, got the two Ben's Deli shopping bags out, sat on the runway chomping a salami on rye for Joe, and a bologna and cheese for me. As we are washing down the first bite with our cream soda, the jeep comes up to our picnic site. The driver yells out in a southern drawl,

"I aint never seen anything like this in my life! You Yankees; don't give you a minute after you get out of New York and your sucking down those lousy salami and bologna sandwiches with pickles, mustard, and that funny lookin' "sodie water"
"Say, there is not much going on at this field, why don't you come and join us, I think I have a sandwich with your name on it."
"Why this is mighty kind of y'all, I'll have that kind of sandwich your friend is eating."
"Oh, you mean the salami sandwich. Here have a pickle."

When we finished he got back in his jeep, happy as a bird, and we followed him to the refueling pump, which I think was a holdover from the First World War. You had to crank it until the indicator shows the amount pumped into the tank, then you crank it again and again until the tanks are topped. Taking turns, it took the three of us over an hour to get refueled. And there still was not one other plane at the airport except ours. We waved goodbye, put our goggles down over our eyes, and the crazy yanks were on their way.

We spent the night in Savannah, Georgia, and the next day our arrival was on the money. We took a taxi to the Hialeah track where there was quite a reception waiting for us. After dinner, the track manager drove us to Dinner Key, where our captain and brand new Chris Craft was at the dock ready for boarding. What a beauty that boat was and it was completely stocked with food and beverages as well as all brand new fishing gear. The captain wished us a good nights sleep and said we would get underway at 9am after we grab breakfast at a small cafe just a short walk from "our yacht". After we got underway on a beautiful day, we were on the Gulf Stream about fifteen miles off shore, sitting in our two brand new fishing chairs, in our underwear and sucking down a cold beer completely oblivious of life elsewhere, when all of a sudden Joe turns to me and asks, "Did you call your wife yet?"

"No, did you?"

"No."

After a short silence, Joe says, "Stud, I'll toss a coin, heads you call, tails I call"

I lost, and had to be the first call. Now you have to fully appreciate the situation. We left our wives three days ago in a small single engine Cessna for Florida, twelve hundred miles away. Joe rarely ever flew long distance in a small plane and further we were both known to be a little off the path of sanity. These factors left a big question in our wives mind whether we were still alive or did we perish in a horrible crash. If they knew we were cruising the gulf and drinking beer relaxed in our underwear while taking in the Florida sunshine, they would be seething mad. I do not know how Joe's wife would react, but I knew my wife would be "off the wall." The transatlantic telephone took about a half an hour to connect. The captain received the call, and passed the phone to me. Immediately Joan starts off with,

"YOU SON OF..."

I stopped her from going on any further and said, "Joan, do not complete that sentence, you are on the air. This is a live broadcast; this is radio telephone!"

"I am?"

"Yes you are"

Now as hard as it may seem to believe, but she starts to sing, "Some Enchanted Evening" from the famous Broadway show South Pacific, (a la, a female Enzio Pinza). Every note was clear and her perfect melody was thus carried live to all via the radiotelephone. Since our radios were set up on the same frequency, Joe and the captain could hear it plain as day and they were in convulsions. It was the funniest thing Joan ever did and to this day we have people laughing about it.

Of course as soon as she completed her rendition we returned to the usual array of questions. In this case, she was absolutely right to be mad, but at the same time she could not resist her artistic temperament, the show had to go on!

A postscript to our fantasy flight to Florida. Joe flew home from Miami via on Eastern Airlines, and I flew solo, a la Lindbergh, back to Teterboro, New Jersey. Joe never again brought up small plane flying.

Please recall at the beginning of this chapter I said there were two stories in 1967 that were worthwhile recording. When I separated from Joan, I left Teaneck, New Jersey and I relocated to Manhattan. My apartment was quite nicely located in the Murray Hill section of New York City, on Thirty-seventh Street and Lexington Avenue. When the day of my impending move to Chicago arrived, a huge Greyhound moving van arrived. It seemed all I had was a brass bed, a marble top dresser and my trophy fish, which was the white marlin cut in half (I had the good half with the long bill). Other than some clothing, my household goods did not fill up a quarter of the moving van. The crew then asked me where Three Mile Harbor was located in Long Island, for the second pickup, which was my boat. After an exchange of information, they were on their way and so was I. It was at this point of time that I suddenly realized despite my move to New York due to my separation I was now making a much bigger move and leaving behind my children, Ken my bother-in-law and close friend, all my pals, etc. etc.

After the 1967 flight to Miami, Florida, the next phase that took place that year will give the reader some idea of what was involved in entering my new life in moving to Chicago as well as the early difficulties of adapting to the large corporate world of Greyhound.

During a pre-move trip to Chicago to look for an apartment, I was lucky in locating one on Lakeshore Drive. It was a ten minute walk from Belmont Harbor where again I was lucky in getting dock space for the Aquarius II, my aforementioned nineteen foot Cape Dory sail boat. You recall I had advised my new boss Herb DeGraff; he must accept the responsibility and assume the cost of shipping my boat to Chicago as a condition for me to undertake the new position with Greyhound. About a week after arriving in Chicago, the giant Greyhound moving van arrived at my apartment. The driver and his assistant open the back doors and I was astonished by what I saw inside the van. They built a structure that supported the hull of the boat with its' nine hundred pound keel. The driver asked, "Do you want to unload the boat first?"

(I thought to myself, where does he think I'll put it...in my bathtub?) No, absolutely not. Please just take everything else up to my apartment and then deliver the boat to the harbor master at the Belmont Harbor Marina."

You cannot imagine, how snuggled that boat was inside the huge truck and in the front of the truck was the rest of my very minute belongings.

The move of Elliot Heit to Chicago became the subject of a small story. Despite my manor of insistence with Herb DeGraff, "no boat, no me", he was able to some how ship all I owned, including the boat, as household goods. About two weeks after I moved, Raymond Schaffer, the President of the Greyhound Corporation calls me on the phone and bellows that I should drop what I am doing and haul myself immediately into his office. To appreciate the situation that was unfolding, one must take into consideration the likes and dislikes of Mr. Schaffer. One is he did not like my boss Herb DeGraff. Herb had a very strong friendship with the chairman of the board, Gerry Trautman. The second point is Mr. Schaffer, again did not like Herb because Herb received permission direct from Trautman to take me out of Gray Line New York and transfer me to the corporate headquarters staff, basically as Herb's assistant. Mr. Schaffer was furious about this and told Herb, "How can you take a hunk of the management from Gray Line New York after we just paid over four million dollars for that company?" It was a pretty good question and the result was I was going to be living inside a virtual tennis ball, being batted back and forth between Herb and Mr. Schaffer. Welcome to corporate politics, example one.

I enter Mr. Schaffer's office totally unaware of the subject matter. He begins, "Heit, you are a bachelor, is that correct?'

(I do not believe he ever used neither my first name nor the title, Mister) I reply, "Yes sir, that's a fact."

He continues, "According to this report on my desk, as a bachelor, you had close to six thousand pounds of house hold goods shipped from New York to Chicago. How do you explain this?"

Now I knew where he was going with this inquiry. He was trying to pin the blame on Herb for allowing my boat to be shipped as household goods. To cover Herb, I told Mr. Schaffer other than the fact that I am now a bachelor, I was married for seventeen years; when "the division of spoils" took place, I got mine, which was considerable and she received hers (of course mine included the boat which Joan did not want anyway, which I omitted from the list of my spoils). My statement appeared sufficient and I was released from bondage (there will be more Shaffer tidbits but I will limit them to only the funniest).

It was not long after they showed me my very nice office and I was introduced to my secretary, then they gave me the key to the men's room, and I knew I was moved in. The next thing that happened was my interview by a magazine called Sales Management. The article was complete with artistic rendition of "Greyhound Corp.'s Heit". (There were a few times I felt "Corp.'s" could have phonetically been spelled "corpse"). The recognition that really caught my attention was "the who's who" listing in the Wall Street Journal.

Now all I needed to do was to make a success out of this new life. That was not going to be easy, but I was building up what I thought was my best shot. It turned out to be one of my initial mistakes. I made a phone call to the chairman of the board, of the forty-third largest company in the country, Gerry Trautman. My inexperience as a corporate executive prompted me to ask for a private meeting. It was my intention to get him to see me "up close". To make matters worse, he granted the meeting and it took place in his private residence. This was in order to provide a comfortable atmosphere for whatever secret formula I was going to tell him about that would increase the fortunes of the corporation. When the meeting took place and it

THE GREYHOUND CORP.:
A Magic Distance

People in Sacramento like to visit San Francisco, and vice versa; New Yorkers like trips to Boston or Washington, and the same travel affinity exists between St. Louis and Kansas City, Seattle and Vancouver, and so on. "There's a magic distance between two points 150 to 300 miles apart, and we're about to capitalize on it," says Elliot E. Heit, the new corporate vice president for sales of the Greyhound Corp., Chicago. "City Pairs is what we call this kind of intercity travel. We're now in the process of marketing it. Greyhound is, after all, a pioneer in intercity and leisure travel."

Although Greyhound owns restaurant chains, food service companies, an insurance company, a computer outfit, and is in several other businesses, including van lines, limousine services, car rentals, and tours here and abroad, about 65% of its revenues, totalling over $620 million, comes from bus operations. "I keep asking myself, 'What more can I do with buses to generate extra revenue?'" Heit says. One method is what Greyhound calls its intermodal system by which a passenger can buy a single through ticket combining air and surface transportation from his departure point to his final destination. This includes bus service from home or office to the airport, an airline ticket, plus service to wherever he's headed, even if it's a small town several miles from an airport. It also takes in the portal to portal transportation of his luggage. "Intermodal travel will also help decentralize airport operations by enabling a passenger to check in for his flight at his point of departure," says Heit. "And there's another thing. Remember that the new 747 jumbo jets, which accommodate 350 people, will also involve almost 350 people who come to an airport simply to see people off. In a few years there won't be space for their cars; in fact, there isn't enough space at many airports now. Summing up my job, I'd say that, one, I expect to exploit the leisure travel market fully, and, two, exploit intercity travel on a conventional basis as well as through luxury travel."

Heit, a suave, dark-haired, good-looking man of 45, joined Gray Line of New York in 1953 as a sales representative. He became sales promotion manager two years later. For the last eight years he's been sales vice president. Last November, Greyhound acquired Gray Line of New York, although Heit maintains that this has no bearing on his joining the parent company in Chicago. "We'd been talking a while before that," he insists. Divorced and the father of two daughters, he moved recently from New Jersey, bringing along his 18-foot sloop, Aquarius, which he'll sail this summer on Lake Michigan. A graduate of West Point, he also attended the University of Pittsburgh and Amherst.

Greyhound Corp.'s Heit

ended up with me playing "show and tell" about myself, his disappointment was obvious and I lost a good bit of his respect. I learned an expensive lesson, "If you have nothing to contribute, keep your mouth shut until you have something substantial to talk about." Mr. Schaffer was made aware of my meeting with Mr. Trautman and aside from severely criticizing me for "jumping channels"; he gave me my first assignment. He wanted me to do a study of the viability of the bus company's "See America" ticket. (This was the special ticket for international travel by Greyhound bus anywhere in the USA and Canada for 99 days and the cost was $99.00. It was first introduced in 1961 during that Pan Am, Greyhound, and Gray Line promotion where we took the Greyhound scenic-cruiser though Europe and it became stuck on top of the Swiss Alps). As far as the numbers sold, the ticket was a huge success, but the company was not making any money. I submitted my study and the recommendations were reviewed and accepted. Imagine me, one person, being responsible for changing the pricing of a ticket that was sold all over the world. My final recommendation was to keep the price at $99 but to reduce the validation period to a month instead of three months. This improved the profitability but in some countries like England it practically created a riot. In one case, the British Student Travel Club (BSTC), our biggest single source of the See America ticket sales wrote me threatening letters. Later on, I found our own overseas staff encouraged the BSTC organization to complain vehemently. Little did the Greyhound overseas staff, realize that they would soon be taking direction from me, and their whole culture would be changed under the new name I gave our overseas activities, namely, Greyhound International.

Prior to the birth of Greyhound International, what was the position of Greyhound overseas? For ten years prior to my arrival in Chicago, the Greyhound Bus Line operated overseas sales offices in London, Paris, Frankfurt, Switzerland and even one in Tokyo. They were set up as Greyhound Lines Inc. Sales offices under management of Jim Cunningham. Jim was quite a nice fellow and a fairly good friend but he had a narrow picture of where to go with these offices. I immediately saw an opportunity to use these offices as a springboard to getting Greyhound fully involved in my favorite subject, "Visit USA". I concluded we could make more money if we expanded the image of Greyhound overseas by providing what I called "a total concept of service". This meant, going way beyond just bus tickets, by selling all types of services to be used by the growing traffic to the United States from primarily Europe. This required two basic steps. First one, drop the name of Greyhound Lines Inc. and change it to Greyhound International, the total concept of service. Second step; build up a network of sales representatives, worldwide. An office domiciled in the United States would manage this network of international sales representatives and Greyhound International offices. The USA office would also coordinate all activities undertaken by our international network. Finally, the office would aggressively "network" to solicit and operate as a receptive tour operator for large overseas tour operators requiring ground services anywhere in the USA and/or Canada. This covered airport reception and transfers, sightseeing arrangements, hotel reservations, charter bus movements, language assistance, and the preparation and operation of group services for many of the prominent overseas companies engaged in Visit USA business. This entire project for Greyhound International, the total concept of service, was comparatively speaking a revolutionary change to the way Greyhound did business overseas. When you undertake a strategy of such dimension you must be prepared; in a large corporation like Greyhound, for a lot of doubters and a lot of seething jealously against the author of such imaginative projects. Most of all, it needed my own determination to persist and succeed. Every problem you can imagine, was thrown at me, but after four years of seemingly endless effort, it started to happen and by the time I left Greyhound in 1979 to become Executive Vice President of the second largest receptive operator in America, Greyhound International grew from a five million dollar operation to a thirty-seven million profitable set up. I am getting a wee bit ahead of myself. Let us go back to the first year of my presence at the Greyhound Corporation.

I was amazed at the number of divergent subjects brought to my attention and the promotional presence required by my office on a worldwide basis. Here is one example of the vast variety of my job. At one point, I was informed that American Airlines was about to inaugurate air service to Australia. The initial flight would be exclusively composed of senior travel executives like the President of Hertz Rent-A-Car, the executive vice President of American Express and many others, including Elliot Heit.

One of Eight

A few weeks after my return from Australia, I received a personal call from Diego Suarez, chairman of Oremar Travel, a very large tour operator from Sao Paulo, Brazil. He wanted me to arrange a meeting with the President of Greyhound and staff to discuss a possible arrangement, and he was prepared to leave for Chicago as soon as I could set this meeting up. I was somewhat surprised to discover Mr. Schaffer, our President agreed to do this. The meeting took place in the corporate boardroom, with Mr. Schaffer and all staff members present. However there was one big thing wrong, Mr. Suarez could not speak a word of English! Fortunately, he brought along Ilyia Hirsch his very reliable assistant. We managed to conclude the meeting with an agreement to set up Mr. Suarez of Oremar Travel as our first Greyhound International representative in South America. (From 1970 to 2000, Oremar was the general sales agent for Greyhound in Brazil. We continued business when I later relocated to Allied Tours, and finally with Tauck Tours – a total of thirty years of strong loyalty and productive business).

The next illustration of variety to my Greyhound function really deserves a reward for its uniqueness. Herb DeGraff turned over to me, a gentleman who had flown from New Delhi, India to discuss an adventurous plan to promote visitors to the USA from India. Mr. Nari Katgara was the managing director of the Travel Corporation of India, one of the largest organizations for travel in that country. He was small in stature but large and extraordinary with ideas. First of all, as far as I knew, the economics at the time in his country was miserable; most people, who left India to travel abroad, had only one thought and that was to leave India forever. Mr. Katgara countered my impression by stating, "If you are not familiar with the market, and I am intimately acquainted with it, don't you think it would be worth while to listen to me?" I listened. He explained, India like most third world countries, has a divided population between "the haves and the have not". Unquestionably, he explains, there is a huge difference between the quantity of people who are the "have not" compared to those that "have". He continued, instructing me that India was a country of 800 million people; the overall possible market for what he had in mind, could be one thousandth of one percent of this population and that represented 80,000 persons. As for me, I was much more conservative when we estimated there could be a market of as much as 10,000 booking travel to the USA. However, he cautions, the product to be promoted for travel to the USA would have to be designed on the most severe economic scale. He described, it would be a series of group departures each year that would cover the entire United States in thirty days by a Greyhound bus towing behind a food trailer with cook to assure compliance with his countries dietary restrictions. Finally, he explains my quotation must be based on four persons to a room and the cost of <u>each room</u> should not exceed $25 per night!

One other important factor was the extreme difficulty his countrymen who travel abroad have in securing visas. Unfortunately India had a very bad "track record" of people who traveled and were issued visas that were illegally used to avoid ever returning to their homeland. Well there you have the concept. I told Mr. Katgara to give me a day or two and I would call him in New York where he has an office that develops programs for Americans who desire visiting India. After several days I called him and right off, I explained the food trailer and cook towed behind the Greyhound bus were out of the question. The bus and routing were no problem, and I was planning a trip to New York City to evaluate the hotel requirement. (I knew most of the hotels quite well from my Gray Line New York experience; the price level he was looking for would make this a significant problem.)

When I visited New York to test the hotel reaction, I went to many of the cheapest tourist hotels like the Dixie, The Times Square, etc. I also "took a shot" at one that was slightly more upscale, namely the Taft Hotel. I explained to each hotel manager that India up to this point has a little or no legitimate visitors to the USA, and TCI was planning, with myself, to open up a brand new market. I described what Greyhound was willing to do and now; it is time to find our what would be the reaction from the hotels. Everyone expressed strong interest. The rates they quoted were not as low as Mr. Katgara would accept, but I was amazed how low the hotels went. The cheapest hotels quoted thirty dollars per room per night and the Taft Hotel of somewhat better quality quoted forty dollars. (Remember this would be forty dollars a night divided by four persons. Ten dollars a night for a room in New York; I was amazed and encouraged.) Mind you, I had to gather rates from all over the United States that would cover the itinerary of the Greyhound charter bus. At least I was now convinced it was doable. When this major obstacle was overcome there was still one more to solve. This brings us to the subject of visas. The issuance of visas is the responsibility of the commercial attaché in our embassies and consulates. These attaches were more inclined to deny visas and avoid the consequence of someone "jumping ship" during their holiday to America. This problem had my congressional and close friend Jack Murphy's name written all over it. Jack did not fail me; I was set up with a meeting in Washington with the head of our immigration and naturalization services. Off I went to Washington. The meeting had some "bumps" especially with the main concern for the "jumping ship" possibilities. I explained to the director, the project was a totally legitimate promotion by one of the largest and highly regarded travel organizations in India. Furthermore, the promotion would be directed to the upper class sector of India's society who had a standard of living far beyond what yours and mine together would amount to; certainly they were not looking toward "jumping ship". In the final analysis, I stressed this would be a dramatic development for our Federal government's support of "Visit USA". I left the director of immigration and naturalization feeling confident that some headway was made. After this meeting ended all operational planning from my office was finished; the rest was up to TCI. In time Mr. Katgara did notify me that the Bombay embassy was ready to cooperate on the visa issue. The green light for the project was on, but it still took three years of promotion before the first group ever from India arrived on the shores of the Untied States. It was a small group, but it was a start. Within a period of three years we were carrying over a thousand people each year and the same was true to some extent of other India tour operators who started to offer similar arrangements. Altogether the total amount from all U.S.A. companies seeking this business totaled around five thousand. While we did not hit the mark of ten thousand that was estimated, it was a "good chunk" at five thousand. (From what I heard, TCI never has a bad incident with the visa situation.)

I know it has been a lengthy explanation of what it takes to design, build and establish a new niche in world travel markets. I had two reasons for doing this. First of all, I wanted to give the reader and idea of what it is like to "build a wheel" in opening international markets. The second reason for the detailed description has more to do with the very close association that resulted between the Katgara family and myself. It led to Nari Katgara calling me one day and extending his hospitality to me and to my wife Carol to come to India as their guest. All expanses paid, including first class travel with Air India Airlines. This trip was one of my best-remembered experiences, and I believe, as you read on you will discover why.

Before leaving for India, I had occasion to meet with Joe McCrane, the other half of my sense of humor. By this time Joe had gone though quite a few career changes, such as general manager for the three hundred room Cherry Hill in south Jersey, then on to general manager of Garden State Race Track of New Jersey, State treasurer of New Jersey, founder of the well known sports complex in New Jersey called The Meadowlands, and finally, Vice President of Sales for Hess – Eisenhart, maker of bullet proof cars. (Since President Franklin Roosevelt, limousines, made from prototypes like Cadillac to protect our presidents have been made by Hess-Eisenhart). What made Joe's position really adventurous was the need for these special vehicles due to the political upheaval going on throughout the world ever since the end of the Cold War. (In one case six cars at a cost of $150,000 each were sold to the ruler of Angola, Africa). When I explained my upcoming expedition to India, Joe told me that he had in mind some time ago to get in touch with me about "opening some doors" in my ongoing travels throughout the world. He was right about the prospects for doing this. Any significant tour operator from abroad, must for survival, maintain very close liaison with the politics in their country of origin. After meeting with Joe, I called Nari Katgara. He told me, he would go to work on it right away. He further stated that I would get an update upon my arrival in Delhi. I had no idea what to expect.

It was a long flight from the States to New Delhi, India; we were required a stop in Frankfurt, Germany for refueling. When we left Frankfurt it was still a long flight. The amenities on board Air India's first class were top notch and removed most of the monotony. We finally arrived at New Delhi's airport, but quite fatigued. Please be reminded that this visit to India took place in the mid-seventies. India only became independent from the British Empire less than thirty years before our arrival and there were many difficulties to overcome with its massive population. A very small example of this was the scene at the airport. There was no baggage claim section. They just unloaded all bags and piled then "mile high" right in the main concourse of the arrival building. Can you imagine how high that pile was from all the baggage of a 747 aircraft that carries over three hundred passengers? Much to our relief, Ram Kohli an executive from TCI met us and together with the chauffeur they went though the maze of luggage while we sat in the lounge bar. After our bags were taken care of, we were whisked off by some kind of foreign made limousine to our hotel, which was the best hotel in the city. A lovely room awaited us; flowers were delivered along with a bottle of good French champagne. All we really wanted was take a hot bath in the sumptuous tub and then "hit the sack" in the also sumptuous bed. The Katgara's were very thoughtful about not contacting us until sometime the next morning. When the phone did ring, it was Nari Katgara to officially welcome us. He notified us that all expenses, meals, entertainment, and miscellaneous charges would be taken care of in New Delhi as well as all other hotels in India during our visit including Nepal. Further more, he made arrangements for both Carol and I to meet a very important government official for lunch in the hotel, where we would carry on with the discussion concerning the armored car project.

The gentleman we met with was exceptionally tall, quite handsome and well attired. Initially, he told us about himself. He was a recently retired general of the army who was in charge of all India troops along the border between India and China. He did not reveal his present position. I was told later that he was Prime Minister Indira Ghandi's personal bodyguard. We briefly discussed the Hess-Eisenhart security company. I told him my information about the company was limited to what I was told by my friend and classmate from West Point, who was the vice President of sales for the armored car company. The reference to the academy put him more at ease with our meeting. When we finished, he said I would be contacted again. Carol and I then went to the very elegant spa in the hotel. As we checked in, the receptionist remarked there were two gentlemen in the lobby waiting to see me. Carol went to our room and I went to the lobby. The two men introduced themselves as representatives from the ministry of Tourism that were sent to interview me. In about five minutes of conversation, I got the distinct impression that neither one of these men knew the first thing about tourism. It was my conclusion that I was being "checked out" by some government security service. This became more apparent, when I returned to our room where I found Carol close to tears and dismayed by the condition of our hotel room. Bureau draws were opened and articles were all out of place. The closet where we hung our clothing and kept our luggage was ransacked and left in disorder. I continued to calm Carol down and explained my own puzzling lobby meeting. Again, I told Carol I believe it has something to do with the luncheon we had with the General. I called Nari and he confirmed my suspicion.

The next morning the front desk called to announce that a government car was waiting for me at the front of the hotel. I reassured Carol, I would be okay. The awaiting car was an army sedan painted with traditional full camouflage colors and the driver was an officer who assisted my boarding the vehicle. I was taken to a large Victorian house in a residential area of the city. The roof of this home had about ten different antennas indicating some type of military specialists occupied it. I was escorted up to a living room where tea and crumpets were served in perfect English style. At tea, a senior officer in uniform introduced himself. After tea, he took me over to a table where he had some blueprints and he began to describe the kind of vehicle they had in mind for Hess-Eisenhart to develop. They showed me the blueprints; I recognized the car immediately as an English Morris Minor. I told them at one time I owned one of these tiny Morris Minor cars. I could not imagine a car like this carrying around armored protection with an engine the size of a Singer sewing machine. He twitched his mustache and gave away the real reason for the project. Before doing so, he reminded me that India became independent in 1947 of the British Empire. At that time the Morris Minor plant was taken over by the India Government and the new name for the car was the Hindustan.

"Okay", I said, "the Hindustan will have the same trouble carrying the extra load of amour reinforcement."

His replay pinned the matter down very effectively. I quote his reply,

"The person who will be driving in this vehicle does not wish to appear ostentatious as would be the case if she were driven in a Cadillac or similar vehicle."

The give away word was "she". "She," meant the car was for the Prime Minister of India, Indira Gandhi. The gentleman in charge of the meeting asked me to have the chief executive of the Hess-Eisenhart Company contact the India ambassador in Washington; from then on, the ambassador will be the pivot for communication. He further told me to have Hess-Eisenhart evaluate the practicality of using the Hindustan as proposed. All this was taken care of by a phone call to my friend Joe McCrane. When we arrived back in the States, there was a message that Joe and his President were flying to meet me in New York, to, "tie things up." We had our meeting and Hess-Eisenhart stated to the India Ambassador that the Hindustan car could definitely be modified to suit the purpose. The very next day there were huge headlines in the newspapers describing how Indira Gandhi was assassinated!! The country was in complete chaos and, of course the Hindustan project was dropped.

We ended our time spent in New Delhi touring via automobile. The Katgara's sent a car with driver and tour guide all in one person and we departed on a fabulous journey of five days traveling to Agra and Jaipur. Once you are out of the city, it is like riding though the pages of the bible. You feel like the car you are riding in is a time machine or magical carpet, going back a thousand years ago. Watching farmers pumping water from a well with a pump activated by oxen tied to poles attached to a rotating wheel at the center of the well. Occasionally you brought back to the twentieth century by a creaky old passenger/freight train coming along on a single rusty track and overloaded with sixty or seventy persons perilously riding on the roof of the cars.

We arrived in Agra and our hotel was very well done. Of course Agra is the site of the Taj Mahal. Most people have seen many pictures of the Taj Mahal in textbooks at school, but to see it up close is something else. I always thought it was a palace of a Raj, which is the equivalent of a prince or a person of royalty, it did belong to a Raj, but it was built for his lady friend!

Our chauffer was excellent in driving and describing history; he was masterful at showing us all the sights to be seen. He was a proud member of the respected Sikh religion. In Agra, Carol could not resist buying some ivory jewelry. Ivory was practically growing off the trees. Anyway, she buys this ivory silver and jade bracelet, which was so immense, in a figurative sense, an elephant could have worn it on his trunk. She could not wait to show it to our escort for his approval. He asked her how much she paid for her "good buy". When she told him, he politely asked if he could borrow it for a little while. When he returned he gave her back half of what she paid! A lesson was learned that our chauffer parks the car and goes shopping with us at all times.

From Agra we went on to Jaipur, the city of castles. Jaipur is noted for having magnificent palatial pink colored homes; most of which were built during the affluent period of the Maharajah's or Indian princes. No doubt the abuse of power, by these princes, led to the emergence of leaders like Mahatma Gandhi. He was the symbol of freedom for much of the former lower caste system that literally imprisoned India.

You may recall in previous chapters, there was mention of Tiger Tops in Nepal. After we finished seeing quite a bit of India, the Katgara's sent us on to Nepal, where Tiger Tops was situated. We spent some time exploring this high corner of civilization; such as it was, before returning to India for our long flight back to the states.

Our trip to the Far East was definitely not a "package tour"; to us, it will always be a trip of adventure, education and very well remembered.

At this point it is necessary to retrace my corporate path, which took a sharp turn in a different direction after only a year in Chicago. The chairman decided it just was not practical to have a marketing department at the corporate headquarters level. How could a marketing department at that level be useful to one hundred and thirty six different companies from Dial Soap to leasing jet aircraft? It was impossible to be effective, and although I was caught in a "tug-o-war", it was the right decision. The chairman of the board gave my boss and good friend Herb DeGraff a fantastic new title, Vice President of "Australasia". He was transferred to Sydney, Australia and represented the entire Greyhound corporate activity. As for me, I had a choice to either be assigned as the Vice President of sales for the bus line or continue the development of Greyhound International. It was an easy choice to make. Thus I packed and left Chicago with my boat and a few other belonging for New York to set up a new entity, a headquarters for Greyhound International. (At the time of this transfer, it amazed me how little it mattered to Greyhound, whatever I did to establish for the corporation's brand new direction to take on international tourism).

The first item of importance was to locate an office. I naturally went initially to my brother-in-law, but he had no space. (He may have felt I would become some form of competition). If that were so, it was wrong, as my activities in some respects complimented his company, Gray Line of New York. To me my brother-in-law Ken has been one of my closest friends and despite little differences here and there we shall always remain close friends.

Back to the search for the new offices. The Greyhound Corporation had a number of different subsidiaries in New York, such as Greyhound Food Management, Greyhound Consultants and Designers, and Greyhound Leasing and Finance, located at Fifty-Seventh Street and Park Avenue. I tried them all, but the only one that showed immediate promise was leasing and finance. The senior executive in charge said he would have a thousand square feet available. I was "tickled pink", but I told him I would have to clear it with our esteemed President of the Greyhound Corporation, Raymond Schaffer. I called Mr. Schaffer and told him that after looking into other subsidiaries, the only one with space was Greyhound Leasing and Finance. To this he bellowed his response, "What gave you the idea that you would locate an office on Park Avenue with Greyhound Leasing and Financing? Heit, get that silver spoon out of your posterior and get over to the Port Authority bus terminal with Greyhound Bus Lines where you belong".

I was reeling with despair after that blow off, but I dutifully went to see the Regional Vice President of the bus line located in the Port Authority terminal. Despite the threats from Mr. Schaffer I found the Vice President to be a really fine chap. He showed me quite a large area, which was used some years ago as a lost luggage storage area. The entire space was covered in dust and filth, and I again started to feel quite depressed. He saw me shaking my head and said, "Don't you worry, give me three weeks and a plan for your office layout and we will have you up and running".

He did just that; eventually I had a very nice large private office with additional office space to house my staff, which soon became 10 persons. The regional manager did a magnificent job in overhauling a totally decrepit location. It was interesting that even though I was now sharing space with the Greyhound Bus Line in the Port Authority basement, I was a totally separate entity; I had nothing to do with them. Greyhound International was on its own just as though it was my own company. It was just the way I wanted it to be. I was so isolated from the rest of Greyhound I actually shopped and bought my own office furnishings including a beautiful second hand enormous wooden desk for my office. The regional Greyhound Vice President gave me an excellent secretary and transferred Udo Koch, a young German immigrant, to add to my growing staff. Udo was sort of a "fifth wheel" in the Greyhound bus system, but for me he became invaluable to my plans for expanding our international business. Finally Greyhound gave me another person, who was the son of one of the old guard terminal managers. His name was Richard Waldron. I made him, sort of, our office manager and liaison for the bus line, which we used, for various bus charters. Udo Koch, our German specialist, I assigned to the German market where he did very well. Additionally, I hired, Ingrid Burgdof, who was a specialist in what we used to call Technical Study Tours. Study Tours were actively used in the international markets, preceding the big expansion of Visit USA business. Most European governments, particularly Germany did not allow a free flow of travel out of the county of origin; they considered that kind of travel spending to be non-contributory to the home economy. What they did support was Technical Study Tours, especially to the USA where the study groups could bring back new ideas for their recovering economies. Ingrid was an expert in this field and her section was very profitable for Greyhound International. Another very productive individual was Casper Kranenburg who was born and educated in the Netherlands. Casper was a devoted multi-lingual staff member with excellent credentials for the kind of business I wanted to develop from Europe. One other key staff member was Aixa, who came from Columbia, South America. She was well educated with excellent language skills and a quick learner. Lastly, I had two or three multi-lingual escorts, who were not permanent staff, but were very involved with our various and frequent needs for freelance, but they knew Greyhound International was very active in the market place. For this reason, they relied on us for contract work, and we depended on them as well.

Due to the excellence of the staff and my strong background in the Visit USA industry, Greyhound International gained quick recognition in the Europe markets. Many of my competitive USA receptive operators, as they were called, did not think the giant Greyhound Company has the required flexibility to handle the minutiae of complex group itineraries. On the other hand, the foreign tour operators knew immediately the name Greyhound was an American company known throughout the business as the world's largest bus company. (When you are doing business on a global basis, you must prove reliability; Greyhound did not have to do this. Whenever I was abroad I was always impressed with the fact that Greyhound's image was in many cases much stronger and more positive than it was in the USA.)

One of the first contracts I signed was with a company in Germany called Neckermann. The parent of this company was the owner of the largest number of department stores in Germany all with the name, Neckermann. They decided to go into the group travel business in a big way, with massive advertising and promotion. They developed one of the largest and most successful VISIT USA programs ever in Europe. They chartered two or three Boeing 707 jets, which at the time, were the largest jet aircraft flying, and they scheduled two departures a month for six months per year. Their itinerary in the United States was made deliberately very simple in order to keep the price down. Each time they flew a group of about three hundred to only New York City. They would stay in the USA one week. On the day of their arrival, in the early evening, they would hold a meeting in the hotel. The meeting would cover a variety of activities they could subscribe to and I was allowed to address them in detail about each activity. The services included sightseeing in New York; yacht cruises around Manhattan Island, a three-day excursion by motor coach to either Montreal and Niagara Falls or Washington, D.C. and Mt. Vernon. I was set up with a desk and a German-speaking staff member from my office, who would book all services including German-speaking escorts. Each group that arrived, usually had at least three hundred persons and ninety percent of them booked "on the spot" one or more of these services. This meant we were servicing over five hundred persons a month for six months totaling three thousand Germans a season from just this one account. (We held on to the Neckermann account for six years and won the respect of the twelve major USA receptive operators, as well as the word of mouth among the German tour operators.) Greyhound International took in over $1,000,000.00 each year from just the Neckermann account.

There were many other similar type accounts from other countries. For example, England has a unique operator who established the "G.I. Brides Association"! I still remember his name, Roger Milbanke. Roger's genius figured that many G.I.'s, who served in World War II, fell in love with young English ladies. After the war ended they married, and the G.I.'s took their brides back to America. By the nineteen seventies, these marriages were at least twenty-five years ago. Roger thinks further and promotes not only a reunion in the United States with the daughters, but how about seeing their grand children for the first time and possibly the last time! These air charter groups always arrived and returned to the U.K. from New York. They were jammed to capacity. Incidentally most families living in the USA would come to New York to meet the in-laws coming from England for the first time since the end of the war. They would stay about ten days before returning to England. What was interesting was the amount of household items they loaded into the tour buses when leaving the hotel for the airport, towels, bed linen, brooms, vacuum cleaners and such. It is hard for U.S. citizens to realize the World War II blitz and it's destruction wrought upon factories in Europe producing household goods. The blitz effect on England's economy was so complete that even in the seventies there was still difficulty in purchasing theses consumer goods.

The G.I. Brides Association of England, for most of the seventies, sent thousands each year for this rare type of migration and reunion.

Not only was my office and staff swamped with work orders, additionally, the Greyhound International offices in Europe were getting some effect from our spreading reputation as a "total concept of service". The business of Visit USA overall was also growing and Greyhound was getting "a good hunk". What was very satisfying was to experience the wonderful espirit de corps displayed by my staff. It was as though it was my own business; they were delighted to be a part of a strong winning team.

The next area of development was to expand Greyhound International's presence overseas, by developing representatives. I began this with visits to Malaysia, Singapore and Hong Kong. Then into Central and South America. In the Middle East, ELAL Airlines was our representative (although not effective; I had to replace them with what turned our to be a very productive general sales agent). In South Africa, we had a representative that was set up by my director in England. Ron Blakley, a great person, who ran his business well. All of a sudden, I find out the representative in South Africa under his control has an outstanding balance of $65,000.00 (in 1974, this was a lot of money, and I did not need this kind of publicity with the Greyhound head quarters hatchet men who were itching to bring me down a peg). I called Ron Blakey in England an told him in a very firm tone, to get on the first plane to Johannesburg, and do not come back without the money, (I reminded myself of the way my father-in-law Sidney Engelhardt, used to act with some of the money problems we had in Gray Line). Ron Blakey did go and did come back with the money. He also cancelled their agreement and had a replacement in one week. The new representative was a very large firm and produced excellent results for years until their currency "took a dive." Each year we used to have over two hundred persons a year visit the USA from South Africa.

Allow me to detour from the business side of South Africa. On one of the many sales development trips I made to that unusual country, our representative set me up for weekend safari, taking place in Botswana. I have never been on a safari, and I was quite excited about going. To get ready, as a typical "yank", I went to a safari outfitter store and bought everything except an elephant. Then as a group including my "rep", we went out for dinner and they "pump me up" with all kinds of wild stories involving snakes and enormous bugs of all types. They also told me, I would probably sleep in a tent, (where is the door; I want out of this safari stuff). The next day I'm picked up at the hotel, taken to the airport where I am squeezed into a six-passenger twin-engine Piper Comanche. With a full load we are off to Botswana. Our airfield was a fairly short dirt runway. The landing was fine and then we taxi up to "open seater" army type truck with a driver, a native helper, and a guide. A rifle is strapped across the hood and the guide stands on a little shelf attached to the truck where the rear bumper is located. His job is not only to spot game but to make sure we avoid surprises. Off we go in a cloud of dust over a makeshift road. There is not another human being in sight, other than the five of us in the truck.

We finally come to some kind of oasis. Up to this point we saw nothing other than the countryside which was absolutely flat with tall sun burnt grass for miles on either side of the road. At the oasis the "Jungle Jim" driver very slowly approaches a small stream where there were about six elephants including mom and dad and little one. The driver turns the car away from the herd and then slowly backs down toward the stream. The driver explained we were backing in just in case he needed "the edge" to get out of the oasis in a hurry. (We have only landed about forty minutes ago and I'm already getting nervous with all these precautions). The big bull elephant suddenly lets his huge ears extend and that makes him look even more ferocious. Then he starts trumpeting and menacing to charge our vehicle, our driver presses the pedal to the medal and we are out of there.

As we approach the safari campground, I was impressed with the high concrete wall that surrounded the living area. We entered through a gate and there before us, to everyone's surprise, was a very attractive tile swimming pool surrounded by tables, chairs and an outdoor circular bar built around a large banyan tree. Nearby to the pool were sidewalks leading to about ten well built circular huts with hatched roofs.

We were unloaded from our truck and each party had a young attractive female escort us, along with our baggage to our individual safari huts. By this time, I was completely sure; the evening before with my friends was completely exaggerated to throw me off guard. The door to my hut was opened and again I was pleasantly surprised by the amenities, especially the bathroom complete with toilet, which according to my friends was supposed to be a rough and ready squatter type. The young lady left me in my hut and I started putting way some toiletries in the cabinet above the sink when I saw four hairy legs about two or three inches long sticking out from behind the cabinet. I dropped everything and ran our to find the girl who checked me in. As I approached her at breakneck speed, I slowed to a casual gate, and asked her calmly if she would kindly return to my hut to check something out for me. When she saw the legs still sticking out from the medicine cabinet, she said, "Oh, that is just a tarantula, they don't bite. They are good to have as they feed on the other bugs in your hut!" I inquired to how big she thought this tarantula was. She holds up her two hands which where about ten inches apart and says, "No bigger than this, but remember they do not bite humans." That may be true, but I would hate to have one crawling on my face looking for bugs, while I am trying to sleep.

We had a meeting that afternoon to talk over the safari plans, which start at four A.M. and finish about eleven. The rest of the day you have time to lounge around the pool and bar and review your experiences with other guests. The reason for the early start is the heat of the day is almost unbearable (by the way, the huts are not air conditioned and they do not suggest keeping the windows open at night.) They supply you with insect powder to spray the insides of your shoes. They further advise that in the morning, a good practice is to "shake out" your shoes, for small snakes and other critters. With all these survival instructions in mind, I went to the circular bar around the banyan tree, and ordered several rounds of cognac before retiring to bed. While I was sipping the second round, I noticed what appeared to be a rope, quite large in diameter dangling from one of the tree limbs. I pointed this out to the bartender. He looks, then excuses himself and calmly takes something like a colt .45 revolver from the cabinet and shoots the rope. The rope turns out to be a seven-foot baby boa constrictor. (The shot got him in the head and it fell from the limb of the tree to the top of the bar about a foot from my drink). One more cognac was needed before I headed down the path to my hut. Once in my abode, I lock the door, close the windows, and hop into bed. The beds were made simply with sheets and an army wool blanket, which I "tucked in tight" to my body. The temperature was over 100 degrees and I was perspiring like I was in a Turkish bath. I do not believe I slept "five winks", but I would not budge out of my cocoon until the call for safari action - 3:30 AM.

Finally, 3:30 arrives and my body appeared to be intact. Off we went on my first safari. It was quite spectacular, with zebras, giraffes, elephants, gazelles, springbuck, and water buffalo.

Most wonderful of all was the absolutely amazing assortment of beautifully colored birds. By eleven in the morning, it was all over and the rest of the day was spent poolside where fifteen or so baboons spent hours looking at the crazy humans sunning or playing in the water. (Strangely enough, they stayed in the trees. They kept to the outside wall of the campground.)

The next day, we left Botswana and flew back to Johannesburg. The following day it was time to fly home; the safari was short, but left an indelible impression.

Not too long after returning from South Africa, I began working on setting up representatives in Malaysia and Singapore. Since there is a social aspect attached to these types of visits, I told my new and beautiful wife, I would like to take her a long if I could get our air tickets from Pan Am. She was very excited about the possibility. The first trip was to Singapore and it stated off with a funny incident. When you fly "on a pass", you never know when you will be "bumped". Bumped means either you will fly economy instead of first class or the aircraft is sold out which results in no flight and you are rescheduled to fly at an alternate time. The strange thing is that once you experience several flights in a row with first class seats, you sort of expect to fly forever on first class. Such was the case with our trip to Singapore.

It started with first class from JFK, New York to San Francisco. The second leg was San Francisco to Tokyo; this was first class as well. Tokyo to Singapore would be the same aircraft, but as we had a two-hour layover in Tokyo, all passengers were to told to disembark and wait for the re-boarding announcement for the continued flight to Singapore. As we left the plane, we were handed two red coupons, which I just casually placed in my pocket, not realizing the red coupon meant we lost our first class seats. Despite much effort to regain status, it looked like we were headed for "the unwashed section" (economy seats). As we entered the aircraft for boarding, I noticed the last row first class seats, which were once occupied by us from San Francisco; A further revelation revealed that the male passenger "in my seat" was none other than Brendon Byrne, Governor of New Jersey, and his wife was in my wife's former seat. Governor Byrne was a good friend of my close friend, Joe McCrane and also attended several meetings of the

"Sundailers", a social group that Joe and I put together some years ago. It is important to mention this history, so you can understand the brazen act I was about to commit, was undertaken with a person I knew fairly well. Before we turned and went down the aisle to the rear end of the cabin to the economy section, I passed the back of Governor Byrnes seat and tapped him on the shoulder. He said, "Hey Stud, what are you doing on this plane?" I said, "I am trying to get to Singapore. I want you to know your sitting in our seats since the flight started in San Francisco, but don't get up; we'll head down towards the tail of the plane, (at least it was close to the restrooms). See you in Singapore."

As it turned out, there was a terrible thunder and rainstorm that was still going on as we landed in Singapore and taxied to the terminal. At the terminal the situation with Brendon Byrne reversed itself.

I had previously mentioned how overseas countries have such a high regard for Greyhound. Here I am Vice President of Greyhound International arriving in Singapore to discuss and designate a well-known leader in the Singapore travel market as the new general sales agent for Greyhound. All their senior executives were on hand to receive us. Our luggage was silently and quickly picked up and loaded in one of two Mercedes limousines waiting for us outside the arrival building. Where it was still engulfed in a very violent rainstorm. Umbrellas sheltered us as we were escorted to our car. As we got under way we were about to pass two figures with their collars up waiting their turn by the taxi stand. I could not resist this scene, so I lowered my window and yelled out, "Brendan, hopefully we will bump into each other; see you".

We went to the Mandarin Hotel, a magnificent property (the stay in Singapore was paid for by our host). The next morning, I had a meeting down town and Carol went to the roof where she relaxed by the swimming pool. In the pool she spots Brendon Byrne in a red white and blue bathing suit that looks like he is wearing the American flag. The Governor emerged from the pool and walked to his chair where a very attractive blonde was now seated in his deck chair. He told her in a disturbed voice that she was in HIS chair. The blonde completely ignored him and the Governor searched for a new location.

I could never figure out why he was not treated more appropriately, as Governor of New Jersey, at the airport and hotel. He certainly was treated properly by the airline when Pan Am bumped my wife and I from our first class seats.

Singapore is a city and a country at the same time. The city is the cleanest city, I have ever seen, and there is an explanation for this. The prevailing government was extremely strict; any person caught discarding refuse of any kind on the street was fined $500.00!!

The business was successfully completed and my wife's charm and attractiveness at several of the parties helped to make it so successful.

About three months after Singapore, we had to make a similar trip. This one took us to Malaysia. We prepared for another long air flight with Pan Am; this time, no seating problems.

Pearl Upsher was the General Manager of AA of Malaysia (a subdivision of the Automobile Association of Great Britain and one of the prominent fixtures in the Malaysian travel industry). She married a successful English civil engineer and they lived in a wonderful Victorian home in Kula Lumpur, the capital city of Malaysia. Pearl had a strong grip on the national travel picture; she knew everybody and everybody knew her.

We began our visit to Malaysia with a sumptuous cocktail party held on the lawn of her home and followed by a meeting held in her very large living room (there were close to one hundred persons attending). The cocktail portion included four or five authentic sidewalk food carts dispensing hors d'oeuvres and cocktails for quite a while. Pearl finally gives the word a to adjourn to the grand living room, where there was a dais for Pearl, the Prince of Malaysia, several government officials, myself and two opened seats. The audience of seventy-five or more sat before us in an array of chairs. The house was not air-conditioned so that Pearl had all the French doors leading to the lawn area wide open. Nowhere inside the room, could I see my wife Carol or Pearl's engineer husband, but as soon as the Prince finished some remarks and I was introduced. I knew exactly where the two of them were. How did I know? Very simple, as I started to speak, my rather deep penetrating tones lofted throughout the French doors and on to the lawn and then into the ears of my wife who was having a cocktail or maybe two, or even three with Pearl's husband. As I spoke to the audience, I maneuvered myself closer to the French doors so there could be no doubt with the two of them that I was addressing the group. Their loud laughter was an impediment to my remarks. A clue that I was getting though to my wife was her message she gave to Pearl's husband, which could be heard by the audience, "Shhhhhhh, I think Elliot is talking to the guests."

Quiet follows their discovery and the two miscreants enter the room and thereupon take seats as far in the back as they could go. Actually, despite that interlude, the party was quite a success.

One of the government people I met was the head of security and ex-hunter of communists who roamed the jungles of Malaysia to avoid detection. They would hide only to make an appearance when their target areas were clear enough for them to stage an attack. The communists were so effective the government posted rewards of $300 for each communist, killed or captured. You had to deliver "the evidence" to the appropriate military facility before getting paid. One of the stories he told me occurred on such a hunt. The group he was leading ware all new hunter recruits. One of then gets a communist and kills him on the spot. He drags the corpse to their jungle camp and they discuss the situation of how they can get the prey all the way back to the military facility, so that they can claim their reward. My new friend, the head of security and ex-hunter of communists, tells them to cut off the head and put it in a bag. This would make it easy to carry. Our headhunter arrives at the headquarters, goes to his office and puts the head in the office refrigerator until the next morning. On the next day, his secretary goes to the fridge to get the milk for her coffee. When she opens the fridge, her eyes meet the eyes of the decapitated head and she lets out a scream and faints. The noise of the scream reminds the group leader to take the head to the "head person" for the reward. If this anecdote sounds unreal; you would only have to meet the chief of security once, and you would change your mind. He has a peculiar shaped head that looked like that of a rattlesnake and he thought like a snake as well.

The following day, Pearl and I went to her office to brief the staff on the duties and responsibilities of Greyhound representative. That afternoon she announced plans for a government car to take Carol and me up to the Penang Club, in Penang, an exclusive spot in one of the Malaysia resort areas. Guess who was driving the government limousine? It was the Head of Security! When he learned of Pearl's plan to send us to Penang for a few days, he requested he would, as a precaution, escort us. (During those days the communists were very dangerous and would attack targets such as a government car operating on roads in the open country and nearby jungles.) With his experience I felt perfectly safe and besides which he was immensely interesting to listen to. By the way, about a year after we left Malaysia, their government sent a promotional group to the U.S.A., with Pearl, the Royal Prince, and of course, the Head of Security. When they arrived in New York we invited them to spend the day at our house in Wilton, Connecticut. There were about eight in the party. They took the train from Grand Central Station in New York and we picked them up at the railroad station with our Jeep and Mercedes. They could not get over the thickness of the foliage, which reminded them of the jungles in Malaysia! We had a great time including a novelty for them, to enjoy an American barbecue with hamburgers and hotdogs, corn on the cob, and cold beer.

When I returned to New York from Malaysia, I found my staff fully engaged in all kinds of Visit USA business. I made it a policy to give them as much as they could handle and sometimes more. When you have a staff whose skills were growing quickly with the overall growth of the business, they felt the responsibility to protect the reputation of Greyhound International, and it made for a strong esprit de corps. Each one felt they owned a part of the business. This attitude made it possible for me to devote time to the expansion of the team of overseas representatives. It also allowed me to assist marketing activities overseas, coming through our sales offices in various countries throughout the world. Finally with the fine staff it allowed me to engage myself fully with organizations like the Travel Industry Association of America (TIA) and the U.S. Government Tour and Travel Agency (USTTA). With respect to TIA, I was recognized as one of the "founding fathers" of Visit USA. I served eight years on their planning committee and five years on their International

Marketing Plan and Development Committee. This lead to my selection as a member of a further subcommittee, of senior travel executives, that traveled around the world twice to collect data from the overseas offices of the federal government and compose the data into a marketing plan for the department of commerce. I was also a personal consultant to Langhorne Washburne, under secretary for the U.S. Department of Commerce on matters pertaining to further development of inbound business to the United States from the rest of the world.

THE FLAG
OF THE
UNITED STATES OF AMERICA

This is to certify that the accompanying flag was flown over the United States Capitol on December 20, 1983, at the request of the Honorable John W. Warner, United States Senator.

This flag will be presented to Elliott Heit from the Travel Industry Association of America.

George M. White, FAIA
Architect of the Capitol

The aforementioned "I was and I was" gives the appearance I was an "I Was" fellow, well simply put, I was.

Every year, I made sure Greyhound International held a meeting in London with our six overseas offices and as many as twenty of the general sales agents would come from all over the world to attend. The integration between our offices and the general sales agents was critical to the growing importance of what we were trying to accomplish. Ron Blakley, my marketing director for Europe would take care of all arrangements and he did a masterful job. (He also was most dependable in getting excellent sales results with all of our own Greyhound offices in Europe.)

Believe it or not, I still found time to do quite a bit of skiing in places like Gstaad, St. Moritz, Davos and Kitzbuhl, Austria. Whenever it is possible, I would take Carol with me. She was not a great skier, but she managed to do quite well and she was fun to be with. There were two stories that are worth mentioning. Let us start with Gstaad, Switzerland, a very chic ski resort in the western part of the Swiss Alps. Ari Drbal of American Express in their New York headquarters arranged a very nice size apartment with a kitchen and all amenities. It was far from fancy but it was most conveniently located over a local tavern. For the price it was a real bargain and its location in town put everything in "Glitzy Gstaad" practically at our front door step. Skiing in Gstaad is of two types. You either "socially ski" which means you do a lot of sunning and gabbing on the terrace of the restaurant located at the lower slopes or "you ski" which is where you take a gondola with several changes before you are on top of the meanest mountain called Diablo Rey. On the second day of our stay, I suggested to Carol we take the gondola up to the top of Diablo Rey; just to see what the mountain looked like from the top. I further added we would take our skis along so that after we visit the top, we can go down to the "bunny slopes" and have some fun. She agreed and up and up and up we went. It was so high, we went through a cloud deck and then suddenly the sun burst out with a cloudless sky. After we dismounted from our gondola it was a short walk to a very attractive restaurant, which had a beautiful terrace. We were having a glass of champagne when we met an American fellow with his teenage daughter. The daughter was begging the father to ski down Diablo Rey. Her father turned to me and asked if I cared to join them. I looked out at the snow in front of the restaurant and it was as flat as a pancake and it stretched our as far as you could see. Did I bother to ask the father if he had skied Diablo Rey before; no, I just assumed he did and he would certainly not want to endanger his daughter's life. Did I ask how difficult it was? No, because it looked so flat and the day was outstanding. Carol wisely said she would wait for my return and off we went, me with the father and the daughter. When we got underway, it was so flat that we had to use the technique of cross-country skiing. This mean pushing ahead by 'digging in" your ski poles and sliding along instead of skiing downhill. This went on for about an hour. We took a break and looked back at the restaurant, which by this time appeared to be a small dot off in the distance. So far this was quite boring, until suddenly, the end of this snow plateau appears and we are looking down on a very steep mountainside. Several hundred feet below where we were standing was a huge cloud that prevented us from seeing the rest of the mountain. Once again, we looked back at the dot of the restaurant and rather than do the boring trip back, we decided to push on ahead. The slope immediately became very steep and before we could think, we were enveloped in the thick massive cloud. Inside this monstrous cloud it was snowing so hard we could barely see each other. It was like being in a dark closet with the door shut and we all began to get disoriented with vertigo. You could not tell if you were up or down. The daughter became completely panicked and lost all control. The father and myself were not far from feeling the same way. We were huddled together wondering what to do. I suggested that we should stop trying to ski, and instead just fall down and roll until we come out below the cloud to see where we are going and regain our balance so we could continue skiing. We had to hold onto the girl at all times for fear she was going to have a total breakdown. We fell and fell until it looked like our fate was doomed. Amazingly, we suddenly popped out from under the cloud and beneath us was a steep endless mountainside of hip deep snow covering Diablo Rey. As far as I could see there was not one other skier or ski track on the mountain. The daughter recovered somewhat from her deep depression, but she was so nervous her skiing was more falling than skiing. (I could have kicked myself for being so stupid. Normally when I ski a new area, I hire a guide to show me the way, then I can usually handle it on my own.) Anyway, we continued flopping and skiing for at least another hour. Then off in the distance there appears to be a small village. This encourages us, and we feel we are not so alone on the mountain, and we press ahead. Much to our dismay, the tiny village is not a village; instead it is a bunch of shelters for snow bound skiers, offering them protection from the elements. There was not a single person around, and we were still isolated from the rest of the world! In looking around the shelter area, I spied a lift line that strangely enough was operating without anyone in charge. The lift did not go up and it did not go down. It went straight ahead, to what appeared to be another dot in the distance. The lift was quite strange, there were only single chairs, without safety bars and there was not a bar to rest your dangling skis on. The father and myself were unsure of where this lift would take us, but it could be no worse than where we all were. I reasoned while we did not know what was on the other side, these chairs will take us somewhere so we could possibly find out where we were. I took the lead and then the daughter and the father. I cautioned them not to look down the abyss we were going to cross, instead to focus on the dot in the distance which will get larger as this "rinky dinky" chair lift creeks ahead. I did sneak a peek down the abyss and it was like crossing the Grand Canyon! You felt like you were slipping out of the chair especially with nothing to hold you in and your skis dangling in space. One thing for sure the dot in the distance was getting larger. I could now see it was the way station for the gondolas that started us up the mountain over five hours ago! I hopped off my single seat and waited for the father and daughter. We all looked like we had just escaped death, and I think we really had. I told my companions, I was not under any circumstances going back up to the top where I assumed Carol was waiting for me. The daughter went with me down to the bunny slope and we parked ourselves to review this great escape from the unknown. Her father went back up to the top and found Carol, who was nearly out of her mind with fear for us. She rushed to the gondola with the father and we were all finally reunited at the bunny slope lounge. I told Carol if somebody gave me a quarter I would give them my skis, poles and boots plus my perspiration soaked ski suit. Nobody offered a quarter. Within a relative short period of time, the palpitating Diablo Rey experience receded to a more normal heartbeat and I was glad I did not sell my ski equipment for a quarter.

The next ski trip took place about a year after Diablo Rey. Our friends Eddie and Doug Jacobsen had plans to go to St. Moritz for a week and we decided to go along. We would meet them in St. Moritz but then we would go on to Austria to visit Vienna and Salzburg.

One of Eight

The skiing in St. Moritz was great; we had a wonderful week. Carol was making very good progress. So much so, that I suggested to Carol that instead of going to Austria that we spend a few more days in St. Moritz skiing. Doug and Eddie would be leaving at the end of the week, thus we could be on our own to enjoy ourselves. I also told Carol that her progress was so good I would like her to join me on one of the ski runs called Pince Ney, which I usually ski with Doug. This run was considered an advanced intermediate slope. The day we went up was warmer than usual which tends to make the snow softer and somewhat slushy to handle. It was such a beautiful day we over looked the less than perfect snow conditions and hopped on the next gondola. The view from the top of the Pince Ney was a lot different than the Diablo Rey. I was sure Carol could handle it, and we began our descent. We got about a quarter of the way down; I was leading the way, when suddenly, I heard Carol scream. I brought my skis to a braking stop. I looked around and there she was about twenty yards from my position. She was crying and completely unable to stand up. She complained about a pain in her left knee. Before you could say "Jack Robinson", this rather short husky old man is skiing down with a stretcher sled. The stretcher sled was a homemade rig made of two poles attached to it and the old man in-between. He pulled up to our scene and in broken English blurts "Doctor Goode or clinic?". Believe it or not, at the same moment of his arrival, a helicopter is flying directly above us and is dragging a big cloth sign that reads, "Doctor Goode...Only the Best". Obviously, for my darling, it must be Doctor Goode. With our approval the cherub-faced old man loads Carol onto the stretcher and I followed him down the ski trail to a gondola mid station stop. Carol was all tucked into the stretcher and she was only able to look upwards. I thanked God for that, because, if she could look down she would have fainted. The workers detached one of the gondolas from the main cable and replaced it with a rectangular five by eight sheet of plywood. Each of the four corners of the plywood board had a cable connected from the corner to the main cable of the gondola's main cable wire. Carol was then placed on the piece of plywood. I was in a gondola directly behind her, watching her dangling on the plywood platform. We were about two thousand feet above the base of the ski lift, descending the steep angle of the mountainside. If she could look around from her stretcher she would observe herself on a flimsy piece of plywood and dangling two thousand feet above the base. I had a feeling that the pain in her knee would be nothing compared to her hysteria suspended high up there on that plywood contraption.

When we arrive at the base of the gondola, there is what looks to be a brand new Mercedes ambulance with a driver and medical attendant waiting for us. Carol is loaded into the ambulance and we are rushed off to a very glamorous hospital where Carol is wheeled into an equally charming private room with a vase of fresh flowers and a window facing the Alps. Dollar signs were beginning to replace my eyeballs. I am brought back to the situation at hand when, not one, but two doctors enter the room to examine Carol's injured knee. One doctor takes a surgical scissors from his pocket and starts to cut Carols brand new one piece ski outfit she had just purchased for the trip at Bloomingdale's. He cuts from the bottom of her leg to well above the injured knee, thus destroying Carols new very chic ski outfit. Both doctors examined her knee and then they order x-rays. They take me aside and advise me it would be best for Carol to spend a few days at the hospital and that I should check back in the morning for further information regarding her condition. I leave my unfortunate sweetheart and return to the hotel alone.

If only we went on to Vienna and Salzburg as planned, then none of this would have happened. While sitting contemplating the days events and worrying about Carol, suddenly my "cash register head" started to estimate the cost of "Doctor Goode...Only the best" vs. the clinic. How much for the old man helper who suddenly appeared on the ski slope to begin the rescue operation? How about the ride down the plywood contraption they put together. Then there was the beautiful Mercedes ambulance and medical crew that took Carol to the lavish hospital. Lastly what about the beautiful private room and the two doctors to attend to Carol? Finally, the replacement cost of the chic ski suit. I was visualizing how expensive it was to be injured while skiing in St. Moritz. I made up my mind that unless Carol had a serious injury, she would get discharged from the hospital and if necessary recuperate in our hotel.

The next morning at the hospital, the doctors reported that nothing was broken or required a caste. They agreed she could leave on crutches and rest at the hotel. She had torn the ligaments in her knee, recovery would be slow, but a hospital stay was not necessary. Now came the dreaded bill. For all the services and treatment described, the bill came to only forty dollars!! Back home, it would have cost forty dollars to rent a bedpan. I could not get over it and I was ashamed of taking her somewhat prematurely out of her luxurious hospital room, but there you have it.

Now for my last ski story, which occurred during one of my many business trips to Europe. When ever I made such trips to Switzerland or Germany I would try to arrange my itinerary so that the weekend would be convenient to a ski area. This happened on one trip to Germany that included a stop in the southern German city of Munich. Munich is about a two-hour train ride from famous Kitzbuhl Austria. It is one of the best ski areas in all of Europe. It was not as chic as Gstaad or St. Moritz, but it is most certainly, a skier's paradise. I had never skied Kitzbuhl, but with its proximity to Munich, and the weekend coming up, I could not resist. I was close enough; my luggage already contained ski knickers, heavy ski stockings, sweater, gloves and jacket. Skis, poles and boots could always be conveniently rented at the ski site.

I took the two-hour journey via an old locomotive, puffing smoke like it would be its last trip before retirement. Behind the steam engine were five or six old-fashioned coach cars. It was very quaint and upon arrival fitted perfectly into the 19th century mode of the town of Kitzbuhl. One of my German clients had arranged my stay at an inn, which exceeded all my expectations for authenticity and comfort. After I unpacked I found a ski shop where I rented all my equipment for the following morning. I brought all my equipment back to my room so that after breakfast the next morning I would be ready to meet the Kitzbuhl Mountain without any delay. I asked the innkeeper when was breakfast served, he advised that dinning room opened at six thirty. I advised I would be waiting at the dinning room doors. I pre-ordered my breakfast of a large sirloin steak, two eggs, toast, potatoes, orange juice and tea with honey.

At six thirty the following morning I was at the dinning room door; dressed in my knickers, heavy wool stockings, ski sweater, along with my rented skis, boots and poles. I was the only one in the dinning room, which was just as well, as my appearance, and menu for breakfast would, at the least, raise some eyebrows and question about who was this character. I quickly gobbled the feast in front to me, grabbed my ski equipment and off on a short walk to the mountain I went.

Upon my arrival I was unable to understand a lot of the signs posted as everything was in German. I did not have to read the signs to observe the chair lifts were operating, but oddly without any staff, just like the Diablo Rey experience in Gstaad. Also similar to that experience, I took no heed of how one finds their way up or for that matter down the mountain. Blame it on my enthusiastic glee to "taste the Kitzbuhl Mountain". I managed, with skis on to get on the next chair. The chair could seat two persons, which would have been better for safety, but I was the only one on the mountain so away I went. I came to the end of the lift line, at which point I got off and followed the arrow to the next lift going higher. I repeated this procedure two more times, which brought me apparently to the last lift. This would take me to the very top. The last lift was one of those single chair set-ups, which again I was able to mount. Why did I not think about what I was doing? When I finally got to the top and looked down from THE PEAK OF KITZBUHL, it appeared to be similar to what one would observe from the window flying at cruising altitude in a jet airliner. In other words I was very high. It could also be said, I was the highest person on the mountain because I was the only person on the mountain. Another peculiarity about the peak of Kitzbuhl was that it actually was a peak. To get down from the peak, you had to ski down on a narrow trail that circled the peak maybe five or six times. Each time you circled, you would get a little lower from the top and the circular ski run would become larger circles as I descended to the broader part of the peak. The ski trial was similar in shape to the conical thread rolls they used to have mounted on the top of old-fashioned sewing machines. In somewhat the same way the ski trail was "etched" into the side of the mountain peak like an imbedded shelf. To gain an idea of my extreme concern; if I fell during this process to get down to the broader part of the mountain, I would fall to the next circular level below the one I was on, if I was lucky. This situation made is a strong temptation to lean against the peak as you slowly proceeded down the narrow ski trail.

At last, I managed to get off the peak onto a broad plateau of powder snow that extended from the base of the peak for a couple of hundred yards. It was a magnificent day, crisp and dry air and brusquely cold. Moving across the plateau, I was still amazed that there was not one single person anywhere to be seen. I suddenly began to realize that once again, I have no idea where I am, and the best thing I can do is ski down the gigantic slope to get to it's end. There were no signs to indicate direction. It actually didn't look too steep, but the powder snow was deeper than anything I had ever skied. You had to ski faster than usual and sit back on your skis to avoid sinking into the snow. I did the best I could but there were a few times, I felt I was sinking and would bury myself until a spring thaw came around. After a while the snow seemed to harden and I could resume normal skiing.

Still not one human being to be seen, but I was making progress. In fact, quite a ways below, I spotted a road. I decided this is what I would head for. I stopped for "a breather" and looked at my watch, it was eleven thirty. I had been on Kitzbuhl Mountain for over three hours and I was very lost. It took another hour to get to the road. I knew I looked like something that fell off the back of a truck. The buckles on my knickers were broken, my heavy wool stockings were down around my ankles and I was sore and wet with perspiration. I managed to flag a truck on the road, but all I could say was, "Kitzbuhl?" The driver said "Ja" (phonetically Ya) and I got in. It took us almost an hour to get to the center of town. I thanked him profusely and found my way back to the inn.

Upon entering the inn, the innkeeper saw me. He was bewildered by my exhausted appearance. He takes me into the bar where the story unfolds. He offers me two cognacs which I quickly down while I describe my harrowing Kitzbuhl adventure. I then excused myself, went to my room, took a hot bath, and went to bed. I woke up at six in the evening, dressed and had a light dinner and went directly back to bed.

While the Kitzbuhl episode had some very scary moments, little did I know that my skiing days would soon be over. Very shortly after I returned home, I took the family skiing at a nearby location. I was coming down a simple run and all of a sudden my right leg gave way. I fell and could not get up. Robert, Susan and Carol got me up and I managed to get down the slop. We drove home and about two weeks later I had a complete right hip replacement. That finished skiing, but I was glad it did not happen before Kitzbuhl, as it was a wonderful way to finish my skiing days.

A funny story worth mentioning, took place with my attendance at an exclusive dinner party arranged by Congressman Jack Murphy for his close friend, Anastasio Somoza, the President of Nicaragua. Jack took over the entire second floor of a well-known French restaurant in New York City. He called me in Connecticut and requested my wife and I attend. Carol was initially reluctant to travel all the way to New York City for dinner. I told her if Jack says, "the word" and the head guest is the President of Nicaragua, we are going.

We arrived by taxi from Grand Central Station. Outside in front of the restaurant there were about six very stocky men lined up shoulder to shoulder all dressed in white panama suits. (It was a hot summers day and their clothing was typical for Central American climate). After seeing these six men, Carol asked me, "Do you think they are going to put on a show during dinner?"

I replied, "No Carol, they are President Somoza's bodyguards."

Upon entering, we were ushered upstairs and Jack grabbed us quickly so we would be in the line up of the reception committee. Carol, my dear wife was beginning to sense this was not going to be an ordinary "dinner on the town". When the reception was completed, Jack strongly suggested that Carol and Jack's wife go up on the stage to the head table and take their places for dinner on either side of the President. As for Jack and myself, we were seated at one of the regular tables reserved for other guests. About midway through the dinner, Carol comes running over to me and bursts out, "He is very charming, but he is also very aggressive!"

(I am not totally surprised because my wife was a model during her younger years and still remains to be very attractive. She was stunning in her fashionable attire). I told her it would be an affront to leave the presidents' honored table, besides which Jack's wife would be uncomfortable without her presence. I am not sure how many readers were aquatinted with the Nicaraguan political situation. At the time the Somoza family ruled the country. Just about all of Central America were experiencing uprisings. Leftist revolutionary cells such as the Contra in Nicaragua sponsored most of these. I believe it was difficult for the Untied Sates to openly show support for the Somoza regime even though the Somoza leadership was holding the Contra forces at bay. President Somoza was a constant target for assassination and you can now understand why he had that squad of bodyguards in front of the restaurant. Also to note, most of the people attending the dinner were influential persons from New York and Washington. Later on, there were articles in magazines and newspapers describing the Somoza family as a hard-nosed dictatorship even though they were supporters of the United States effort to offset the growing threat of communism in Central America.

Let us return to the dinner party, and the speech of President Somoza. When the President rose to make his informal speech, he started off by saluting Jack Murphy, as a good friend even though Jack was a member of the Democratic Party (actually Jack, with his aggressive nature, was known as a hawk democrat). Then the President went on to say "As for myself, quite a few of you think, I am a dictator...well, I am."

It was said in such a way it caught the audience off-guard. The audience burst into laughter as a reaction to his disclosure. The rest of what was said was a quiet rebuke of the press that should spend more time on aiding the Somoza stand against the spreading revolutionaries of Central America, rather than undermining his position and strong support he has shown for the United States Government policy in Central America.

At the close of the dinner we established, once again the reception line, only this time the President was going down the line to thank the host and the reception committee. Carol, was the first one to whom he said goodnight. He graciously kissed her hand and Carol remarked to him, "That is the first time I have ever been kissed by a President."

So he kissed her again, but this time, it was more in the style of a Hollywood screen hero. Carol did not make any further remarks.

President Somoza was obviously not popular with everyone, but never the less; it was a most interesting evening.

Unfortunately, in 1980, Anastasio Somoza was assassinated in Asuncion, Paraguay during an official visit to that country.

Chapter 8

Leaving Greyhound & A New Career

The seventies can best be characterized by dramatic changes in the business world of Elliot Heit. Despite excellent progress with my international activities for Greyhound, there seemed to be a growing number of rumors concerning the overall management of the Corporation. Taking rumors at face value is a dangerous past time, but if you accept rumors as "smoky suspicions', you are at least on guard for what ever lies ahead. The Vice Chairman of Greyhound was a youngish, good-looking Irishman, Jim Kerrigan. Very aggressive and very confident, he made a spectacular rise through the ranks to become President of the bus line. He continued upwards after gaining entrance to the "corporate management club" but Jim's ambition was still not satisfied, even when he was named Vice Chairman. His direction was to go for "the big chair."

The only indication I had to substantiate my "smoky suspicion" was a private lunch he invited me to. Now occasionally, he would drop into my office during one of his "fly by" visits to New York, but a private lunch with the Vice Chairman is something else. So was the subject matter discussed during lunch? He was considering a special ad hoc committee composed of some of the ranking executives of the corporation headquarters and he was considering including me. While we did not go into specifics, I was flattered. I stated I would be glad to be of service. Actuality, that was as far as it went, but it seemed an indication of some serious developments shaping up in the near future

In the meanwhile, there were other unusual events developing in my own bailiwick. Stanley Fisher at the time was President and owner of Allied Tours, which was basically a competitor to Greyhound International. We knew each other for many years and he was impressed with what I was able to get done with the Greyhound giant. He was impressed to the extent that he offered me the position of Executive Vice President of Allied Tours. I did not bite on this, but I put his offer in my back pocket just incase my suspicions about Greyhound turned real.

Then there was my good friend Eddie Hartnett. He graduated a year later than I did from West Point. He was a fantastic athlete. Even though Eddy weighed only one hundred and forty eight pounds, he was an outstanding halfback for our "B" squad football team. He was so athletically endowed, that upon graduation he accepted an offer to participate on the Olympic pentathlon team. It literally took Eddy only five minutes to catch on to any new sport. Tennis, handball, squash, wind surfing; he would not only "catch on", he would be "tops". When he left the army he became an FBI agent and at the same time went to night school to study law. When he became a lawyer, he left the FBI and got started being an entrepreneur. From a guy who came from a poor family up in Buffalo, New York, he certainly got on the "A" train in a hurry. It did not take long for him to buy the big house at Sand Point, Long Island, a condo in Florida, a thirty-six foot power cruiser, and his first Cadillac.

We stayed close friends. He was always "pushing" me to get out of Greyhound so he and I could start our own travel business. This really caught my attention especially since things seemed to be going in the wrong direction at Greyhound. I told Eddy that my financial situation with Carol, her kids needs, my alimony and child support, the hassle from Carols ex-husband, our new house in Wilton, Connecticut and on and on, did not leave me much room financially to start a new business. I suggested that he keep me in the background where I felt I could help him with such essential things as securing a federal interstate license to operate tours from New York to any state in the country. I also asked him to allow me to speak to my top German tour specialist to see if he would be interested in leaving Greyhound for an opportunity that could lead to him becoming general manager with equity in the new business. Eddy liked this idea very much. I then spoke to Udo Koch, my Greyhound German specialist, and he went ballistic with enthusiasm. The new company was called Transamerica with Eddy President, and Udo the manager. I was able to secure the license and they were off and running. Udo did, as expected a wonderful job.

Eddy developed cancer and died within three years, and Eddy had Udo listed in his will as the heir apparent to the business.

During the seventies I had other offers and opportunities to provide me with a change of venue. One was an unsolicited "headhunter" who narrowed down to three possible candidates for filling the vacancy to become the President of PATA (Pacific Area Travel Association). I was one of the three finalists. Another possibility was an offer from Stella Barros Tourismo of Sao Paulo, Brazil. Her son Luis took over her business and he would do most anything to get me to move the family to Rio De Janeiro to run one on his subdivisions. Carol received permission from her ex husband to move the children to Brazil. Luis agreed to ship all our household goods to Brazil and guarantee the return incase the move did not work out. We knew the apartment we wanted for our residence and even checked on the schooling for the kids. Just before the contract was to be sent, I received a phone call from mother Stella. She begged me not to accept, and I listened to her. In the final analysis, she was right, her advice was, "Do not leave the USA. This is your base of power. If you go to Brazil, you will lose that power."

One other offer was more humorous than real but it is worth mentioning. Ted Halligan graduated from West Point in the class of 1945. He was a wonderful individual who I met while attending a meeting of the West Point Society of New York. He was just elected to the presidency. It was the start of a long friendship with Ted and his charming wife Irene.

After he graduated Ted spent some time in the eighty-second Air Borne division, subsequently he received his masters in journalism. Ted then completed an assignment at West point as an English instructor before resigning from the service. A big handsome hulk of a man that played varsity football at the academy, Ted was extremely intelligent and at the same time humorous and charismatic. Ted went head on into the stock brokerage business and was at one time Managing Director of the Piper Jaffray Company. Socially he was a complete bon vivant, there was always something going on. To illustrate an incident, while I was in Chicago, I received a call from him asking if I had any interest in becoming a commissioner for John

Lindsey, then mayor of New York City. I asked Ted, "Commissioner of what?"

"Commissioner of Sanitation, with 18,000 collectors under your command."

"Ted are you serious? If you are, how much does it pay?"

He was dead serious but the answer to the payment question found Ted to be at his funniest.

"$50,000 a year plus all you can eat!"

After I finished crying with laughter, I told him the project was not for me. He had been completely serious about the position.

It was also Ted Halligan who got me on the list to fill the vacancy for Vice President of the West Point society of New York. Additionally he was instrumental in my selection as a member of the Board of Trustees for the Military Academy. It was an exceptional honor serving with such distinguished graduates. The members included, General Leslie Groves, who headed the initial development of the atomic bombs that we used for the first atomic raid on Japan. General Mcauliffe, hero of the Battle of the Bulge, who told the Nazi's who surrounded him to "Take a walk", Mark Clark who led the invasion of Italy, etc, etc. Unfortunately, Ted contracted cancer and passed away while I was out of the country. Ted was a magnanimous person who always will be remembered.

I did go ahead with Stanley Fisher of Allied Tours. I signed a five-year contract as Executive Vice President. For the financial arrangement he agreed to twenty percent more than I was receiving from Greyhound. On the subject of incentive, he also agreed to pay me two percent on gross sales after the first $300,000 increase in business. I brought with me two of my staff, namely Ingrid Burgdof for technical study tours and Aixa as a senior touristic specialist. According to Stanley's accountant the current fiscal year ended with $3,500,000 in sales (Greyhound International's sales for the same period were $37,000,000). I do not believe Stanley Fisher understood the full financial impact of what he agreed to. He woke up in a hurry when my first year sales ended with a $2,000,000 increase! (This meant after subtracting the first $300,000 increase, he owed me 2% on $1, 700,000 or $34,000). He waited until three months passed and I brought the matter to his attention. We argued and settled on 1% instead of 2%, which cut my bonus to $17,000. At the end of the second year, sales increased another $2,000,000 (in two years he doubled his business) once again he "fudged" on payment, but finally paid me a $15,000 bonus. Aside from this difficulty, Stanley in business is not the Stanley socially. To further complicate the situation he had two sons in the business. The eldest was not happy with me having a higher title than him and in general I could not find the right managerial rhythm with him or his father. I suppose he was always king of the hill and found delegating functions were not to be his forte.

One day we went to lunch and he brought up the sales incentive subject. "Elliot, if your bonuses continue, you will be making more money than me. I read our contract carefully, and it contains a clause that states as owner, I can void the contract by giving you one years salary and that is what I plan to do."

My initial reaction was relief; because I got to dislike him and the unprofessional way he handled business. I went home to Connecticut and after dinner I sat out on our screened in patio facing the forest that bordered our property and pondered my future. Carol was with me, (she too was relieved I was out of Allied Tours). I told her we certainly do not have any immediate financial problems, but the fundamental issue was where am I, at age fifty-five going out and getting started again in my own industry or any other industry. For the next couple of weeks I pondered and I pondered. I came up with an idea and reviewed it with Carol.

There was one person in the travel industry that I deeply admired and respected more than anyone else I have ever met, and to this day my opinion is still the same. That man is Arthur Tauck. We initially met at one of the many travel circuit meetings we were both participating in. In 1925 his father founded what was then called Tauck Tours, (the company was renamed in 1995 to Tauck World Discovery). His son Arthur Jr. began to work for his father before he was even a teenager. His father was a tough taskmaster in pioneering what became known as a tour operator.

Before I go ahead with my own story involving Tauck, it would prove helpful to devote some attention to the history of this top-notch company. Prior to July 13, 1925, the date that marked the departure of the first Tauck operated tour, Arthur's father worked as an inauspicious bank clerk. One of his duties was to separate the different denomination of coin, fold them in wrappers, and load them on a tray, which he then placed on a dumb waiter. He would then lower the tray by rope to the basement for further sorting. Each day Arthur's father performed this duty without a hitch, until the one day when he opened the door of the dumb waiter, but he failed to check if the platform was there to place the tray of coins upon. Instead he placed the tray with no platform underneath, in the chute of the dumb waiter and down fell three hundred dollars worth of coin. The coins hit the basement floor and were scattered in every direction. His father was told there would no longer be a need for his services.

It is here the unique nature of and inherent quality of the Tauck family determination comes to the surface. Arthur senior went home and designed a better coin tray. He created an aluminum sample of his invention and managed to get a meeting with the head of the bank he was just fired from. The manger advised him that they had no use for his coin tray. Arthur senior was still not ready to give up.

The solution was to start small. He would avoid the big sophisticated city banks, and instead bring his coin tray invention to the smaller country banks. He built himself a large supply of aluminum coin trays and headed off to New England. His idea of going to country banks was the thing to do and his invention was well accepted. But the visit to the New England region showed him something else. It was the mid twenties; in those days there were no McDonalds and very few gas stations. The lack of touristic infrastructure left the area of New England wide open for tour development. Mother Nature covered New England with beautiful forests, rolling hills and lakes, and there were delightful villages, with quaint wooden bridges traversing rivers and streams. Seeing all this beauty brought home to Arthur senior that a lot more people should see and learn about these treasures. (Not to be overlooked is the fact that New England and its history contained the very soul of early America, with many roads of dirt, and few gas stations and hotels.) There was no question; people avoided New England due to the lack of touristic structure. All this wonderment circulated in Arthur seniors mind and he decided he could do something about it. On July 13, 1925, the "something" took place. As the driver, escort and guide, he loaded his Studebaker sedan and left Newark, New Jersey with a supply of aluminum coin trays for the banks and five curious people who signed up for his promotion to "open up" New England tourism. This was all discovered due to the loss of Arthur's fathers job at the bank and became the first step in the history to organize a company that has blazed a remarkable path of progress and innovation for over eighty years.

He knew all the good hotels and country inns; he knew his geography from the many trips he had made to sell his invention to the banks, and he knew New England's history. Additionally, Mr. Tauck did something else to make this first escorted tour unique. He included only the best available hotels, a la carte individual dining, inclusive of all tips and admission fees. With this "all inclusive" formula, his tour was a great success and Tauck Tours was in business. There were many roadblocks along the way to becoming recognized by the entire travel industry as one of the best tour operators in the world.

Many problems beset them. They survived the 1929 depression, but not before going out of business and coming back in 1934. Then they had to cease and desist during World War II. One of the truly remarkable chapters in their history occurred in the fifties, when the Greyhound Bus Line legally objected to the Interstate Commerce Commission, that their federal franchise was being continuously violated by Tauck Tours, a non-licensed company, operating many tours over their route systems. No tour operator anywhere in the United States, had a tour operator's license; the matter became a cause celebre for all motor coach tour operators throughout the entire country, who were also operating tours without proper license. The case became known as the "Famous Tauck Case", and went all the way up to the U.S. Supreme court. After eight years of the Tauck family stubbornly fighting the case, the Supreme Court finally ruled in favor of Tauck. Once again their convictions and determination came to the fore. Tauck was awarded the number one license as an interstate motor coach tour operator. Thus the company set the standards for all interstate motor coach tour operators in the United States. The company earned the respect of the industry for achieving this landmark decision and Tauck continues to this day with the same diligence and operating philosophy.

In 1958, Arthur Tauck junior was given the reins of the company. By that time Arthur senior felt his son was ready to assume the responsibility of maintaining the basic premise of a Tauck experience, which leaves guests feeling their expectations have been exceeded.

Now that you have a bit of background on the company, let us return to my desperate situation. I was reviewing my situation with Carol on the back patio of our home in Wilton Connecticut. I mentioned to Carol that maybe it would be a good idea to call Arthur Tauck who was nearby in Westport and discuss the possibility of getting Tauck Tours started in my end of the travel business. To the best of my knowledge, most of Tauck's guests were Americans. Very little business was coming from other countries abroad, which was my area of expertise. I certainly had nothing to lose; Carol agreed. I called Arthur and asked for an appointment to discuss what might be a new dimension that could be added to their market. He was readily agreeable.

In August of 1981, I unfolded my concept and my qualifications for this new business venture. Arthur had a very positive reaction. (It was helpful that he was somewhat aware of my history). "I do not do contracts. Instead I will give you a hand shake for three years, and if it does not work our by then we will still stay friends."

That handshake turned out to be far better than any contract I ever signed. I told him the three years was enough to prove my case. Arthur then said he would like to have me present myself to his executive staff so that I could give them a picture of what I had in mind. Within a week or so, a meeting took place with Arthur's accountant, Vice President of operations and three or four staff members. I presented myself in some detail with a history of my success with Gray Line New York, Greyhound International and Allied tours. As I got more involved in explaining how we open markets abroad, and the international techniques used to advance the business, I could see they had little or no idea of what I was talking about, and how I was going to get Tauck involved with the international business organizations in the overseas markets.

Arthur was not present at this meeting. Subsequently I requested an additional appointment with him to make him aware of my opinions and game plan. I told Arthur, it was very obvious to me that to make this new source of business a success, I must have full control. This included, not having his staff, which knew little or nothing about my business, trying to supervise or influence my decisions. He agreed to this and left me in full control for fourteen years! I would start by working alone and would only ask for my own personnel as the business demands required. I did not want any of the annual company bonuses or pay raises, until I see the kind of progress I expected. At the proper time I will knock on his door and ask for a salary adjustment. It turned out, I never had to "knock" because his response to the progress we made was always more than I expected.

I was given the title of Director of International Markets. Along with this, I was given exclusive responsibility to implement my plan with one of the finest companies in the tour operator industry. My goal was to establish for them a worldwide market for their service. It was an honor to undertake such a task, it gave me dedication, strength, and determination to do it. I took an oath to myself to "leave no stone unturned" to make this work.

Tauck had a partially unused office in New York on Fifth Avenue, located almost across the street from the New York Public Library. I explained to Arthur that we would now be dealing with many international interests, who had offices in New York and overseas, therefore it would be beneficial if he allowed me to set up the vacant portion of his New York office space. He agreed quickly, and on the following weekend my son and I went to New York, to clean up and paint my new office space. On the following monthly statement received after moving in, I noticed an item, $425.00 for New York office rent. I called the accountant and told him that I would be closing the offices, and I would be working from the Westport office rent-free. {Plus no commuting expense to New York City made it even more logical.)

In Westport there was no office space readily available for me, so I made due by using one of the many chairs set up around the large table in the conference room. The conference room also doubled as a lunchroom at the appropriate time of day. Very often during lunch hour I would be on the phone with various managers of large tour firms in England or elsewhere while food odors would waft across my desk, (conference table). This continued for three or four months.

It was at last time when I needed an administrative assistant; it was also decided to assign us to an office, though it was very small and cramped. In 1981, the Tauck office did not have a fax machine or e-mail, and limited availability for copy equipment. It practically took an act of congress to secure these for my office. Arthur ran a "tight ship." As an example, at the time, Tauck Tours was carrying about 65,000 guests and the entire office staff to administrate the business was only sixty-four persons (including Arthur Tauck).

Back to my administrative assistant; getting the right one took ten different attempts with each one lasting about a month. My office must have been the graveyard for anybody Tauck was trying to get rid of. The eleventh prospect was a young lady by the name of Shelia Thompson. Due to her inexperience, I suspect she was handed over to me. I liked her alertness and enthusiasm. I explained we would be dealing with countries all over the world. This picture of innocence from a Nebraska farm lit up like a Christmas tree. She became invaluable to me. We shared a fax machine, but she had her own typewriter. She was always amazed to see so many papers coming out of the fax machine from, England, South and Central America, Australia and many other countries of the world. This coupled with my incoming global calls heightened the intensity of her interest. Shelia definitely left the farm.

There were three areas of the company that we had to collaborate with. First there was Arthur Tauck. This also included his secretary and very sweet lady, Dotty Ahearn, who guided me many times, regarding the politics of the company. The second person was Don Selesko, the accountant, who knew his numbers and was often a source of advice. Finally, there was Charley Wanska. He worked out of a small separate warehouse, across the street from the headquarters building. He was the iron-fisted custodian for all distribution of all Tauck brochure supplies. I could not have survived without him.

Before I left for England on my first trip, I received a call from Ed Button, Managing Director of North American Travel in Leeds, England. Through my work with the Travel Industry Association of America, we had met several times. He invited me to be the main speaker at a Waldorf –Astoria breakfast he was hosting for about twenty of his top producing agents, who had been invited to New York for the weekend with hotel accommodations at the Waldorf Astoria. I, of course said that I would be delighted. The breakfast was my first exposure to English agents for Tauck Tours, and my presentation was warmly received. After the breakfast Ed came over and shook my hand and said he will include Tauck in his brochure. I asked how many brochures he printed; he advised 50,000. Can you imagine, that this one deal put Tauck on the map with over five hundred active English travel agents that North America Travel dealt with? Furthermore because Ed Button would include us in his brochure, I did not have to "smuggle" any Tauck brochures out of Charley Wanska's warehouse. I told Ed Button I would be coming over to England shortly and I would then show him how to display Tauck effectively in his brochure. Ever since then, North America travel has been a loyal supporter of Tauck and continues to be to this day.

I finally made that trip to England and met with North American Travel. I also met with many more operators, in an effort to make similar agreements like the one with Ed Button. This is not an easy task; some companies required a year or two before they bore fruit, but I never gave up until an agreement was reached. Incidentally, while I was Director of International Marketing for Tauck for over fourteen years, I would say that over ninety percent of my air travel was as a guest of carriers that I have known for many years, prior to joining Tauck. This advantage allowed me to substantially reduce the cost of my travel expenses.

The duration of the England trip was three weeks, and I visited about fifty target companies. The trip was an excellent learning experience. The biggest disappointment was my alma mater, Greyhound International. Ron Blakey, the Managing Director was polite but firm in refusing to promote Tauck in England. It required three years to get him to see the light, but it finally happened. Greyhound was perfect for Tauck. Who in England knew the USA better than the largest bus system in the world? "To prime the pump," I suggested a mail campaign to the Travel Agents of England, which would explain Greyhound's endorsement of Tauck. To do this I wrote the letters and Ron

Blakey mailed them. Within two years Greyhound was making almost a thousand bookings a year, and was our single largest source of business in the world.

My next accomplishment was getting Kuoni, the "crème de la crème" tour operator in England to come on board with us. As soon as this became known within the U.K. travel industry, I was able to negotiate agreements with many of the other top up-market operators throughout England. I told every one of these major players that I was not satisfied to get only a handshake; I wanted to teach and preach Tauck to their selling agents. To further achieve the deepest penetration of the minds of these selling personnel, I suggested they set up a number of seminars where the sales agents with their clients are in the same learning room. I figured if I could impress the clients of the agents, the agents would be more inclined to sell Tauck to their other clients. To do this effectively I included skits where I would pick one of the clients to come forward on the stage. There I had a table for one, set with a full formal place setting (linen tablecloth, napkin, plates, and silverware), and of course a candelabra. I would escort my guest to the table and seat him or her properly. I would announce to the audience that this lovely lady is on a Tauck Tour of the Canadian Rockies and has arrived at the Monarch dining room of the Baronial Banff springs Hotel. As her waiter, I showed her the authentic menu from the Banff hotel. I continued with reciting the menu to her and the audience, and then ask that she select an item. I then request that she jot down the price with the pencil on the pad already in place at the table. As the waiter in the sketch I continued with the following,

"Would madam care for an elegant shrimp cocktail as an appetizer? Good, write $11.95. Thank you. For your entrée would madam enjoy a filet mignon? Good, write $29.00. Would madam care for a salad, possibly a Caesar salad? Good, write $9.95. Now for desert, the specialty of the house is chocolate soufflé. Good write $10.95. Coffee, that will be $4.50, please write that down as well. Thank you."

I would then turn to the audience and say, "Can you imagine this petite femme consuming a dinner for $61.85, this would be before adding on a gratuity of 9.28. Ladies and gentlemen, all of our services along with the price of meals such as this, are included in our price. Other tour companies will say we are inflating prices; we are not; we are creating value for your money."

Preach I did, and all over the world, with hundreds of seminars, and always with me, was my little cardboard box, with all my props to set the stage.

The seminars plus the formulas for getting Tauck into the overseas tour operator's brochures was largely responsible for my initial success. At one time during the eighties, in just the United Kingdom, there were close to 3,000,000 brochures from most of the top quality operators that carried our best selling tours.

It was now time to move onto the continent. I decided with certain countries, to modify the method of presenting Tauck to the market place. I returned to my prior habit of designating general sales agents in the Netherlands and Switzerland. In both cases, I was able to reach an agreement with American Express to be our representative. Germany was more like the English market. Even though we had no tours with Germany speaking escorts, we still carried almost a thousand Germans a year!

I now turned my attention to Australia and New Zealand. (When you do business with Australia it is a given that you also take in New Zealand only 400 miles away) In Australia, I had been getting a handful of bookings, prior to Tauck, through a lone wolf by the name of Ran MacDonald. He was actually an exiled Scotsman (without kilts). He was a very difficult and stubborn individual, but it was a promising start for Tauck Tours in Australia. In my search for a better setup I came across Tony Millmore of Venture Holidays, a very aggressive member of the travel industry in the state of New South Wales. He understood what I wanted to do; expand sales by promoting Tauck throughout Australia instead of confining it to New South Wales. I introduced Ran MacDonald to Venture Holidays, but "Mac" was such a loner, he gave up and left. Tony continued to follow the plan to open offices in other coastal states of Australia. It did not take long to blossom into four or five hundred Tauck guests each year.

It is a falsity that Australia and New Zealand are "nearby" each other; the islands are in actuality an ocean apart. The natives of New Zealand in this down under country are called Maoris. It is believed that they originally migrated from Polynesia. Their history shows that seven Maori canoes originating from Polynesia crossed the huge expanse of Pacific Ocean to finally arrive in New Zealand. The relationship between the Maori's and the white settlers from England was not a cozy one. Largely through the efforts of their own chiefs, the Maoris have reemerged as an economically self-sufficient minority in New Zealand, and their population today is more than 500,000. The Maori maintain their own cultural identity apart from the general New Zealand community, while at the same time sending representatives to parliament and participating, at least to some degree, in most national issues. Legislation passed in the early 1990s provided for the settling of Maori land claims going back to the 19th century, when land was seized by British colonists. Carol and I learned about the Maori's during a semi-business trip to New Zealand, to search for a suitable representative for Tauck.

We stayed at a hotel owned by a Maori family in Rotarua, which is the center city of Maori culture. While having lunch one day in the hotel restaurant, our table was approached by the sales manager and the owner of the establishment. They were already aware that I was associated with Tauck and they invited us to a cocktail party, to be held that evening for the Minister of Lands for New Zealand, who was a Maori. We graciously accepted their invitation.

At the party we met Maori lawyers, politicians, artists and a very accomplished professional pianist. (In respect to the Maori's they were treated much better than their counterparts, the Aborigines of Australia). The cocktail party proceeded a dinner to which they also invited us to attend as their guest. We were getting along so well, we eagerly accepted. We were seated at a very long table accommodating at least twenty persons in a private dining room. The Minister of Lands was seated at the center of the table, flanked by some of the politicians. Carol and I were separated; I was seated at one end of the table next to the pianist and Carol on the other end of the table was seated next to the legal counselor for the Minister of Lands. Once we were all seated, the Minister stands up and welcomes everybody, and then points to me and says, " Elliot, it is a Maori custom, whenever a new member joins an occasion such as this, that person must get up and sing a song for us. Would you please do us that honor?"

Surprised as I was, I stood up and had the good luck to bring to mind a song my ex father-in-law used to sing, it goes like this,

> *"It's a good time to get together,*
> *It's a good time to know,*
> *Who the pal is who sits beside you,*
> *So smile and say hello.*
> *Goodbye to that lonesome feeling,*
> *Farewell glassy stare,*
> *Here's my hand,*
> *I'm mighty glad to meet you,*
> *So put your right there."*

With that and upon completion of my song, I turn to the person next to me and shook his hand. The table went wild with laughs and applause. The Minister of Land rises, and thanks me profusely. He then proceeds to take off his parliamentary cufflinks, which he hands to me as a gift. I still have them to this day.

After dinner there was still more to come. They again ask Carol and I to join them and we adjourned to the empty ballroom. They push a piano to the center of the dance floor and the pianist starts to play with all of us surrounding the piano. A few extra bottles of wine found there way into the room and the glasses were once again filled. The pianist was perfect; she could play any kind of music. Everyone was asked to perform, even the Minister sang Pavarotti's favorite aria (it was pretty bad but he got an "A" for effort). I asked her if she knew "Give my regards to Broadway". She got right onto it, and I grabbed Carol and then we not only sang good and loud, but we even threw in a little soft shoe, which seemed to delight everyone. At one in the morning we thanked ever one for an unforgettable evening and said good night. According to some survivors we met the following day, "good night" for the rest of the group did not occur until three thirty in the morning.

Shortly after returning from New Zealand, I made several trips to Argentina, Brazil and the Central American countries setting up representative arrangements. When my trips were finally completed I had a worldwide network of representatives in thirty-six countries in addition to England and Germany. In each country I was able to set up separate trading agreements with many of their most powerful travel companies. In England, there was one company by the name of Thomas Cook. I tried for three years to get them to join with us, but to no avail. Thomas Cook & Sons, was a premier company, over a hundred years old and had over three hundred and fifty travel shops throughout the United Kingdom and the Irish Republic. Unfortunately English bureaucracy burdened the company and I could never get to first base. That is until Arthur Tauck successfully became the first tour operator in the world to start booking tours using the technology of the first two automatic reservation systems operated by the airlines. United Airlines named its new technology Apollo and Northwest Airlines named theirs Worldspan. Tauck was once again in the leading edge of reservation technology. These two exclusive booking services made it possible to book an airline or a Tauck Tour, from anywhere in the world with any member of the travel industry who had an agreement to use either one of these automated systems. Can you imagine what this would mean? Instead of sending faxes or expensive phone calls, you could "punch in the right numbers" and INSTANTLY receive a confirmed reservation from anyplace in the world.

My mind lit up like a Christmas tree and I immediately thought of Thomas Cook. I called Peter Gidley, General Manager of Travel for the mighty Thomas Cook and explained I had a revolutionary facility to lighten the burden of expense and time in the booking tours for clients touring the United States and Canada. I was prepared to fly out immediately to discuss this system directly with him. BINGO! He was astonished, and the next day, I flew to London and then by train to the town of Petersborough to Peter Gidley's office. This was Thomas Cooks headquarters where there were one thousand five hundred personnel employed. The meeting took place with just the two of us in his office. He was absolutely intrigued with my description. He advised that Thomas Cook had its own system, which he was desperately trying to "interlock" with Apollo or Worldspan systems. Regardless of what he did, it did not work. In desperation he called on his intercom set, "Get Simon Laxton to come to my office immediately."

Simon immediately entered; he was a skinny built young man with thin-rimmed glasses and a prematurely balding head. He seemed the type that everything he did, or for that matter said, was done with a fanatic energy. Peter explained the problem and Simon attacked the Thomas Cook automatic system in a frenzy. In a matter of minutes he was "interlocked" with the Apollo reservation system. I gave them a few sample Tauck bookings to create. When they were instantaneously confirmed they were both astounded.

Nothing very significant followed that Thomas Cook meeting except to say Peter Gidley was shortly succeeded by Simon Laxton as Managing Director of Thomas Cook Holidays, the tour operation arm of the largest travel enterprise in the United Kingdom. That initial meeting with Gidley and Saxton marked the beginning of one of my strongest and long lasting business relationships. Simon Laxton had absolute confidence in me to initiate and develop the sales of Tauck service with all appropriate Thomas Cook travel ships. To get things started, a communication was issued to all shops announcing the introduction of Tauck and myself. Needless to say, it opened the door to a very strong productive association. I took the 100 best shops and spent more than a year to sermonize them into the "Tauck Clan". Each one was given the "Heit Seminar" including the now famous dinner skit. Thomas Cook Holidays became the second largest account in the world and held that position for a number of years.

The phase of developing a healthy productive and profitable overseas marketing division was almost complete except for proper staffing. Before getting onto that subject, I would like to expound a bit on the importance and the improvised Heit way of distributing Tauck brochures worldwide. Regardless of what I previously said about getting Tauck Tours included into 3,000,000 international brochures, which were produced by tour operators domiciled in the United Kingdom, it was not enough. I needed to find a way to satisfy the demand from the big operators for the "complete" Tauck brochure. This demand also included the thirty-six representatives from the rest of the world that were under my direction.

Due to this heavy demand, International brochure distribution ranked as one of the highest priority functions of the international marketing division. I think you will appreciate the development of my cunning and deceptive methods in acquiring sufficient brochure distribution to satisfy the craving masses of my overseas army of agents. To give you some idea of the problem I faced; for the second year of my Tauck employment, I was allotted 10,000 brochures for the entire world! This was why getting the Tauck product into the tour operators brochures was so important. Furthermore these Tauck brochures were not available until January or February. The overseas operators usually publish their brochures in August or at the latest September. These early publications are necessary to catch clients who normally book there "holidays" six to eight months in advance. If I wait until January of February to get my brochures and then mail them, by the time they get into the hands of the overseas market half the business will be over for the year. Having said all this, I must say Tauck did however slowly adopt a much more significant improvement in the timely release of this material.

Back to my skullduggery, fortunately, I would work long hours and, for the first couple of years I usually spent seven days a week at the office just to keep the paperwork humming. Charley Wanska, the Supreme Ruler of Brochures, enjoyed my fierce loyalty to Tauck and also to my stubborn conviction; Tauck can be successful in overseas markets. He entrusted me with a key to the brochure warehouse and quite frequently each year at brochure distribution time, after everybody left work, I would back up my jeep to the big doors of the "brochure fort", pull out my key and open the doors revealing these treasured articles. My jeep could hold at least twenty cartons, which meant about a thousand brochures. In the course of a year I probably kidnapped ten to fifteen thousand copies.

Arthur Tauck was a hard worker. He too, would most always be in his office by seven in the morning and would not leave until after six. His office was located in a tower of the main building that had a window that circled the tower and gave him a three hundred and sixty degree view of everything outside the building including Charlie's fort. About the middle of the second year of my acts of contraband, one early morning, on my arrival to the office, my phone rang, and its Arthur, "Ok Elliot, how many did you take last night?"

I was shocked because it then occurred to me that he probably knew from the first day I started, about this clandestine operation to fill the brochure needs of my hungry army of agents. What a great guy!

As mentioned, we became quite friendly. Some of this was due to the similarity of his family upbringing and my bus business background on the business side. He was and still is quite an athlete. I am about five years older. Arthur was still pedaling a bicycle all over Europe, skiing, and roller blading. He was a blue water sailor and a wind surfer. The last sport really caught my attention. So much so, that my determination to windsurf led to a couple of private lessons. For the rest of the technique, I taught myself.

Arthur lived on an island in a very contemporary house located on the beach at the mouth of the Saugatuck River, in Connecticut, where the river meets the Long Island Sound. The salt water of the Sound starts from New York, proceeds past the Saugatuck River, and then further for, another eighty miles to the Atlantic Ocean. The reason for this detail is a story about my windsurfing.

When Arthur discovered he has a contemporary to windsurf with, he insisted I keep my board at his house. This way we could enjoy the sport together, which we did. I used to keep my board in a storage area with the garden tools, so that I could have access to it without disturbing the family. On one very fine weekend, in late September, my daughter Susan came up from New York for a visit. I suggested she might like to see me windsurf, and perhaps, if she liked it, I, the Ancient Mariner at sixty-seven years, would teach her. She agreed and off we went to Arthur's house.

I grabbed my board from the shed, rigged the sail and off I went to demonstrate my skill. She was quite impressed and so I started my first lesson with her. During this session, Arthur Tauck comes out of his house and tells me he will get his board and join us. I told him not to bother that he could use mine. He agreed, and while Susan and I watched, off he went. Arthur executes every sport he indulges in with great skill. My daughter was so impressed that I became envious. Arthur returns and we both compliment him on his performance, and he returned to his house.

    I get back on the board to show Susan more of my style. To do so, I sail a good distance (close to a half a mile) out from the beach to give myself plenty of room to maneuver. All of a sudden a very strong southwest wind comes on like "a clear day wind squall." I am tossed off my board and despite ten or so efforts to get back on the board; this heavy wind kept knocking me back in the water. To complicate the matter, I was beginning to tire, so I straddled the board, but noticed the low tide was taking me from the river route to the channel and into Long Island Sound, which will take me directly out to the Atlantic Ocean! While a few sailboats recognized my windsurfer, the severity of the winds had forced them to concentrate on getting back to port under power and no sails. I was finally able to catch the attention of one sailboat, who threw me a line, which I grabbed, or clutched would be a better word. He helped me on board, took one look at the exhausted, haggard looking wind surfer and said, "Stay right there, I told my wife to go below and get you a good stiff cognac."

    Back on the beach where I left Susan more than an hour ago, she ran hysterically into the house, and explains that she cannot see me and is very worried. Alerted, Arthur runs to the yacht club across the street from the house and grabs a tender. As my rescuing boat enters the mouth of the Saugatuck Harbor, I spot off in the distance, this very tall six foot four inch figure standing in the tender making ever increasing circles and staring into the water. Perhaps he was searching for some facedown body to come floating by! Arthur hears me yelling and comes along side my rescue boat. I hopped into the tender, secured the windsurfer, thanked the captain for the lift, and we were underway to the yacht club.

    Arthur helped me carry the board back to the house. Standing outside were Susan and Arthur's wife Lee, she was quite angry and remarked, "Look at you! You look like a drowned river rat, and NO LIFE JACKET? Are you crazy?"

I just looked at her and said, "If you give me a quarter, I will sell you my board."

We all started to laugh, and that ended that adventure.

Tauck Tours, as originally named, was best known for its fall foliage tours, particularly of New England. It is said within the company walls, "Arthur Tauck Senior invented the leaf." To give you some idea of their popularity, when I first went to England, in pursuit of "getting my foot in the door," I would always suggest for a "starter" (as said in England), "Why not try promoting the magnificent explosion of natures fall colors on the whole northeast area of the United States?"

The most frequent response was, "Are you out of your mind? Do you think that anybody from England is going to purchase a ticket for a six thousand mile round trip air journey to the United States just to look at a bunch of leaves? Least you forget we in England also have leaves!"

"Yes you do, I have seem some, but there is a difference. You do not have the continuous and enormous area that is covered with an amazing variety of multicolored leaves. Neither do you have the historic sites and our version of the American Revolution, and finally, you do not have the extraordinary service of Tauck."

To make a long story short, in two years our fall foliage tours became the number one Tauck Tour selection in England. Additionally the foliage tours led our overseas guests to return for other tours as well. The number of tours operated during the peak foliage period was hard to believe; thirteen or fourteen motor coaches each day during the period from early September to the end of October were dispatched from the forty ninth-street side of the Waldorf Astoria. Arthur Tauck had a standing order that every senior member of staff including himself would take a turn at arriving at 7AM at the scene to manage the departures for five hundred persons each day! As a measure of the grip these tours had on our guests; during one of the busy, busy weeks, a terrible "northeaster" storm hit the New England south coastal area, and New York City. Trees were down; streets were filled with debris and the hard rain would practically bite your skin. We were warned a day before my dispatching turn came about the time the peak of the storm would occur; that morning I had over five hundred persons from all over the country who were scheduled to, "leave for the leaves". We were tempted to cancel everything, but we "rolled the dice". To avoid fallen trees, debris, and back up traffic to New York, I left my house in Connecticut at four in the morning dressed in my yellow sailing slicker with matching trousers. I managed to get to the Waldorf Astoria in two and a half hour. This trip usually could be done in one and a half hours. I was lucky to make it, at that. When I arrived all fourteen motor coaches were lined up and our tour directors were almost all on hand as well. Various company materials for each coach had to be onboard each vehicle. Our pre-tour duties accomplished, we now waited nervously for the eight AM departures to begin. Would our guest's show up? After all, the wind was fierce; streets soaked with rain and heavy clouds hung over the city. Will we have a disaster? To begin with, many of those Tauck guests knowing of the storm, came into New York two nights ahead of time, and they appeared on time in all kinds of rain gear. About thirty minutes later, the most marvelous thing happened, more guests came out of the hotel and were directed to the proper coaches. Then taxi cabs by the dozens started arriving, with passengers yelling, "Are these the Tauck foliage coaches?"

I was yelling back, "They sure are and welcome aboard!"

I was just flabbergasted. Taxi after taxi arrived and out they poured. Do you want to know how loyal these people were to Tauck? There must have been at least seventy cabs that arrived direct from the airport with passengers who flew the "red eye special" from the west coast. All I kept hearing was, "where can I get a quick cup of coffee, and which one is my coach?"

Out of over five hundred passengers loaded with luggage, we only had four no shows or cancellations! It was thrilling to be part of this incident. The final miracle was by ten AM, the storm passed through and the sun came out. I guess five hundred passengers knew more about the weather than we did.

The "eighties" were also dominated by some other events that were not directly connected with my overwhelming efforts to succeed in getting Tauck properly registered in the international markets. One of these events was my general health. While I always believed my concentrated efforts in keeping fit with exercise and sports would offset the likelihood of developing some of the ill's, but there are hidden ailments which do not give one much of a clue as to what is going on inside ones body. Such was the case with colon cancer. Three polyps made it necessary to remove a ten-inch section of my colon. Recovery was quick and after a short period I was allowed to continue my overseas work and to some extent windsurfing as well as a few other sports.

The next circumstance took place in 1983. I was in Pompano, Florida as a guest of my friend Eddy Hartnett. We were playing a match of singles tennis when I reached for a backhand shot. When I reached there was a loud pop, like a revolver shot, and I fell to the surface. My right foot was just dangling. We rushed to a doctor and he said I severed my achilles tendon. I called my doctor in Connecticut who compared notes with the Florida doctor and urged me to leave that day for home. The next day I was operated on and when I regained consciousness, in the recovery room, I found my right leg in a caste from my toes up to my crotch. I immediately called for my doctor, as I was furious. I told him in three weeks I was making a special trip around the world to evaluate the U.S. government tourist offices in Japan, Germany, France and England, for the U.S. Department of Commerce. I was one of a five-member select committee of very senior travel executives designated by the Travel Industry Association of America to do this. "Now doctor, you just tell me exactly what I have to do in the way of exercises because I am leaving in three weeks!"

To begin with I had to learn how to walk on crutches for good distances. I walked everyday in the hills of Connecticut on those crutches and a few days before my trip I was able to walk three miles! To further strengthen my legs he gave me a series of leg lifting exercises from a floor position on my back. My routine consisted of three hundred leg lifts a day. The last session with the doctor included a suggestion that I should take a sufficient supply of large plastic garbage bags. I asked why I needed theses? His reply was, "If you want to take a shower; you will have to put your right leg in the bag to keep the cast from getting wet."

I notified the other committee members of my predicament, and of my determination to make the trip. They notified the airlines of my crutches and I was on my way to Tokyo to meet the rest of the committee. Fortunately, we were provided with first class tickets and the airlines around the world met me at planeside each time with a golf cart. I never even went through customs. When I think about this I could have taken an elephant home with no customs duty, but my wife would not have appreciated that. The first leg of the flight to Japan was via San Francisco, which was about five hours on a jumbo jet. I handled that nicely. In San Francisco I had great assistance by airline ground crew that were able to get me boarded for the next thirteen-hour leg of the flight to Tokyo. I was able to get comfortably seated once again in the first class section. We climbed to cruising altitude, and I suddenly realized that it was time to pay a visit to the rest room. This was a serious problem that I had never given any thought to. I buzzed the flight attendant to bring the other attendant as well and the three of us reviewed the situation. Remember my right leg was in a full-length cast and could not be bent. The configuration of the first class area on the 747 Jumbo had two aisles extending the full length of the section. The rest room was located in a hallway between the two aisles. The attendants decided they would station an attendant on each end of the hallway that connects the two aisles; in this way I would have exclusive use of the rest room. Now I am sure that I do not have to explain how small airplane rest rooms are. It was so small that when I finally managed with the crutches and me to get at last properly seated in the restroom, my leg in the cast was protruding extensively into the hallway. I was so inhibited with all this commotion and protruding leg that my visit to the restroom was a miserable failure. That was one heck of a long trip to Tokyo!

The whole trip was truly a fascinating experience. We collected pertinent facts and data and we had a series of discussions with each of the office directors from the five countries we visited. Upon our return to the United States, a marketing plan by our committee was submitted to the U.S. Deputy Secretary of Commerce that would improve the effectiveness of the Federal governments involvement in promoting travel to the United States. Among the results of the trip, Langhorne Washburne, the then acting Deputy Secretary of Commerce and head of the overseas tourist offices invited me, to informally act as his personal consultant for appropriate touristic matters, pertaining to his office. I also received a flag of the

United States that was flown over our nations capital on December 20, 1983 at the request of John W. Warner, United States Senator.

As stated earlier, "the eighties" were somewhat marred with a few health items. In addition to the cancer and severed Achilles tendon, the medics found it necessary to replace my already once replaced hip joint because I wore it out; this was the second time for the same hip! The result was a slightly shorter right leg that gave me a definite limp. (Believe it or not, I was still able to windsurf until I became seventy-one.)

Everything at Tauck was coming along very nicely. I was beginning to realize it would be wise to hire a person who could learn the business from me and then sooner or later that person could carry on. Mark Lamont became my final choice. He worked as a tour director for Tauck for about five years, and one of the Tauck's suggested him as a candidate for the job. I found him to be quite opinionated, but on the other hand, he had some qualities that offset the negative. Being somewhat of the same nature myself this tended to make his indoctrination more difficult. Despite it all I stayed with him, as he was the best of the bunch interviewed. I had him takeover many of the arduous tasks I handled myself, such as the annual chore of brochure distribution. To me that was almost a religious procedure. To be able to secure air cargo for most of the worldwide distribution of Tauck brochures at no cost to Tauck was indeed a worthwhile accomplishment. To get it done, I would drive to the printers warehouse, park my car and line up five hundred cartons going to various destinations throughout the world. (This came to about 15,000 pounds of material). The truck driver and myself would load the truck with the forklift, in such away that we could unload at the airport in a consecutive sequence. Mark did not like this chore, but I insisted he do it so that he knew exactly "who got what and when." It was also a way for him to learn the business.

Shelia Thompson as mentioned before was the second most important person on my staff. Whereas normally, at least a dozen bookers handled domestic bookings, I made it a practice for only Sheila to handle all inbound international bookings. This job single handedly carried out through one person, Shelia Thompson. (Later on I added another "booker", but Sheila always remained my main vein.) While initial billing ran out of accounting I managed collections and problems myself. It may appear I was overburdening my staff and myself, but international business was so different from domestic procedures, that I felt it was the only way to make it run smoothly, and it did. Shelia worked so hard and for long hours, I decided to do something for her. I had just finished organizing what we call a familiarization tour for one of the most popular tours called Canyonlands. Invitations went out to many of our key accounts in England. We had thirty confirmed reservations. I thought it would be a nice touch to have Shelia go along as our hostess. She has never done anything like this before so that itself made it a pleasant surprise for her, and at the same time it was a good "Tauck Touch", for the invitees. When she returned from the Canyonlands Tour, she was all aglow and asked me for a private meeting. I expected to receive information about how delighted everybody was with the Tauck service. Instead, I received the news that Shelia has fallen in love with an Englishman, Roger Thompson who manages one of the North America Travel offices in Nottingham, England. I was shocked and asked myself, what did I do? Not only is she in love, but also he asked her to get married and he was going to move to the United States! I tried to diplomatically explain to her, (an innocent Nebraskan from a farm life background) that sometimes people from abroad have ulterior motives in getting involved with U.S. citizens. All she said to me was, "Oh no, not Roger!"

    A few months later Shelia announces she was leaving Tauck and was moving to England. This was bad news. For one thing, I did not want to see her hurt by this Romeo and of course, it created a big gap in all the duties that she performed. I was lucky to replace her with Diane Fossi, a lovely lady with good skills. I was determined to get her more involved with the overall business as well as specific functions. Diane was very suitable for this formula, and she enjoyed her work until she too went off a few years later to marry. Several kids later and a very successful husband had substantiated her decision. What I was beginning to realize was two things. Firstly, unless a person finds their work a career building undertaking, they will always be thinking of their job as a "gap filler" until something better comes along. Secondly, regardless of what I do to create a team effort and also to fuel self-esteem and satisfaction, the involved person's own agenda seems to take a higher priority. This was my observation in Tauck as well as many of my prior management situations.

I should have kept the observations closer to my own surface. It would have left me more prepared for some of the coming events that personally affected me. Before getting to the serious side of those events, which took place in the mid-nineties, allow me to close out the eighties with a very unique friendship.

Toon Waltman was President of KLM Royal Dutch Airlines for their North American division, which included all countries from Canada to the United States and Mexico. I initially met Toon when I was invited to be a guest speaker at a special Dutch travel agent society, which strangely enough held a meeting for about two hundred Dutch members in St. Petersburg, Florida. I believe that Toon flew them to St. Petersburg on a special 747 jumbo jet. Toon and I were to be the main speakers. The general manager from American Express, Wim Siebers was chairman of the meeting and he introduced Toon and myself Toon is a very tall man, well over six feet with a slender build; handsome in a fierce sort of way, and always impeccably dressed. After we finished addressing the audience, we had lunch together with Wim Siebers, who as chairman was looking after Toon with close attention. Wim explained my position at the world famous Tauck operation and how American Express was our general sales agent in the Netherlands. I invited Toon, and his lovely wife Carla, to be our guests on Tauck's Canyonlands tour and they accepted. Upon his return from the tour, he called me to laud the Canyonlands as the best experience he and his wife have ever had on a tour. During the call he mentioned that they lived in New Canaan, Connecticut, which was very close to where Carol and I lived in Ridgefield. We invited the Waltman's, along with Arthur Tauck and his wife, to dinner at our home. We all got a long very well and in return the Waltman's invited us to dinner at their New Canaan home.

The dinner at their attractive home included about twenty guests. It was elegantly done and Toon was more like a king than a homeowner. His habit was to introduce each person at the table individually, and required that each one of us give a capsulated "bio" of who we were. There were artists, musicians, philosophers, etc, which made these get-togethers always most enjoyable.

One day we received in the mail and engraved invitation to be the guest of KLM Airlines for a **weekend** in the Netherlands! We were picked up by limousine and taken to JFK Airport where we were met and escorted to Queen Juliana's private lounge. At the lounge we met two other couples, who had been invited. One was the publisher of a well-known travel newspaper and the other was a very large tour operator who did a considerable amount of business with KLM. We chatted a bit and then were escorted to our very comfortable first class seats aboard a KLM jumbo jet. Upon arrival at Schipol Airport in the Netherlands, we did not have to do anything except follow our escort to a waiting limousine. We were taken to the Golden Tulip Hotel, and each couple was assigned a beautiful suite. We had enough time to relax and bathe before we all had to meet back in the lobby. After a sumptuous lunch, we were shuttled by limousine to the famous Ryk Museum. The museum had been closed to the general public and the authorities provided us with a private tour conducted by the museum director. After that it was back to the hotel to relax a bit before dinning at the home of the President of all KLM Royal Dutch Airlines. The next morning, once again, we were taken by limousine to the airport were we boarded a private jet for an air tour of the Dykes of Holland along the coastline. When we returned to the airport we were ushered to the famous tulip festival of Holland. In keeping up with the style of our visit, the tulip festival board of directors personally escorted us with golf carts through the unbelievable blanket of various colored flowers. After lunch we went to one of the best diamond factories in the country where the President met us and invited the ladies to place what ever jewelry they wore on a velvet pillow he was holding and promised they would be cleaned to sparkle like new. Carol was wearing a set of magnificent diamond and jade earrings (that she received from her first husband). Before I could tell her not to do this, the earrings were on the pillow. The reason I wanted to stop her was that one of the diamonds was missing and I did not want the expense of the replacement. I was too late, and off they went with the other ladies jewelry. The tour progressed with the President presiding over it and was indeed very interesting, but my mind was focused on the price of the missing diamond they would in all probability be replaced. The tour ended, and the velvet pillow reappeared. Carol's earrings, as I has dreaded, had the empty space replaced with a new diamond, but no bill was ever given to me!!

To expand on the behind the scene story of the missing diamond. The story started before Carol and I were married and she was still living with her first husband. I had an apartment in the Murray Hill section of Manhattan. I invited Carol one night to my apartment, where I would be the cook and the waiter. My specialty was calves liver sautéed in onions with rösti potatoes. Before dinner we had hors d'oeurvres, martinis, and Louis-Jadot, Puilly-Fuissé accompanied dinner. After completing our scrumptious meal, it was my habit to clear the table immediately. It was also a habit for Carol to remove her earrings and place them on the table. Unfortunately, she was at the time wearing the very same earrings that several years later she placed on the velvet pillow in the Amsterdam diamond factory. When I cleared the table and threw the garbage down the incinerator from my seventeenth floor apartment, neither Carol nor I realized that in the garbage were her magnificent earrings. When she got home, she called me almost hysterical to report the loss. I searched the apartment carefully but they were nowhere to be found. My suspicion was I threw then into the incinerator with the garbage. I knew I had to keep trying, so I woke up the janitor and promised a reward is he could find the earrings in the garbage of the high-rise apartment. The next morning I went down to the basement and there I saw the janitor laboring with a shovel and sifting the garbage through a screen. I did not imagine that his endeavor would be successful but gave him an A for effort. Later that morning I received a call from him, Eureka! He found them. I left the office rushed back to my apartment building, picked up the jewelry and gave the janitor a one hundred dollar reward. A quick glance showed that the incinerator had already burnt them black and they were slightly bent out of shape. I took them to a fine jewelry store on fifth avenue and they advised that they would do they best they could. After a few days I got a call that the earrings were ready. I returned to the store and they were true to their word, except for the one missing diamond. The empty spot on Carol's earring was the same spot the diamond factory in Amsterdam refilled with a beautiful clear diamond free of charge!

Back to Amsterdam, Holland, that evening, we attended a symphony concert where we occupied Queen Juliana's box.

After dinner, it was back to our suite, and we were exhausted. I was happy to "hit the sack" with about ten pillows and my wife. Our last day was leisurely and back to the airport with limousines awaiting our arrival in New York to take us back to our respective homes. When we arrived home, we knew how Cinderella felt when she lost the glass slipper.

I was determined to find some way to "get even" with Toon Woltman. The day he causally mentioned he had never visited West Point nor seen an "American football game", Bingo! My eyes lit up and I told him, "This will be taken care of."

When the football season arrived, I called a classmate of mine, who although retired, was retained by West Point as the protocol officer for visiting dignitaries. He was the most effective person at West point that I ever met. He left no stone unturned down to the tiniest of detail. Here is how it went. We arrived at the south gate entrance to the academy. I explained to the guard that Mr. And Mrs. Woltman were the guests of Mr. and Mrs. Heit. The guard checks his clipboard and comes back to our car, salutes, and states, "Sir, you are cleared to proceed to Cullom Hall, the officer's club where the superintendent has invited your party to attend a breakfast prior to the parade and following that, by attending the football game as the guests of the Superintendent of West Point."

Off we go to Cullom Hall and after parking we continued on our way to the breakfast. The guard at the gate where we were initially stopped must have passed the word that we had arrived, because a special escort was waiting for us at the door to Cullom Hall. The hall is a beautiful building outside and inside as well. The superintendent must have had seventy or eighty people present for this function. Toon Waltman was simply overwhelmed with the interior beauty and the splendid oil paintings of the heavily decorated West Point graduates who served gallantly in past wars. I lost sight of Toon just at the point when I spotted the superintendent, General Goodpaster. I grabbed our two wives and ran over to General Good Paster thinking Toon would spot us and run over as well. I still could not see Toon, so I proceeded to introduce Mrs. Woltman, my wife and myself. I told the General that Toon was indeed looking forward to the honor of meeting him; would he spare me a moment, I know I would find him quickly. I entered the men's room and there he was washing his hands. I grabbed him and explained on the way back to our party that the General was anxious to meet him. At the moment this was about to happen, Toon turned on his magic charm. Both men are tall and both stand very erect. They extended their hands to each other in a strong convincing manner, which was followed by Toon's firm toned voice, "General, this is my first visit to this fine institution; FOR ME THIS IS VALHALLAH."

The word Valhalla was just the most perfect word to describe West Point's impression on a person of Toon's stature. For those readers not familiar with the term Valhalla, it is a Viking word for where all brave warriors are rewarded to spend their eternity in heavenly comfort. The General was overtaken with instant admiration for Toon. He put his arm on Toon's shoulder and they left the two wives with me while the General lead my friend off to the upstairs gallery. The upstairs galley was like a museum with many large oil paintings. The General spent time describing with pride the past hero's of West Point. He spent over an hour before returning our guest, who I thought by this time, was so impressed he was about to make a career change.

When breakfast was over our escort took us over to the marching plain. There were four seats clearly marked with our names and located in the special dignitary section of the grandstand. The parade was a perfect West Point display of the utterly fantastic marching band lead by a major with a plumed hat and four thousand cadets marching behind in unbelievable precision. Our friends were just astounded at the spectacle. After the parade we chose to walk to the football game at Michie Stadium. Our escorts were ready to transport us by a military car, but they agreed to permit us to walk a mile and a half up a very steep hill from the marching plain to the stadium. They also mentioned that our tickets were at the box office under my name. The hike up the hill took us past a beautiful picnic spot by Lusk reservoir. You have to appreciate the day, we had a clear blue sky and it was right at the peak of fall foliage season. We admired the perfect weather and perfect setting of autumn leaves desperately trying to hang onto the trees surrounding Lusk reservoir, which was a short distance from the stadium. While passing the reservoir, we spotted a small group of people on the far side of the reservoir, apparently having a tailgate party. Since these parties are part of the "American scene", I thought the

Woltman's would enjoy a peek. Lo and behold, our very dear friends, Irene and Ted Halligan, were hosting a party of about twenty people. Irene's version of a tailgate party was far from the norm. Linen clothed tables complete with candelabras, shrimp and oyster hors d'oeurvres, tiny one-bite filet mignon sandwiches and a full array of liquid refreshments from champagne to beer! I never saw anything quite like this and needless to say, the Woltman's had a very unexpected surprise, to see what looked like the country version of the posh "21" restaurant in New York City.

Our visit to the Halligan's bash, cut into our schedule a bit, so we thanked them profusely and walked the short distance to Michie Stadium, to watch the football game with Army against Cornell. I picked up our tickets and we were directed to the superintendent glass enclosed private section. Once again, the assigned seats had our names inscribed thereon and once again; Toon was in conversation with his old pal General Goodpaster. We were right on the fifty-yard line and we were so high it seemed we were in a blimp flying directly over the field. After an exciting game, again, we chose to walk down the hill back to Cullom Hall to get the Woltman's car. We would then drive back to a restaurant in Connecticut, where my car was parked. Seeing the restaurant prompted the Woltman's to insist on having dinner as their guest. It was a day that began with a meeting at seven in the morning and ended at nine in the evening upon our return to our home. It left us absolutely exhausted but with big smiles of satisfaction, as not only was it a fabulous day, but we had paid our dues.

I previously mentioned before getting into the Woltman wonders, that there were some serious developments beginning to appear with Tauck. These began in the early nineties when Arthur Tauck felt it was necessary to convert his single person enterprise to a full corporate structure. To do this he engaged a consulting firm run by Gary Youell. Gary was an extremely brilliant person who must have won the confidence of Arthur Tauck to get the process started. While this change was in the pre-birth stage, it was a well-kept secret. At the same time my division was humming along with Mark making good progress in adapting himself to most of the duties that a manager would have to undertake. In noting this, I promoted him to be the Manager of International Marketing. I did have some reservation about his attitude toward certain major accounts in the United Kingdom, but I felt his negativity would disappear when he became manager. He definitely needed to sense the proper responsibility toward all major accounts and not just some.

A month passed, when I decided to bring Mark into my office for a closed-door discussion. I look back at that discussion as the first backward step I took since I appeared on the Tauck doorstep in September of 1981. I described to Mark a plan I was working on but not yet discussed with Arthur Tauck. I wanted Mark to be the first to know, in order for him to recognize the faith being placed in him. If everything went according to plan, I would move to Florida where I would maintain contact with most of the important accounts in the world and Mark would become General Manager and still report to me. When I advised Mark of my plan, he had a very surprised look on his face; I too later on, as the situation developed, had a much bigger surprised look on my face. After our meeting I met with Arthur Tauck and his immediate reaction was, "Are you sure you want to do this?"

"Yes I am."

Before I left for Florida, Gary Youell, the consulting expert, made up a list of the Tauck management personnel to be individually interviewed. I was number one. I answered a series of his questions, which gave me the distinct impression that he thought I was retiring. My short, to the point reply was, " Not yet. When I am ready to retire, it will be in a blaze of glory, we are not yet there."

Mr. Youell who apparently had other ideas for my future did not appreciate that statement by me. Our meeting ended on that note and off I went to Florida. About two weeks after setting up my Florida office, I received a letter from one of the Tauck family advising me that I will have a two-year contract at half the salary to act as a consultant and would be reporting to Mark Lamont! Furthermore, Mark will now report to someone else besides me. I felt completely ambushed by a conspiracy engineered between Mark and Gary Youell. I was inflamed with anger to the point of calling Mark to advise him that I was flying up at my own expense and I wanted him, without fail, to meet me at the Westport Inn, in Connecticut. He was there as ordered and I did not mince my words. Looking at him directly in the eye, "How could you participate in such a scheme without the manhood to let me know what was going on behind my back?"

Mark could not answer, and that reaction to my question made it abundantly clear he did not act alone. I told Mark I had enough deceit to make any further discussion of the matter useless. I returned to Florida with the deepest disappointment.

Epilogue

It was difficult for me to face the reality; my reign at Tauck was over even though I was retained for nine more years as a consultant from 1995 to the end of 2004. About the middle of December of the year 2004, I received a call from Arthur Tauck. He said it so eloquently; I did not feel too badly; "Elliot, I guess we reached the end of a legacy." In January, I would be turning eighty years old, and I guess enough was enough.

A consultant is not part of the management structure; they are like appendages that offer advise without responsibility to enact the advice given.

I could gradually see decay setting in to our international markets. Mark Lamont, the presiding Director of International Marketing lasted as such for another four or five years, then chose to leave Tauck for apparent opportunities elsewhere. The next sad news that hastened the retreat of international marketing abroad was the shifting of responsibility from one unqualified person to another. In each case these people still remained with their other regular duties. Thus, the basic management principle that I lived by of homogeneous assignment, especially for the complexity of international marketing, was voided. My leaving Connecticut and moving to Florida undoubtedly started the slow disengagement of our strong position in foreign markets to a point where the business eventually dropped by fifty percent.

Had I heeded Arthur Tauck's warning the situation might have very well turned out much differently than it did. I quote again, "Are you sure you want to move to Florida?"

Despite the unfortunate turn of events, the fine traditions of Tauck spanning over the same years as my upcoming eighty first birthday, together with my deep fondness for Arthur Tauck as one of the foremost leaders in travel; these will live on in my own personal biography, as the pinnacle of fifty-two years in the travel industry.

Since the book, One of Eight, is not exclusively devoted to corporate life, I would like the reader to know how thankful I am to all my friends who continuously encouraged me to write about all the other adventures and unique situations that life allowed me to experience. Just writing about these has given me pleasure and the chance to revisit in detail what has happened to me during the course of many years.

While on the subject of friends, such as Arthur Tauck, I do want to reserve comment for Herb DeGraff and Ken Engelhardt. Herbert from the moment I entered corporate life in 1953 at Gray Line of New York has been an inseparable part of my conversion from soldier to a modestly successful businessman. In the beginning we had some difficulty in learning what made each other tick. When we got past that; he was the one who got me started "rowing my own boat". From getting me on the board in 1962 for representing the one hundred or more Gray Line sightseeing companies in the best trade promotion ever to Europe with Pan American Airlines and Greyhound. Then practically kidnapping me away from Gray Line New York to become his Vice President of Sales and Planning for the world famous Greyhound Corporation; I could go on and on. What was truly remarkable about Herb was not these things he did for me; more importantly, it was the true friendship that we both felt for each other. This went on right up to the time I, along with many of his close and prominent friends had the honor of eulogizing him as a person we will never forget. Fortunately Anne DeGraff, his absolutely charming widow lives on to share our memories of a great person.

In like manner, Ken Engelhardt who started out as my brother-in-law then through the course of many years in business together we forged a very strong friendship. Our backbreaking experiences with "growing up" the Gray Line business and its' success was an important part of what we mean to each other. It was in that process, that Ken went from brother-in-law to becoming my very close friend. Ken, his wife Bobbie, Carol and I still enjoy great times together.

One of Eight

Quite often in life in the pursuit of economic conquest, we confine ourselves to the point of losing focus for the attention we owe to our loved ones. Such as it was in my case with my daughters Robin and Karen. This is true, as well, to some extent with Carol's children from her first marriage Robert and Susan. I know Robin and Karen received an abundance of love from their mother; as for me, my priorities were mixed with more weight toward making headway in the material world. While things were in a better balance with my second marriage, I was still a bit "light" on time spent with Robert and Susan. This was due to continuous traveling throughout the world to make my promise to Arthur Tauck successful. To all my children, and my wife as well, I apologize for my absence. I know I could have made it better for each of the children during their difficult time of being teenagers.

In closing I am going to miss writing this book, "One of Eight", and being with you, the reader. Somewhere in each of us, lies that vicarious search for the unusual to be experienced. In this regard, I hope reading this book has made it possible for you to enjoy my fortunate circus of life.

The last item I have in my appointment book is dated April 9, 2006. That is the date Carol and I shove off on what should be a very soft adventure. We will cross the Atlantic Ocean in fourteen days, from Barbados to Lisbon, Portugal. Sailing onboard the "Windsurf" is a "Soft" adventure that equals, six hundred and seventeen feet in length with a crew of one hundred and ninety, two electric propulsion motors, two sets of an ACH engineering stabilizer system and over twenty eight thousand square feet of sail. Even though I am not so young that I can enjoy the full thrill of a difficult adventure; still I am not old enough to stop having one or more adventures of this kind.

ISBN 142510444-4